barbri®

AF861809

Multistate Preview

A MULTISTATE ADVANTAGE™ WORKSHOP

Table of Contents

To be used in conjunction with the Summer 2009 and Winter 2010 BAR/BRI Bar Review Courses

PRE

HOW TO USE THE MULTISTATE PREVIEW

What is the Multistate Preview?

The Multistate Preview is the second MBE Workshop in BAR/BRI's Multistate Advantage™ program—an unparalleled set of Workshops that give you just what you need to succeed on the MBE.

What do I get with the Multistate Preview?

The Multistate Preview Workshop consists of questions and lecture analysis for each of the six MBE subjects, plus a 100-question simulated MBE with a subject-by-subject review. This book contains 250 questions, accompanied by full explanatory answers, that cover a broad range of the topics tested on the Multistate Bar Exam.

How do I use the Multistate Preview book?

If your course has scheduled the Multistate Preview as a 5-day workshop, you will do the questions during class time. If your course is offering the Preview lectures online, you should do each set of questions at home and then watch the corresponding lecture video at www.barbri.com.

Why do the Multistate Preview?

The Multistate Preview gives you an unsurpassed head start in your bar review preparation through its topic-oriented approach to answering MBE questions. Together with the other Multistate Advantage™ Workshops, the Multistate Preview is one more reason why ***BAR/BRI is all you need for the Multistate Bar Exam***.

Constitutional Law

Questions and Analytical Answers

barbri®

Constitutional Law

1. Ⓐ Ⓑ Ⓒ Ⓓ
2. Ⓐ Ⓑ Ⓒ Ⓓ
3. Ⓐ Ⓑ Ⓒ Ⓓ
4. Ⓐ Ⓑ Ⓒ Ⓓ
5. Ⓐ Ⓑ Ⓒ Ⓓ

6. Ⓐ Ⓑ Ⓒ Ⓓ
7. Ⓐ Ⓑ Ⓒ Ⓓ
8. Ⓐ Ⓑ Ⓒ Ⓓ
9. Ⓐ Ⓑ Ⓒ Ⓓ
10. Ⓐ Ⓑ Ⓒ Ⓓ

11. Ⓐ Ⓑ Ⓒ Ⓓ
12. Ⓐ Ⓑ Ⓒ Ⓓ
13. Ⓐ Ⓑ Ⓒ Ⓓ
14. Ⓐ Ⓑ Ⓒ Ⓓ
15. Ⓐ Ⓑ Ⓒ Ⓓ

16. Ⓐ Ⓑ Ⓒ Ⓓ
17. Ⓐ Ⓑ Ⓒ Ⓓ
18. Ⓐ Ⓑ Ⓒ Ⓓ
19. Ⓐ Ⓑ Ⓒ Ⓓ
20. Ⓐ Ⓑ Ⓒ Ⓓ

21. Ⓐ Ⓑ Ⓒ Ⓓ
22. Ⓐ Ⓑ Ⓒ Ⓓ
23. Ⓐ Ⓑ Ⓒ Ⓓ
24. Ⓐ Ⓑ Ⓒ Ⓓ
25. Ⓐ Ⓑ Ⓒ Ⓓ

Question 1

By state law, no movie theater may admit anyone under age 18 to any movie classified as "adult" by the state ratings board. In response to a survey on the effect of adult entertainment on people under age 21, the legislature proposed to amend the statute to prohibit admission of any male under age 20 and any female under age 19 to any theater playing adult-rated movies. A theater owner operates a theater showing only adult-rated movies. Since it is located next to a college campus, he stands to lose nearly half his patronage if this statute is enacted. The theater owner brought an action in federal court to restrain its enactment, arguing that it would amount to unconstitutional sex discrimination.

The court should:

(A) Dismiss the action for want of a case or controversy.

(B) Dismiss the action, because it does not present a substantial federal question.

(C) Abstain from hearing the case, pending an authoritative construction of the proposed statute by a state court.

(D) Hear the case on its merits, because the proposed statute would deny males the equal protection of the law.

Question 2

A hairdresser owned a beauty salon employing only male hairdressers and catering only to female customers. A city ordinance made it unlawful for any person to operate a female beauty salon if the hairdressers are male. The hairdresser brought an action in federal court challenging the constitutionality of the ordinance.

If the city moves to dismiss the lawsuit arguing that the hairdresser lacks standing, the city would:

(A) Prevail, because the ordinance does not prohibit the operation of beauty salons per se, but only the right of the male employees to service female customers.

(B) Prevail, because only the employees can raise their rights of association.

(C) Not prevail, because the employees and beauty salon operators have rights that are harmed by the ordinance.

(D) Not prevail, because the ordinance prevents the employees from exercising their First Amendment rights.

Question 3

Congress passed a statute requiring energy consumption be reduced by a specified percentage, to be set by a presidential executive order. The statute provided specific standards that the President must use in setting the percentage, and detailed procedures to be followed.

This statute is likely:

(A) Constitutional, because it creates a limited administrative power to implement the statute.

(B) Constitutional, because inherent executive powers permit such action even without statutory authorization.

(C) Unconstitutional, because it is an undue delegation of legislative power to the executive branch.

(D) Unconstitutional, because it violates the Due Process Clause of the Fifth Amendment.

Question 4

A massive earthquake struck Mexico, causing widespread death and destruction. The President of Mexico made an urgent plea to the President of the United States asking for assistance. Congress was not in session and the President, without calling Congress into special session, ordered extensive military aid, in the form of personnel and equipment, to assist Mexico.

Which of the following best describes the constitutionality of the President's orders?

(A) The action was a valid exercise of the President's position as Commander in Chief of the Armed Forces of the United States.

(B) The action was valid under the plenary powers of the President, inasmuch as the Army units were used for humanitarian, rather than warlike, purposes.

(C) The action was unconstitutional, because the President may not perform acts when Congress is not in session that he would have to ask Congress to approve if it were in session.

(D) The action was unconstitutional, because the President does not have the power to unilaterally authorize this type of foreign aid.

Question 5

A lunarian society believed that intelligent life existed on the moon, but that the government was not interested in searching for it. A wealthy political contributor who was a member of this society successfully lobbied Congress to pass a $100 million bill to investigate this hypothesis, even though virtually all reputable scientists rejected it. The President vetoed the bill, calling it a waste of money, but Congress overrode the veto, and the appropriation was authorized.

If the validity of the expenditure is challenged in federal court, the likely outcome is that it is:

(A) Constitutional, because the spending power of Congress is limited only by the political process.

(B) Constitutional, because Congress could believe that the expenditure is a reasonable measure to advance the general welfare.

(C) Unconstitutional, because the expenditure is inconsistent with the exclusive authority of the President over foreign affairs.

(D) Unconstitutional, because the spending does not directly affect interstate or foreign commerce.

Question 6

Congress enacted a statute requiring colleges and universities receiving federal funds to offer aid to students solely on the basis of need.

Which of the following is the strongest constitutional argument in favor of enacting such a statute?

(A) Power to tax and spend for the general welfare.

(B) Power to enforce the Privileges and Immunities Clause of the Fourteenth Amendment.

(C) Power to enforce the Equal Protection Clause of the Fourteenth Amendment.

(D) Police power.

Question 7

To combat the spread of a dangerous and highly contagious disease, the state passed legislation authorizing testing clinics be set up in major cities. One of the cities, with a population of 25,000 people, had an army base in the city employing 2,500 people and housing 5,000 soldiers. The mayor and the state director of public health determined that the best location for the clinic would be on the base, because that is where the disease had the greatest risk of spreading. When the proposal was made to the base commander he refused to allow it, even though there was ample space available.

Can the state compel the base commander to allow the testing clinic on base?

(A) Yes, because the concentration of service personnel and civilian base employees in one location poses a significant health threat to the citizens of the state if they are not tested.

(B) Yes, because the area of public health has not been preempted by the federal government.

(C) No, because the state has no right under its police power to impose this burden on the federal government.

(D) No, because the state could easily construct the clinic elsewhere.

Question 8

A state law required that state civil service employees retire by age 65. Congress then passed a law making it illegal for states to require anyone to retire prior to age 70, absent valid physical or mental reasons why the job had to be performed by younger persons.

A long-time state employee in excellent physical and mental health who just turned 65 was told by his supervisor that he must retire. He filed suit against the state in federal court, challenging the state law.

The court is most likely to rule that:

(A) The employee must retire, because the federal statute interferes with an integral governmental function of the state.

(B) The employee must retire, because the state is merely trying to promote efficient government at a lower cost to its taxpaying citizens.

(C) The employee must be reinstated, because federal law is supreme and voids inconsistent state laws.

(D) The employee must be reinstated, because age is a suspect classification.

Question 9

After a private plane crashed near the Lincoln Memorial, Congress enacted a law prohibiting private planes from flying over Washington, D.C. An organization representing private plane pilots brought suit in federal court seeking to invalidate this law.

The federal statute could best be supported by:

(A) The Supremacy Clause.

(B) The General Welfare Clause.

(C) Congress's plenary power to make regulations protecting government policy.

(D) Congress's police power over the District of Columbia.

Question 10

Eighty-five percent of tobacco products sold in the United States originate in the tobacco fields of one state. Its legislature passed a law prohibiting cultivation of tobacco in the state, citing severe health risk concerns. In response, Congress enacted legislation specifically authorizing and encouraging cultivation of tobacco by providing tax incentives and federal subsidies for tobacco growers.

If a tobacco grower and state resident is prosecuted under the state statute, will the federal law compel the state court to dismiss the action?

(A) Yes, because the commerce power authorizes Congress to regulate activities of national economic significance and the state statute is inconsistent with the federal legislation.

(B) Yes, because the General Welfare Clause empowers Congress to enact legislation it believes to be beneficial to the people of the United States, making the inconsistent state statute invalid.

(C) No, because the power to regulate to promote the general welfare is reserved to the states by the Tenth Amendment.

(D) No, because the state has a compelling interest in protecting the health of its residents.

Question 11

The President issued an executive order prohibiting exportation to certain countries of specific computer software that, although not useable directly to develop nuclear weapons, would facilitate nuclear weapons technology. Congress had previously passed a law authorizing the issuance of such orders. Prior to the issuance of the executive order, a computer software company contracted with one of those countries for software that is now banned for sale and distribution.

What effect does the executive order have on this contract?

(A) The executive order unconstitutionally impairs the obligation of the company's preexisting contract, which was lawful when made.

(B) The executive order unconstitutionally denies the company a valuable property interest without due process, because it is not limited to computer software used directly to produce nuclear weapons and, therefore, is not necessary to vindicate a compelling national need.

(C) The executive order is constitutional because Congress has plenary powers to regulate commerce with foreign nations and has used that power to authorize such orders.

(D) The executive order is constitutional, because the inherent power of the President to conduct foreign affairs is plenary and, therefore, not limited by the Constitution.

Question 12

A federal statute provided: "No speed governing device may be removed from any vehicle if it was installed by the federal government." The statute also provided for criminal penalties for its violation.

A driver purchased a previously owned government vehicle with a speed governing device at auction and used the car to drive to and from work. The car struggled to maintain speed above 35 m.p.h. on any incline, nearly causing the driver to be rear-ended several times. Deciding that the device was dangerous, the driver removed it.

If the driver is prosecuted for violating the statute, her strongest constitutional defense is:

(A) The statute violates the Due Process Clause of the Fourteenth Amendment.

(B) Because no state statute prohibits removal, the federal statute invades interests protected by the Tenth Amendment.

(C) The statute violates the Privileges and Immunities Clause of the Fourteenth Amendment.

(D) The statute violates the Due Process Clause of the Fifth Amendment.

Question 13

A state statute makes it a crime punishable by fine or imprisonment "for any person to attempt to intimidate or force a state official to discriminate against persons in violation of the Fourteenth Amendment to the United States Constitution."

The statute is:

(A) Constitutional, because the state has a right to punish those who seek to suborn its officials into committing illegal acts.

(B) Constitutional, unless it conflicts with federal civil rights legislation.

(C) Unconstitutional, because the statute deals with acts of private persons and the Fourteenth Amendment requires state action.

(D) Unconstitutional, because states do not have the authority to enforce the Federal Constitution.

Question 14

The state legislature, alarmed by the 50% rise in the divorce rate of its citizens in recent years, enacted legislation requiring applicants for marriage licenses to be interviewed by a state psychologist to determine compatibility and evaluate their likelihood of success in a marriage. An engaged couple had their application for a marriage license denied after the state psychologist who interviewed them decided that they had an 80% chance of divorce within five years.

If they bring an action challenging the constitutionality of the statute, they will prevail if:

(A) They can prove that the state statute is not rationally related to a legitimate state interest.

(B) The state fails to prove that its statute is rationally related to a legitimate state interest.

(C) They can prove that the state statute is not necessary to effectuate a compelling state interest.

(D) The state fails to prove that the statute is necessary to effectuate a compelling state interest.

Question 15

Two adult males set up a tent in a remote and secluded camping area of a state park. A park ranger who happened to be in the area heard them engaging in sexual relations and pulled open the tent flap and arrested them. They were charged and convicted under the state's century-old anti-sodomy statute, which the state still enforced.

If the defendants appeal to the state appellate court claiming a violation of their constitutional rights, the court should:

(A) Reverse the conviction, because the defendants' due process rights were violated when they were arrested in the secluded park area.

(B) Reverse the conviction, because consenting adults are free to engage in sexual activity.

(C) Uphold the conviction, because the United States Constitution provides no right to engage in sodomy in a private setting.

(D) Uphold the conviction, because the defendants were in a state park, a public area.

Question 16

A state retirement system deducts a fixed percentage of an employee's pay each payday. Retirement benefits are paid at age 65 for the life of the employee. Statistics reveal that the life expectancy of a male at age 65 is less than the life expectancy of a female at the same age. Therefore, the state benefits to males are greater than those made to females.

If a female employee challenges the constitutionality of the retirement system, what is the applicable standard of review?

(A) The employee should be required to demonstrate that the benefit standards are not rationally related to the public interest.

(B) The state should be required to demonstrate a compelling state need for the benefit standards.

(C) The state should be required to show that the classification serves important government objectives and is substantially related to the achievement of those objectives.

(D) The state should be required to show a rational purpose for the benefit standard.

Question 17

A state law provided that only citizens of the United States may be hired by any governmental unit within the state. A citizen of the Philippines, who had been a legal resident of the state for five years, was awarded a medical degree from the state university and was licensed by the state to practice medicine. The doctor applied for a job opening in the state government, but despite the fact that she was fully qualified, she was rejected solely because of the statute.

If she files suit in federal court to enjoin enforcement of the statute, her best constitutional argument would be:

(A) The Ex Post Facto Clause.

(B) The Equal Protection Clause of the Fourteenth Amendment.

(C) The Due Process Clause of the Fourteenth Amendment.

(D) The Privileges and Immunities Clause of the Fourteenth Amendment.

Question 18

An attorney was employed by the United States Department of Health and Human Services in a regional office located in a leading tobacco-growing state. A labor contract between the agency and the clerical workers union provided for termination of union employees only for certain specified grounds. The attorney, however, was not a union member. Angered by the regional director's refusal to adopt a no-smoking policy for employees, she posted a notice in the employee cafeteria ridiculing management for the hypocrisy of an agency charged with promoting health allowing people to be exposed to unnecessary health risks. This notice generated substantial debate within the office and upset the regional director immensely, such that she wanted to fire the attorney.

Which of the following statements is most accurate with respect to the right of the agency to dismiss the attorney?

(A) The attorney has a liberty interest in the exercise of her First Amendment rights that entitles her to a hearing to contest the grounds of her dismissal.

(B) The attorney has a property interest as a public employee that precludes her from being fired without notice and an opportunity to respond.

(C) The attorney has no right to a hearing because her statements were not an expression of views on public issues.

(D) The attorney has both a liberty interest and a property interest that entitles her to a pretermination evidentiary hearing.

Question 19

A defendant stood accused of murdering a family of six in a small town. The judge, concerned not only about prejudice to the defendant's right to a fair trial but also about media attention and public opinion in such a small locale, issued an order forbidding the press from attending the trial or publishing any details of the testimony at trial.

If a local newspaper sues in federal court to have the judge's gag order overturned, will the newspaper prevail?

(A) Yes, because the proper way to deal with prejudicial publicity is via a change of venue.

(B) Yes, because of the constitutional right to a public trial.

(C) Yes, because the judge has attempted to impose a prior restraint in violation of the First Amendment.

(D) No, because the judge honestly believed that publicity would be prejudicial and would impair the defendant's constitutional right to a fair trial.

Question 20

A city zoning ordinance prohibited adult theaters and bookstores in areas zoned residential or commercial. The ordinance was enacted to protect surrounding property values and prevent other adverse secondary effects of such establishments. The theaters and bookstores were freely permitted in industrial areas where adverse secondary effects were less likely. A storekeeper who owned a building in a commercial zone was denied a permit to open an adult establishment in the building. He brings suit challenging the constitutionality of the ordinance.

Which of the following statements is most accurate?

(A) The ordinance is valid, because a city may enforce zoning restrictions on speech-related businesses to ensure that the messages they disseminate are acceptable to the residents of adjacent property.

(B) The ordinance is valid, because a city may enforce this type of time, place, and manner regulation on speech-related businesses, so long as this type of regulation is designed to serve a substantial governmental interest and does not unreasonably limit alternative avenues of communication.

(C) The ordinance is invalid, because a city may not enforce zoning regulations that deprive potential operators of adult theaters and bookstores of their freedom to choose the location of their businesses.

(D) The ordinance is invalid, because a city may not zone property in a manner calculated to protect property from the likely adverse secondary effects of adult theaters and bookstores.

Question 21

Due to violence erupting against picketers advocating automatic deportation of foreign persons accused of a crime, a state enacted a law prohibiting all picketing "carried out for the purpose of deterring others from exercising their constitutional rights."

The strongest constitutional defense that can be asserted by those charged with violating this statute is that it denies them:

(A) The Fifth Amendment right to due process of law, because the statute is so vague that reasonable persons cannot ascertain its scope.

(B) Equal protection of the laws, because the statute does not prohibit picketing for purposes other than those specified.

(C) First and Fourteenth Amendment rights of free expression and assembly, because the statute excessively restricts the marketplace of ideas.

(D) Article IV privileges and immunities of state citizenship, because picketing is a fundamental right.

Question 22

In an effort to keep all protest demonstrations peaceful, legislation was enacted which imposed fines and jail time on leaders of unruly demonstrations. The law made it a crime to "aid, abet, incite, urge, or encourage behavior that amounts to a breach of the peace."

A protester led a large group of picketers to a plant allegedly involved in chemical warfare research. He shouted to his followers, "Let's show these murderers what we think of them! Let's stop the poison gas machine now!" A student at the local university, carried away with emotion, picked up a brick and heaved it through one of the plant's windows. The student was arrested for, charged with, and convicted of disturbing the peace, and the protester leading the event was arrested, charged with, and convicted of violating the statute.

If the protester challenges his conviction in federal court, the court should rule that:

(A) The statute is constitutional, because the protester is vicariously liable for the student's activities.

(B) The statute is constitutional as applied to the protester only because the student was actually convicted of disturbing the peace.

(C) The statute is unconstitutional, because it is vague or overbroad.

(D) The statute is unconstitutional, because the state legislature may not limit political protests.

Question 23

A religious group that worships a wine god as a deity celebrates once a year by having every group member, including children, drink a great deal of wine. Investigating the group after complaints by local citizens, a sheriff observed the group's leader giving wine to young children. He arrested the leader, and she was charged under a state statute that prohibits persons from giving wine to minors. The leader defends on the ground that the statute interferes with the right to the free exercise of her religion.

In determining whether the statute can be constitutionally applied to the leader, the court may ***not*** properly:

(A) Require the state to bear the burden of persuading the court that the statute is constitutional as applied to the leader.

(B) Determine the reasonableness of the leader's religious beliefs.

(C) Ascertain whether the leader's religion requires her to serve wine to minors.

(D) Decide whether the leader is sincere in her religious beliefs.

Question 24

A long-standing controversial religious group had several disputes with local politicians. An inspection of its church building by the county fire marshal determined that it failed to meet code because of insufficient fire exits, and proceedings were initiated to revoke the church's certificate of occupancy. The group requested that the county make an exemption from the building code, asserting that it could not afford to make the necessary changes to make the building conform to the code, and that closing the building would hinder their ability to congregate and worship.

If the group's request is denied and the group seeks to enjoin the county from enforcing the building code on constitutional grounds, the decision should be for:

(A) The county, because an exemption for the church would constitute an establishment of religion.

(B) The church, on the basis of freedom of religion.

(C) The church on the basis of equal protection.

(D) The county, because the regulation was not intended to close the church.

Question 25

The state capitol building had fallen into disrepair, so the state contracted with a company for remodeling. After the contract was signed but before remodeling work had started, the state repealed the statute authorizing money for remodeling and notified the company that it was cancelling the contract because of budgetary concerns.

If the company brings suit in federal court against an appropriate state official to enjoin cancellation of the contract, the court should hold:

(A) For the company, because it had a valid contract.

(B) For the company, if it has detrimentally relied on its contract with the state.

(C) For the state official, because the courts will not substitute their judgment for that of the legislature.

(D) For the state official, because constitutionally the sovereign is not liable except with its own consent.

STOP

Answer to Question 1

(A) The court should dismiss the action because no case or controversy is present. Under Article III of the Constitution, federal courts may only decide real "cases and controversies," and not issue advisory opinions. The state law at issue here is a "proposed" statute. Therefore, a federal district court is without jurisdiction to decide its constitutionality. Hence, (A) is correct and (D) is incorrect. (B) and (C) are wrong because the court will not even consider those issues, because there is no case or controversy before it.

Answer to Question 2

(C) The city will not succeed in having the lawsuit dismissed. The hairdresser (as well as his employees) will suffer direct economic harm by the statute and, therefore, they have standing to contest the ordinance. (A) is incorrect. While the statute does not prevent the hairdresser from operating a beauty shop, it does restrict the sex of the employees who are employed to operate it. Such a restriction constitutes sufficient harm to confer standing on the hairdresser because it will seriously harm his current operations. Therefore, the suit will not be dismissed. (B) is incorrect because the right of association is not the only right at issue here; the hairdresser's right to operate his beauty shop without unlawful restriction is also at issue, and therefore, the suit will not be dismissed for this reason. (D) is incorrect because it is a question of fact whether the ordinance prevents the employees from exercising their First Amendment rights, and questions of fact are resolved at trial, not by a motion to dismiss. The only issue here is standing, where the merits of the claim (beyond showing actual harm) are irrelevant.

Answer to Question 3

(A) The statute is likely constitutional. Delegations of legislative power to the executive branch of government are virtually always upheld. The Supreme Court says that there must be some standards to guide the exercise of discretion, but the requirement is very minimal. Here, the statute "sets forth specific standards" and thus is sure to be upheld. (B) is incorrect because, even if the President had such inherent powers, that would not make the legislation constitutional. The question asks about the constitutionality of a statute; an answer about the President's inherent powers is nonresponsive. (C) is incorrect for the reasons explained above: Since the New Deal era, virtually no laws have been declared unconstitutional as an excessive delegation of legislative power, and this statute has sufficiently specific standards that it would not be invalidated on that basis. (D) is wrong because due process claims require that an individual be denied life, liberty, or property without due process of law. The facts of the question do not indicate any such deprivations.

Answer to Question 4

(A) The President as Commander in Chief of the Armed Forces has broad discretion to use American troops in foreign countries. In fact, never in all of American history has a presidential use of troops in a foreign nation been declared unconstitutional. Thus, the President's power as Commander in Chief would justify this action. (B) is incorrect because the Constitution does not limit the President's use of troops to humanitarian, as opposed to war, purposes. (B) draws a distinction that has no support in the text of the Constitution or in Supreme Court precedents. (C) is incorrect because the President may use troops in foreign countries whether or not Congress is in session. Moreover, (C) is based on a false premise—that the President would need prior congressional approval to send the troops to Mexico. (D) is wrong because the President does have the unilateral authority to send troops to a foreign country. Calling the troops "foreign aid" does not change the legality of the President's power as Commander in Chief to use troops in foreign nations.

Answer to Question 5

(B) The court is likely to find the expenditure constitutional. Congress can spend federal monies for the general welfare [art. I, §8] provided the spending is reasonably related to a legitimate federal interest. [South Dakota v. Dole (1987)] Here, Congress could believe that it is in the national interest to determine conclusively whether life exists on the moon. (A) is incorrect because Congress cannot spend for unconstitutional purposes, *e.g.*, to promote racial discrimination. (C) is too broad a statement. While the President has broad authority over foreign affairs, the authority is not "exclusive," as Congress also plays a major role in this area. (D) is wrong because the Spending Clause is not limited by its relationship to commerce.

Answer to Question 6

(A) The strongest basis for the statute is Congress's power to tax and spend for the general welfare. Since the federal government has the power to tax, and since spending for education is for the general welfare, the government may attach any reasonable conditions to the expenditure it desires. (B) and (C) are wrong because the Privileges and Immunities Clause and the Equal Protection Clause do not apply to the facts presented. (D) is wrong because there is no general federal police power.

Answer to Question 7

(C) The state cannot compel the commander to allow the clinic. State governments may not regulate federal government activities. States thus lack the authority to impose regulations on federal military bases. The Supremacy Clause prevents such state control of the federal government. (A) is incorrect because the state lacks constitutional authority to impose regulations on federal military bases. (B) misses the issue because the question is not whether the public health regulation is preempted by the federal government, but rather the immunity of federal instrumentalities from state government regulations. (D) is incorrect because regardless of the ease (or even hardship) of constructing other facilities, states may not regulate federal military bases.

Answer to Question 8

(C) The court most likely will require the employee to be reinstated. The federal law clearly prohibits state laws forcing retirement prior to an employee's reaching age 70. The state's application of a retirement law to a 65-year-old conflicts with federal law. Thus, the state's law is superseded by the federal law. The supremacy of federal law makes the state's action clearly unconstitutional. (A) is incorrect because federal laws are allowed even if they interfere with integral state government functions. In *Garcia v. San Antonio Metropolitan Transit Authority* (1985), the Supreme Court stated that it would not invalidate federal laws on the ground that they usurp state authority. (B) is incorrect because the state cannot violate a federal law regardless of its interests. Federal law is supreme over the state law; thus, states must comply with the federal statute. (D) is incorrect because age is not a suspect classification. The Supreme Court has held that age discrimination receives only rational basis review.

Answer to Question 9

(D) The statute is supported by Congress's police power over the District of Columbia. In general,

Congress lacks police power. Police power is possessed by state and local governments that have the authority to legislate for the welfare of their citizens. However, a major exception is when Congress legislates for the District of Columbia. Congress has police power in such circumstances. (A) is incorrect because the Supremacy Clause refers to conflicts between federal and state laws. There is no federal-state conflict in this case. (B) is incorrect. The General Welfare Clause gives Congress the power to tax and spend for the general welfare. This question does not involve spending of federal funds. (C) is incorrect because it is too general. It is not clear what federal power is deemed "plenary." Also, Congress does not have broad authority to make regulations to protect government policy.

Answer to Question 10

(A) The federal law will compel the state court to dismiss the action. Congress's broad power to regulate interstate commerce includes the power to control production of items having a substantial impact on such commerce. (B) is not the best answer because there is no federal general welfare power except the taxing and spending power, and the challenged legislation does more than spend. (C) is irrelevant. An otherwise proper state enactment may still be invalid if inconsistent with a valid federal law. (D) is also irrelevant. Given the sweeping nature of the commands of the Supremacy Clause, the fact that a state interest is compelling has no bearing on whether state actions predicated on that interest must fall in the face of a valid federal action.

Answer to Question 11

(C) The executive order is constitutional because it was authorized by Congress. For all practical purposes, the power to regulate foreign commerce lies exclusively with Congress. (D) is therefore an inferior answer. By authorizing the issuance of the Presidential executive order, Congress has constitutionally exercised this power. (A) is incorrect because the impairment of the Contract Clause applies to state governments only, not to the federal. (B) is incorrect because the company's contract right would not qualify as a property interest under the Fifth Amendment.

Answer to Question 12

(D) The only possible basis for a successful challenge against the federal statute is the Due Process Clause of the Fifth Amendment, and thus, by process of elimination, (D) must be correct. (A) is wrong because the Due Process Clause of the Fourteenth Amendment limits ***state and local government*** action, not the federal government. Due process limitations are applied to the federal government through the Fifth Amendment. (B) is wrong because the Tenth Amendment is no longer used by the courts as a limit on congressional action that applies to both the public and private sectors. In *Garcia v. San Antonio Metropolitan Transit Authority* (1985), the Supreme Court held that the Tenth Amendment, as a limit on Congress, is enforced by the political process. There is no zone of activities reserved to the states for their exclusive control. (C) is wrong because the Fourteenth Amendment does not apply to the federal government; it only regulates state and local governments. Moreover, the Privileges and Immunities Clause of the Fourteenth Amendment is rarely used as a basis for declaring laws unconstitutional.

Answer to Question 13

(A) The statute is constitutional as properly within the state's power to enact. The state can punish through its criminal law whatever behavior it wishes, provided the state statute does not violate the Constitution. There is no constitutional violation in punishing those who attempt to intimidate state officials. (B) is wrong because the fact that the statute does not conflict with civil rights legislation does not automatically make the statute constitutional. Both (C) and (D) are incorrect statements of the law.

Answer to Question 14

(D) The couple will prevail if the state fails to meet its burden. Since the statute affects the couple's right to privacy of marriage and family matters, the state must show that the law is necessary to effectuate a compelling state interest. (A) is incorrect because it involves an improper test, since fundamental rights are involved here. (B) and (C) are incorrect because they improperly allocate the burden of proof.

Answer to Question 15

(A) The court should reverse the conviction on substantive due process grounds. The Supreme Court in *Lawrence v. Texas* (overruling *Bowers v. Hardwick*) held that a state law criminalizing sodomy between members of the same sex violates the Due Process Clause of the United States Constitution. (C) would have been a correct answer before the *Lawrence* decision. However, the Supreme Court now holds that the state has no legitimate interest in prohibiting private sexual conduct. (B) is incorrect because it is too broad a statement. The sexual conduct must be conducted in a private setting and must not be commercial in nature. Even though the defendants were in a state park, they had an expectation of privacy while in a tent in an isolated location in a park in which camping was permitted. Thus, (D) is wrong.

Answer to Question 16

(C) The state has the burden under the "substantial relationship" test. In *Craig v. Boren*, the Court imposed an intermediate standard of review in cases involving sex discrimination, placing the burden of proof on the state to show that a classification based on gender serves important governmental objectives and that there is a nexus between those objectives and the challenged statute, as stated in (C). (A) is incorrect because it states the standard of review in cases involving economic and social welfare legislation. The challenge to this statute is that it creates a gender-based classification and therefore is subject to an intermediate standard of review. (B) is incorrect because it states the strict scrutiny test applied to cases involving suspect classifications or implicating fundamental interests. Since this statute involves a gender-based classification and not a suspect classification such as race or alienage, it is subject to only an intermediate standard of review. (D) is incorrect because it addresses the rational basis test applied to challenges to economic and social welfare legislation. Further, this choice incorrectly places the burden of proof on the state. When the rational basis standard is applicable, the burden is on the person attacking the constitutionality of the statute.

Answer to Question 17

(B) The doctor's best constitutional argument is the Equal Protection Clause. Since 1978, the Supreme Court has ruled in a handful of cases that a state may require citizenship for important state jobs that directly affect the political process, provided the state has a rational basis for such discrimination. [*See, e.g.*, Foley v. Connelie (1978)—state troopers; Ambach v. Norwick (1979)—public school teachers; Cabell v. Chavez-Salido (1982)—probation officer] This is an exception to the usual rule that state classifications of aliens are "suspect" and subject to strict scrutiny. Serving as a doctor is unlikely to fit this exception. (A) is wrong because the Ex Post Facto Clause only applies to retroactive criminal laws. (C) is incorrect because the doctor does not have a liberty or property interest in the possible government job. Because there is not a deprivation of life, liberty, or property, the Due Process Clause is inapplicable. (D) is wrong because the Privileges and Immunities Clause merely forbids a state from infringing on rights of national citizenship and has essentially been a dead letter since the *Slaughterhouse Cases* (1873). Thus, (B)—the Equal Protection Clause—is the basis for the doctor's strongest argument.

Answer to Question 18

(A) If the attorney is fired, she has a right to a hearing to determine whether her First Amendment rights were violated by her dismissal. Under the Due Process Clause of the Fifth Amendment, a person has a liberty interest in the exercise of specific rights provided by the Constitution, including freedom of speech. A government employee may not be fired for expressing her views regarding public issues, but can be fired for speech that disrupts the employer's policies or undermines the employer's authority. Under the Court's expansive interpretation of what a public issue is in this context [*See* Rankin v. McPherson (1987)], the attorney's statement would probably qualify. At the very least, she can make a sufficient showing that her termination violates her free speech rights to be entitled to a hearing on the issue under procedural due process principles. [*See* Givhan v. Western Line Consolidated School District (1979)] (B) is wrong because the attorney does not appear to have a property interest in her job. A public employee who is subject to removal only for "cause" has a property interest in her job and must be given notice of the charges against her that are to be the basis for her job termination, and a pretermination opportunity to respond to those charges. Here, however, the attorney did not have a property interest in her job. She could have been dismissed for no reason at all. She was not covered by the labor contract between the agency and its clerical workers, and there appears to be no other basis for her to claim an entitlement to continued employment. (C) is wrong because the attorney is entitled to a hearing as long as she can raise a prima facie claim that her speech, which was regarding an important health issue and the perception of her agency, was on a public issue and therefore protected by the First Amendment. (D) is wrong for two reasons. As discussed above, the attorney does not have a property interest in her job. Also, due process does not necessarily entitle her to a pretermination evidentiary hearing; a post-termination evidentiary hearing is probably sufficient. [*See* Cleveland Board of Education v. Loudermill (1985)]

Answer to Question 19

(C) The newspaper will prevail on First Amendment grounds. In *Nebraska Press Association v. Stewart* (1976), the Supreme Court made it clear that gag orders on the press are impermissible as a way to secure a defendant's right to a fair trial. Although prejudicial publicity can pose a serious problem, the Supreme Court held that it virtually always should be dealt with by means other than prior restraints. (A) is incorrect because a change of venue is only one of many techniques available to judges dealing with prejudicial pretrial publicity. Delaying trial and screening and sequestering jurors are among the other means that can be used. (B) is incorrect because the constitutional right to a public trial under the Sixth Amendment belongs to the defendant, not the media or the public. Prior restraints violate the First Amendment rights of freedom of speech and press. (D) is incorrect because such prior restraints are virtually always unconstitutional. Also, (D) fails to indicate that less restrictive alternatives would be ineffective. Prior restraints are tolerable, if ever, only if no less restrictive alternative would work.

Answer to Question 20

(B) The ordinance is a valid time, place, and manner regulation. Zoning ordinances are considered a time, place, and manner restriction on speech when they regulate adult entertainment and bookstores, even though that type of speech is singled out for regulation because of its content. Therefore, this ordinance is valid. Preserving property values in commercial zones is a substantial governmental purpose. If there are industrial zones in the city where property values will not be harmed by adult bookstores and they are reasonably available, then those conditions will sustain the validity of the ordinance. (A) is incorrect because adult bookstores are treated much like commercial speech. There is a very limited right to limit the content of the speech produced by adult bookstores. The city cannot use its zoning ordinance to completely ban or regulate the bookstores to ensure that the messages they produce are acceptable to the neighbors. (C) is incorrect because it is too broad. The city may impose reasonable place restrictions on the speech of adult bookstores to achieve substantial governmental objectives as long as there is a reasonable alternative to the dissemination of the speech. (D) is incorrect because the adverse secondary effects of adult entertainment are a matter of legitimate governmental concern, and it can reasonably regulate those stores and theaters through zoning ordinances to achieve that objective as long as there is a reasonable outlet for the dissemination of the speech.

Answer to Question 21

(C) The strongest defense is based on free expression and assembly grounds. Since the statute regulates content of the speech rather than conduct, the state would need to establish a compelling interest behind the legislation for the law to be valid. This puts the burden on the state to prove the need for the legislation. (A) is incorrect because the Due Process Clause of the Fifth Amendment applies to the federal government, not to the states. (B) is incorrect because any discrimination that may arise from the statute is merely an effect of facially neutral legislation and not subject to the Equal Protection Clause. (D) is incorrect because Article IV prohibits discrimination by a state in favor of its own citizens, which is not the case here.

Answer to Question 22

(C) The court should rule that the statute is unconstitutionally vague or overbroad. Criminal laws that are either vague or overbroad are unconstitutional because they put a chilling effect on free speech rights. Under this statute, it is a criminal offense to "aid, abet, incite, urge, or encourage behavior that amounts to a breach of the peace." Clearly, it is difficult to know what behavior is proscribed. Thus, (A) and (B) are incorrect. (D) is far too broad a statement and is not true. The state may limit political protests as long as the speech restriction is a reasonable time, place, and manner limitation that is not content-based.

Answer to Question 23

(B) The court may not properly determine the reasonableness of the leader's religious beliefs. The freedom to hold religious beliefs, no matter how contrary to society's acceptance, is absolute and no court may inquire into the reasonableness of any person's religious beliefs. If a statute, as written or as applied, interferes with a citizen's religious beliefs, the burden is on the state to show a compelling public interest in the enforcement of the statute against such a citizen. Thus, the trial court can require the state to bear the burden of persuasion in this case, and (A) is not the right answer. Although the state cannot inquire into the reasonableness of the belief itself, it can first determine the nature of a defendant's belief, and, once the belief is determined, whether the defendant has a sincere and good faith belief in the particular tenet which has run afoul of some state law. Thus, (C) and (D) are incorrect.

Answer to Question 24

(D) The county should prevail because the regulation was not intended to close the church. A state regulation promulgated to protect the health and welfare of the citizens of the state will prevail over constitutional objections, as long as the state regulation was not instituted merely to discriminate against a particular religious group. In this case, the building code was enacted to protect the health and safety of the state's citizens and not simply to close down the church. Therefore, the county will prevail over any constitutional objections raised by the church, and (B) is incorrect. (A) is incorrect because an exemption for the church would not constitute an establishment of religion. As long as a special exemption is not made for this organization that would be or has been denied to other organizations (at least those similarly situated), an exemption could constitutionally be granted. This situation is analogous to a property tax exemption for all religious and charitable organizations, which is permissible. As long as this exemption is not allowed to promote this group over others, it should be permissible in this case. That does not mean, however, that an exemption is required by the applicable constitutional doctrines; it is merely permitted. (C) is incorrect because there is no clear equal protection argument made out by these facts. The church has not shown that it has been treated differently from others similarly situated. The fact that this statute impacts poor organizations more severely is not enough to invalidate it, since it is a valid police power regulation and poverty is not a suspect class. Likewise, the church has not shown that the action was brought because it had exercised any of its fundamental rights. Therefore, there is no equal protection argument on these facts.

Answer to Question 25

(A) The court should hold for the company because it has a valid contract. A state violates the prohibition against impairing the obligation of contract when it substantially impairs any contracts to which it is a party and the impairment does not meet the various exceptions recognized by the Court. Here, the state is simply seeking to reduce its contractual financial obligations, and its decision would violate the prohibition. (B) is wrong because detrimental reliance on the part of the corporation is not required. (C) is wrong because, while states have great latitude in purely economic and social matters, the state may not act in violation of a constitutional prohibition. (D) is wrong because, while the Eleventh Amendment provides that federal courts do not have jurisdiction in suits against the states, that functional equivalent of sovereign immunity does not prohibit suits alleging that state officials have violated the Constitution.

Contracts

Questions and Analytical Answers

barbri®

Contracts

1. Ⓐ Ⓑ Ⓒ Ⓓ
2. Ⓐ Ⓑ Ⓒ Ⓓ
3. Ⓐ Ⓑ Ⓒ Ⓓ
4. Ⓐ Ⓑ Ⓒ Ⓓ
5. Ⓐ Ⓑ Ⓒ Ⓓ

6. Ⓐ Ⓑ Ⓒ Ⓓ
7. Ⓐ Ⓑ Ⓒ Ⓓ
8. Ⓐ Ⓑ Ⓒ Ⓓ
9. Ⓐ Ⓑ Ⓒ Ⓓ
10. Ⓐ Ⓑ Ⓒ Ⓓ

11. Ⓐ Ⓑ Ⓒ Ⓓ
12. Ⓐ Ⓑ Ⓒ Ⓓ
13. Ⓐ Ⓑ Ⓒ Ⓓ
14. Ⓐ Ⓑ Ⓒ Ⓓ
15. Ⓐ Ⓑ Ⓒ Ⓓ

16. Ⓐ Ⓑ Ⓒ Ⓓ
17. Ⓐ Ⓑ Ⓒ Ⓓ
18. Ⓐ Ⓑ Ⓒ Ⓓ
19. Ⓐ Ⓑ Ⓒ Ⓓ
20. Ⓐ Ⓑ Ⓒ Ⓓ

21. Ⓐ Ⓑ Ⓒ Ⓓ
22. Ⓐ Ⓑ Ⓒ Ⓓ
23. Ⓐ Ⓑ Ⓒ Ⓓ
24. Ⓐ Ⓑ Ⓒ Ⓓ
25. Ⓐ Ⓑ Ⓒ Ⓓ

Question 1

A weather vane collector placed the following ad in a newspaper: "I will pay $300 for information as to where I can purchase a Connecticut copper weather vane with Victorian Serpentine Motif in good condition." The ad, which included contact information, was placed on Friday, December 5, and was to run a full week, starting on Sunday the 7th. A friend of the collector's knew of his quest for the weather vane, but she did not see the newspaper ad. On Sunday morning, she saw at a swap meet the exact type of weather vane the collector sought and called him to tell him about it. The collector hurried down to the swap meet and got his weather vane at a good price.

On Monday, December 8, the friend saw the collector's ad in an open newspaper. She called the collector and asked him to pay her $300 for the tip. After he declined, saying the offer was revoked when he purchased the weather vane, she sued the collector for her reward.

Will she prevail?

(A) Yes; the collector must pay his friend because he bought the vane based on her tip.

(B) Yes; the collector must pay his friend because his revocation was ineffective.

(C) No; the friend cannot collect because she did not know of the offer when she accepted.

(D) No; the friend cannot collect because the collector's ad was not an offer.

Question 2

On June 1, a homeowner sent a letter to a painter that stated, "I will pay you $8,000 for painting the exterior of my home, provided you commence painting by July 1 and finish by July 10." On June 5, the painter sent the owner the following letter, "I am available to paint your house, but I cannot do the work for less than $10,000." On June 10, the painter sent the following letter to the homeowner, "I have changed my mind. I will do the work for $8,000. I will start on July 1 and finish painting before July 10 unless I hear from you differently." The homeowner never responded to the painter's letter. On June 30, the homeowner left the country for a one-month vacation in Europe. Unknown to the homeowner, the painter commenced painting the house on July 1.

At this point, does the homeowner have a contractual obligation to pay the painter $8,000 upon completion of the painting?

(A) Yes, provided the painter completes the painting by July 10.

(B) Yes, because the painter accepted the contract before the homeowner materially changed his position in reliance on the painter's rejection.

(C) No, because the painter rejected the homeowner's offer to paint the homeowner's house for $8,000.

(D) No, because the homeowner left the country without ever accepting the painter's offer to do the work as originally requested.

Question 3

A dog owner owned a mongrel of little monetary value. One day, the dog disappeared, and the owner placed the following advertisement in the newspaper: "I will pay $500 to anyone who returns my dog." A man found the dog the next day. Knowing to whom the dog belonged, the man took the dog home, intending to return it that night. Before he returned the dog, the man read the dog owner's advertisement in the newspaper.

Assuming that the dog owner's advertisement was an offer, the man who found the dog:

(A) Can recover $500, as he has accepted the offer.

(B) Can recover $500 if he returns the dog to the dog owner.

(C) Cannot recover the $500, even if he returns the dog, because he did not have knowledge of the offer when he found the dog.

(D) Cannot recover the $500 because the dog owner's promise was not represented by a signed memorandum.

Question 4

A homeowner mailed a letter to a prospective buyer on January 15 offering to sell her house for $25,000. The letter was delivered to the buyer on January 17. The buyer mailed a letter to the homeowner on January 19 stating that she accepted the offer.

The buyer's letter of January 19 operates as an acceptance even if:

(A) The homeowner telephones the buyer on January 18 telling Buyer that she is revoking her offer.

(B) The buyer's letter is lost by the post office.

(C) The buyer misaddressed the envelope and, as a result, it was not delivered to the homeowner until February 1, after the homeowner had sold the property to a third party.

(D) The buyer knew that the homeowner had sold the property to a third party on January 18.

Question 5

After a series of arsons, a city council adopted a resolution on January 5 providing that the city would pay $15,000 for the arrest and conviction of anyone found guilty of any of the arsons committed in the city. The city council proceedings on January 5 were telecast live over the city's local public-access cable channel. No other publicity was given by the city.

Thereafter, concerned about budgetary problems, the city council by resolution on January 25 repealed its reward offer. That meeting was not telecast by the local public-access cable channel. The repeal resolution was contained in the minutes of the city council meeting, which was published in the legal pages of the local paper.

On February 1, an eavesdropper overheard a conversation in a barroom implicating a known arsonist in the arsons. He informed the police about the conversation. The police then called the suspect in for questioning, and after properly being advised of his rights, the suspect confessed. The suspect was subsequently convicted of the arsons.

In a suit by the eavesdropper against the city for the reward:

(A) The eavesdropper will prevail if he knew of the January 5 resolution at the time he talked to the police, unless he also had actual knowledge of the January 25 repeal.

(B) The eavesdropper will prevail, provided that he had no actual knowledge of the January 25 repeal.

(C) The city will prevail, because the January 25 resolution effectively revoked the offer.

(D) The city will prevail, because the offer was not accepted in a reasonable time.

Question 6

A large dairy regularly supplied milk to local grocery stores located in the same city. A large grocery store in the city which had not previously done business with the dairy sent a written order to the dairy for 50 cases of homogenized whole milk at the wholesale market price of $10 per case for prompt shipment. The warehouse clerk at the dairy facility negligently shipped 50 cases of low-fat milk instead of the grade which was ordered.

When the milk is delivered at the grocery store by a common carrier, which of the following is the most appropriate statement of the parties' rights and duties?

(A) The store must accept the delivery, even though it is nonconforming, because a contract was formed when the dairy shipped it.

(B) A contract was formed but breached by the dairy when it shipped nonconforming goods, which the store has no obligation to accept.

(C) Because the goods are nonconforming, the store can treat the delivery as a counteroffer and refuse acceptance.

(D) The dairy's shipment of the milk is a counteroffer, but the store is under an obligation to reship it to the dairy at the dairy's expense if it decides not to accept the delivery.

Question 7

On September 1, an art collector offered to sell one of his expensive paintings to a buyer. The buyer, who was a friend of the collector, wanted a few days to make up her mind, so the collector and the buyer decided that the collector would keep his offer to her open until September 8 in exchange for a payment of $5. Later that week an art investor tendered to the collector double what he was asking for the painting. On the morning of September 8, the buyer telephoned the collector to tell him that she wanted the painting but his phone was out of order, so she wrote out a check for the agreed-on amount and dropped it into a mailbox before leaving town. On September 9 the collector, not having heard from the buyer, sold the painting to the investor.

Who owns the painting?

(A) The buyer, because she had a valid option contract with the collector and effectively accepted the collector's offer to sell the painting.

(B) The investor, because $5 is inadequate consideration for an option contract involving an expensive purchase such as this one.

(C) The investor, because the collector sold the painting to the investor on September 9 before receiving the buyer's check.

(D) The collector, because a sale of goods priced at $500 or more must be in writing to be enforceable.

Question 8

After a difficult divorce, a mother wrote to her son and daughter the following:

> In consideration of your emotional support for me during that trying time and your love and affection for me, I promise to divide my estate between you in equal shares. You know you can count on your mother's word.

The daughter thereafter continued her usual practice of calling her mother once a week and visiting her at Christmas and on her birthday until her mother died three years later. Shortly after the funeral, the daughter learned that the mother's will made the son the sole legatee.

If the daughter sues the executor of the mother's estate for one half of that estate, based on the mother's letter to her, she will:

(A) Win, because she relied to her detriment on her mother's promise by visiting her mother.

(B) Win, because her emotional support of her mother during the divorce proceedings constituted valid consideration for her mother's promise.

(C) Win, because even though her mother's letter is a promise to make a gift in the future, the promise is in writing and intended by her to be enforceable and therefore needs no consideration.

(D) Lose, because the mother's promise was not supported by consideration.

Question 9

A young girl was 10 years old when her parents died and her aunt took her into her home to care for her. The aunt became very attached to her niece and after a couple of years told her niece that she would be well cared for and that she would inherit everything that the aunt had.

When the niece was 17 years old, her aunt told her that she should go to college and promised to leave the niece $10,000 in her will. While the niece was in college, she lived with her aunt, who paid her tuition and gave her $10 a week.

Soon after the niece graduated from college, her aunt died. Her will, which was dated a year before her death, contained a $500 bequest to the niece and left the rest of her property, valued at about $35,000, to a charitable institution.

In a suit by the niece against her aunt's estate for $10,000, based on her aunt's promise to pay her that amount, the best defense would be that:

(A) There was no offer and acceptance.

(B) The promise was not in writing.

(C) There was no consideration for the promise.

(D) The promise is unenforceable because the niece was a minor when it was made.

Question 10

A large producer of bread wrote to a distributor of flour, asking, "How much will you charge to supply my needs for flour for the next year?" The distributor replied in writing that it could supply the producer with all the flour it would need next year at a specified price per pound. The producer wrote back, "Your offer to supply me with flour is hereby accepted, provided that you agree to a 10% discount if payment is made within 10 days from date of billing."

The producer's reply concerning a 10% discount would probably be characterized as:

(A) An acceptance with a proposal for an additional term, provided both parties are merchants.

(B) An acceptance with a proposal for an additional term, whether or not both parties are merchants.

(C) A counteroffer, but not a rejection.

(D) A rejection and counteroffer.

Question 11

A debtor owed $50,000 to a creditor. One week before the statute of limitations was to expire, the debtor's mother sent the creditor a letter stating that she was sure that her son was about to pay the debt, and that if her son did not pay, she would. Relying on the mother's letter, the creditor allowed the statute of limitations to expire without bringing an action to recover the money. The debtor refused to pay the creditor.

If the creditor brings suit against the mother for the $50,000, will he prevail?

(A) No, because the statute of limitations has run against the son's debt.

(B) No, because the mother received no bargained-for exchange to support her promise.

(C) Yes, because the creditor reasonably and foreseeably relied on the mother's promise.

(D) Yes, because of the main purpose exception to the statute of limitations.

Question 12

The proprietor of a men's shop contracted on May 1 with a wholesaler of shirts to buy 300 men's long-sleeve white cotton shirts for $4 per shirt, or $1,200. The parties each signed a purchase order calling for delivery of the shirts to the proprietor's place of business and payment of the purchase price on July 1. Two days later, the wholesaler discovered that he had made a mistake in his price quote. He told the proprietor that, unless the proprietor paid him $8 per shirt, or a total price of $2,400, he would not be able to deliver the shirts. The proprietor refused to pay anything more than $1,200. When the wholesaler failed to deliver the shirts on July 1, the proprietor purchased 300 comparable shirts for $8 per shirt and brought suit against the wholesaler for damages.

In this lawsuit,

(A) The wholesaler will prevail because he made a unilateral mistake.

(B) The wholesaler will prevail because of the doctrine of mutual mistake.

(C) The wholesaler will prevail if the proprietor had reason to know on May 1 that the wholesaler made a mistake in quoting the price of $4 per shirt.

(D) The proprietor will prevail.

Question 13

A purchasing agent of a steel company invited bids from several coal companies for 10 lots of metallurgical coal. The coal company with the winning bid offered $750,000, which was substantially under the market price for metallurgical coal. The agent immediately made a written agreement with the coal company to carry out the purchase, but several weeks before the coal was to be delivered, the coal company notified the agent that it had made an arithmetical error in pricing the coal and that the price should have been $1 million. The coal company requested a price increase to $825,000, which the agent approved in writing.

If the agent had no reason to believe that the coal company had made an error in its initial calculations, the modification by which the steel company agreed to pay $825,000 is:

(A) Enforceable, because the request for the modification was made in good faith.

(B) Enforceable, only if the coal company can establish that enforcement of the contract at the $750,000 price would be unconscionable.

(C) Unenforceable, because the coal company was under a preexisting duty to sell at $750,000.

(D) Unenforceable, unless the arithmetical error is tantamount to changed circumstances.

Question 14

A ski-shop operator ordered by telephone 12 pairs of lined ski gloves from a glove manufacturer at its list price of $600 per dozen; delivery in 30 days. The manufacturer orally accepted the offer, and immediately faxed to the ski shop operator this signed memo: "Confirming our agreement today for your purchase of a dozen pairs of lined ski gloves for $600, the shipment will be delivered in 30 days."

Although the ski-shop operator received and read the manufacturer's message within minutes after its dispatch, she changed her mind three weeks later about the purchase and rejected the conforming shipment when it timely arrived.

On learning of the rejection, does the manufacturer have a cause of action against the ski-shop operator for breach of contract?

(A) Yes, because the gloves were identified to the contract and tendered to the ski shop operator.

(B) Yes, because the manufacturer's faxed memo to the ski-shop operator was sufficient to make the agreement enforceable.

(C) No, because the agreed price was $600 and the ski-shop operator never signed a writing evidencing a contract with the manufacturer.

(D) No, because the ski-shop operator neither paid for nor accepted any of the goods tendered.

Question 15

A parks and recreation association placed an order for 100 12-inch softballs with a softball manufacturer. The order stated that the association would pay the current market price for the softballs and requested prompt shipment. The manufacturer promptly shipped 100 16-inch softballs to the association because the manufacturer's shipping director negligently misread the size listed on the shipping instructions.

Which of the following best describes the association's rights and duties upon arrival of the 16-inch softballs?

(A) A contract was formed by the manufacturer's prompt shipment of the 16-inch softballs and the association must accept the softballs and offset its damages against the purchase price.

(B) A contract was formed by the manufacturer's prompt shipment of the 16-inch softballs, but the association is not required to accept the softballs and may sue the manufacturer for its damages.

(C) The manufacturer's prompt shipment was a counteroffer and the association can accept the softballs or reship them to the manufacturer because it has a duty to mitigate damages.

(D) The manufacturer's prompt shipment was a counteroffer, and the association can refuse to accept the softballs, but has no cause of action for damages.

Question 16

A catering company entered into a written contract with a dish supplier to purchase 5,000 plastic dishes at $.10 per dish. The contract called for the supplier to deliver the 5,000 dishes to the caterer on or before October 1. On October 1, the supplier delivered only 3,000 dishes to the caterer. The supplier informed the caterer that it was experiencing manufacturing delays and would deliver the other 2,000 dishes by October 31 at the latest. The caterer accepted delivery of the 3,000 dishes, but because it had a number of catering jobs lined up for early October, the caterer was forced to purchase 2,000 dishes from another supplier at a price of $.12 per dish. The supplier demanded that the caterer pay $300 for the 3,000 dishes delivered, but the caterer refused to pay anything.

If the supplier sues the caterer for breach of contract, the supplier will recover:

(A) $300, the price under the contract for the 3,000 dishes that were delivered, with no deduction for the caterer's extra cost, because the caterer waived its right to cover when it accepted the supplier's tender without expressly reserving its rights.

(B) The reasonable value of the 3,000 dishes that were delivered less $40, which is the extra cost incurred by the caterer to obtain the balance of the dishes.

(C) $260, the price under the contract for the 3,000 dishes that were delivered less $40, which is the extra cost incurred by the caterer to obtain the balance of the dishes.

(D) Nothing, because the supplier is in material breach of the contract until it tenders delivery of the last 2,000 dishes.

Question 17

A gourmet food company entered into a long-term contract with an airline, under which the food company would supply the airline with 5 million Chicken Kiev gourmet dinners over a five-year period at a special rate of $2 per unit. The food company insisted as a term of the contract that the airline agree to purchase from a microwave supplier, and to install in each of its planes, a microwave oven specifically designed to heat Chicken Kiev frozen dinners, in part because the food company owned considerable stock in the microwave supplier. The contract between the food company and the airline had a clause that authorized "oral modifications by the contracting parties."

One month after the contract was signed but before any dinners were delivered, the airline informed the food company that it would have difficulty complying with the provision requiring purchase of the supplier's microwaves because the supplier's products had increased dramatically in price. Subsequent negotiations between the food company and the airline led to an oral agreement to increase the price per dinner to $2.08 per unit and eliminate the supplier's microwave requirement.

If the supplier sues the airline for enforcement of the contract, the most likely result will be:

(A) Judgment for the supplier, because under the U.C.C. the oral modification is not valid and the supplier's rights vested when it brought suit.

(B) Judgment for the supplier, because it was a third-party beneficiary to the original contract and it did not agree to the modification.

(C) Judgment for the airline, because the contract was between the airline and the food company, and by its terms an oral modification was permissible.

(D) Judgment for the airline, because the supplier's rights had not vested when the modification took place.

Question 18

A dealer in oriental rugs acquired an antique rug measuring 24 feet by 36 feet. A banker inspected the rug and orally agreed to buy it for the asking price of $65,000, providing he was successful in purchasing the house he was trying to buy, because it had a living room large enough to accommodate the rug. The sale agreement was later reduced to writing, but the provision concerning the purchase of the house was not included in the written agreement.

If the banker is unsuccessful in acquiring the house he wants because the owner decided not to sell, and the dealer sues the banker for the purchase price:

(A) The dealer will prevail because the original oral agreement need not be in writing to be enforceable.

(B) The dealer will prevail because of the parol evidence rule.

(C) The banker will prevail because he was unable to acquire the house he wanted.

(D) The banker will prevail because the dealer is not entitled to specific performance.

Question 19

An owner of a piece of waterfront property contracted in writing with a contractor to rebuild the owner's dock in accordance with plans and specifications prepared by the owner. The agreed contract price was $50,000, $25,000 of which was payable on May 1 when the job was to commence and the balance due upon completion of the work.

On March 1, the contractor notified the property owner that the contractor would lose money on the job at that price, and would not proceed with the work unless the property owner agreed to increase the price to $80,000. The property owner did not respond to the contractor, instead making a written contract with a third party to repair the dock, commencing May 1, for $60,000, which was the fair market cost of the work to be done. On May 1, both the contractor and the third party showed up at the dock to begin work, the contractor telling the property owner that he had decided to take the loss and would repair the dock for $50,000 as originally agreed. The property owner dismissed the contractor and allowed the third party to begin work on the dock.

In a contract action by the contractor against the property owner, which of the following would the court decide?

(A) The contractor will win because the property owner did not tell him before May 1 about the contract with the third party.

(B) The contractor will win because he attempted to perform the contract as originally agreed.

(C) The property owner will win because the contractor in legal effect committed a total breach of contract.

(D) The property owner will win because the third party's contract price was $20,000 lower than the $80,000 demanded by the contractor on March 1.

Question 20

A golf pro entered into an employment contract with a country club to be its golf pro. The agreement specified that the golf pro would run the pro shop and provide private instruction to members from April through September of each year for the next five years, at a monthly salary of $5,000, plus instructional fees. During those months, the club's other instructor was playing on the professional tour and was unavailable.

On March 15, the club's manager received an e-mail from the golf pro, stating: "Made the final cut in Sarasota Winter Open. May not be able to get to club by April 1. Could be delayed until 5th if playoff necessary." The club's manager asked his attorney whether he should bring an immediate action against the golf pro for breach of contract.

Which of the following is the most accurate advice for the manager?

(A) Do not file suit; a repudiation must be in a signed writing to be of legal effect.

(B) Do not file suit; the golf pro has not repudiated the contract.

(C) File suit, but only if the club has changed its position to its detriment in reliance on the e-mail.

(D) File suit, because the golf pro has repudiated the contract.

Question 21

A manufacturer and a buyer entered into a written contract for the manufacturer to produce and sell to the buyer 1,000 whirligigs at a price of $10 per whirligig. The contract expressly provided that the buyer shall have no liability under the contract unless 1,000 whirligigs are delivered to the buyer at his place of business no later than May 1. Nine hundred whirligigs, meeting the buyer's specifications, were tendered by the manufacturer on May 1. The remaining 100 whirligigs were tendered on May 3. The buyer refused to accept any of the whirligigs.

In an action by the manufacturer against the buyer, which of the following would best support the manufacturer's case, assuming it can be proven?

(A) The buyer had orally agreed, just prior to the time the written contract was executed, to accept and pay for partial deliveries of the whirligigs.

(B) Whirligigs are a unique product produced only by the manufacturer and in a size and tolerance that varies with the needs of each purchaser.

(C) Delivery of the 100 whirligigs on May 1 was delayed by a storm which disrupted the shipper's activities, and was not the manufacturer's fault.

(D) A drop in the buyer's credit rating from good to fair had caused the manufacturer not to produce and tender the full 1,000 whirligigs on or before May 1.

Question 22

A patient owed a physician $25,000 for professional services. The physician orally assigned this claim to her adult daughter as a wedding gift. Shortly thereafter, on suffering substantial losses in the stock market, the physician assigned by a signed writing the same claim to her stockbroker in partial satisfaction of advances legally made by the broker in the physician's previous stock-market transactions. Subsequently, the patient, without knowledge of either assignment, paid the physician the $25,000 then due, which the physician promptly lost at a horse track, although she remains solvent.

Assuming that Article 9 of the Uniform Commercial Code does not apply to either of the assignments in this situation, which of the following is a correct statement of the parties' rights and liabilities?

(A) As the assignee prior in time, the daughter can recover $25,000 from the patient, who acted at her peril in paying the physician.

(B) As the sole assignee for value, the broker can recover $25,000 from the patient, who acted at her peril in paying the physician.

(C) Neither the daughter nor the broker can recover from the patient, but the daughter, though not the broker, can recover $25,000 from the physician.

(D) Neither the daughter nor the broker can recover from the patient, but the broker, though not the daughter, can recover $25,000 from the physician.

Question 23

In a single writing, a painter contracted with a farmer to paint three identical barns on her rural estate for $2,000 each. The contract provided for the farmer's payment of $6,000 on the painter's completion of the work on all three barns. The painter did not ask for any payment when the first barn was completely painted, but she demanded $4,000 after painting the second barn. The farmer rightfully refused the painter's demand for payment at that time.

If the painter immediately terminates the contract without painting the third barn, what is the painter entitled to recover from the farmer?

(A) Nothing, because payment was expressly conditioned on completion of all three barns.

(B) The painter's expenditures plus anticipated profit in painting the first two barns up to a maximum recovery of $4,000.

(C) The reasonable value of the painter's services in painting the two barns, less the farmer's damages, if any, for the painter's failure to paint the third barn.

(D) The amount that the combined value of the two painted barns has been increased by the painter's work.

Question 24

A contractor agreed to build a power plant for a public utility and solicited bids from subcontractors. A subcontractor agreed with the contractor to lay the foundation for $200,000. The subcontractor supplied goods and services worth $150,000, for which the contractor made progress payments aggregating $100,000 as required by the subcontract. The subcontractor then breached by refusing unjustifiably to perform further. The contractor reasonably spent $120,000 to have the work completed by another subcontractor.

If the subcontractor sues the contractor for the reasonable value of benefits conferred, and the contractor counterclaims for breach of contract, the court should rule that:

(A) The subcontractor recovers $50,000, the benefit conferred on the contractor for which the subcontractor has not been paid.

(B) The subcontractor recovers $30,000, the benefit the subcontractor conferred on the contractor minus the $20,000 in damages incurred by the contractor.

(C) The contractor recovers $20,000, the excess over the contract price that was paid by the contractor for the performance it had bargained to receive from the subcontractor.

(D) Neither party recovers anything, because the subcontractor committed a material, unexcused breach and the contractor received a $50,000 benefit from the subcontractor for which the subcontractor has not been paid.

Question 25

A high-volume pleasure-boat retailer entered into a written contract to sell a customer a power boat for $120,000. The retailer could obtain from the manufacturer, for $90,500, as many of these boats as it could sell. As the contract provided, the customer paid the retailer $40,000 in advance and promised to pay the full balance on delivery of the boat. The contract contained no provision for liquidated damages. Prior to the agreed delivery date, the customer notified the retailer that he would be financially unable to conclude the purchase; the retailer thereafter resold the boat that the customer had ordered to a third person for $120,000 cash.

If the customer sues the retailer for restitution of the $40,000 advance payment, which of the following should the court decide?

(A) The customer's claim should be denied, because, as the party in default, he is deemed to have lost any right to restitution of a benefit conferred on the retailer.

(B) The customer's claim should be denied, because, but for his repudiation, the retailer would have made a profit on two boat sales instead of one.

(C) The customer's claim should be upheld in the amount of $40,000 minus the amount of the retailer's lost profit under its contract with the customer.

(D) The customer's claims should be upheld in the amount of $30,500 ($40,000 minus $500 as statutory damages under the U.C.C.).

STOP

Answer to Question 1

(C) The friend cannot recover because she did not know of the offer. Although the collector's placement of the ad was an offer, his friend did not accept by giving the requested information, because she did not know about the ad when she gave the collector the lead on the weather vane. The general rule on public offers is this: an offer of reward is an offer to enter into a unilateral contract, and if made to the public generally, it may be accepted by anyone to whom it becomes known. One who performs the requested act has done all that is necessary for acceptance, but if he does not intend that his acts constitute an acceptance, no contract results. Thus, where he has no knowledge of the offer, no act of his can be deemed an acceptance. [*See* Restatement of Contracts §§23 comment (c); 51 comment (a)] (A) and (B) are incorrect because they reach the wrong result; there is no contract with the friend for the reasons above. The fact that the revocation may have been ineffective begs the issue, because even though the offer was still in existence until effectively revoked, there can be no contract without the proper form of acceptance as noted above. (D) states the rationale incorrectly; the friend loses because she did not accept, not because of a defect in the offer. This ad was specific enough to constitute an offer.

Answer to Question 2

(D) The homeowner is not obligated to pay the painter. The painter's June 5 communication was a rejection of the offer for employment by the homeowner on June 1. The painter's June 10 communication, therefore, created a new offer that would require some further manifestation of acceptance by the owner in order to form a contract. Note that the language "unless I hear from you differently" has no effect on the outcome. Thus, (A) and (B) are wrong. (C) is not as good an answer as (D) because it does not go far enough. While it is true that the painter rejected the homeowner's offer, what is relevant is whether the homeowner accepted the painter's subsequent offer. The painter may have a cause of action against the homeowner under an unjust enrichment theory. However, the question asks if the homeowner has a ***contractual*** obligation to pay, to which the answer is clearly no.

Answer to Question 3

(B) The man can recover $500 if he returns the dog. The man has not accepted the offer until he performs the requested act, *i.e.*, returning the dog. Once he returns the dog, he has not only accepted the offer but fully completed his performance. At that point, the dog owner must perform his obligation under the contract to pay the man who found the dog $500. (A) is incorrect because it fails to make clear that the man who found the dog must return the dog before he has a right to the money. Finding the dog alone does not entitle the man who found the dog to the reward money. The dog owner has made a unilateral offer, *i.e.*, one that requires acceptance by the doing of an act. The act required for acceptance is the return of the dog. Until the man who found the dog actually returns the dog, he is not entitled to the reward money. (C) is incorrect because the finder's knowledge at the time of finding the dog is not material; only his knowledge at the time of performing the act required for acceptance (*i.e.*, returning the dog) is relevant. Performance of an act requested by an offer made before the offeree has knowledge of the offer does not form a contract; however, where, as here, the offeree has only partially completed performance (finding the dog), completion of the requested performance (returning the dog) with knowledge acts as acceptance. If the man who found the dog had also returned the dog without knowing of the dog owner's offer of a reward for his return, he would have no contractual claim for the reward money. (D) is incorrect because this contract does not fall within the Statute of Frauds. The Statute of Frauds provides that certain contracts are enforceable only if they are evidenced by a written memorandum, signed by the party to be charged. The Statute of Frauds would cover a contract for the sale of goods where the price is $500 or more, but this question does not involve a sale of goods, because the man who found the dog does not have title to the dog. Neither does this transaction come under any other provision of the Statute of Frauds. Therefore, no written signed memorandum is necessary to the dog finder's recovery.

Answer to Question 4

(B) Even if the post office loses the acceptance, a contract is formed. Under the mailbox rule, the acceptance becomes effective when the letter is put out of the possession of the offeree, *i.e.*, when it is properly posted. This is true if the offeror at least implicitly authorized the offeree to use the mails in accepting and the mails are a reasonable means of responding to the offer. Here, the homeowner's mailing of her offer authorized the buyer to use the same method in accepting. (A) is incorrect. If the homeowner telephones the buyer on January 18, revoking the offer, the revocation is good and the attempted acceptance on January 19 is too late. The mailbox rule applies here, and stands for the principle that the acceptance takes effect as soon as it is put out of the possession of the offeree. Thus, the buyer's acceptance would only become effective when she mails it on January 19, which is too late under the additional facts presented in this choice. Unless the offer is irrevocable or a firm offer, the offeror retains the right to revoke the offer at any time prior to acceptance by the offeree. Such revocation is effective upon receipt by the offeree, which is January 18 here. (C) is incorrect. Under the mailbox rule, the acceptance becomes effective when the letter is properly posted. However, where, as here, the envelope is misaddressed, then the rule that the acceptance becomes effective at the time of posting no longer applies. In such a case, the acceptance becomes effective only when received, which is too late in this case. (D) is incorrect because an offeree cannot accept the offer when the offeree knows or has reliable information that the offeror has done some act, usually selling the property, which is inconsistent with an outstanding offer. Revocation of an offer may occur prior to the time of acceptance when the offeree acquires information which would indicate to a reasonable person that the offeror no longer wishes to keep the offer open. Here, the buyer's knowledge that the homeowner sold her house to a third party before the buyer accepted the offer means that the offer was revoked, and the buyer's power of acceptance was terminated.

Answer to Question 5

(A) The eavesdropper will prevail if he knew of the first resolution but not the second. The January 5 resolution was an offer for a unilateral contract which could be accepted by anyone knowing of that offer. The January 25 resolution revoking the earlier offer was not publicized in a manner comparable to the offer. Therefore, there was no revocation except as to those who had actual knowledge of the revocation. (A), which incorporates both of these concepts, is the correct answer. (B) is incorrect because it does not indicate that the eavesdropper had to be aware of the offer before he could claim the reward, which is the applicable rule of law. (C) is incorrect because the January 25 meeting was not televised. Thus, the purported revocation did not get publicity comparable to that of the January 5 offer and therefore would not revoke it, except as to those persons who had actual notice of the revocation. (D) is incorrect because the offer was accepted within four weeks of the time it was made, which is a reasonable time for a reward offer to remain outstanding.

Answer to Question 6

(B) A contract was formed and breached by the shipment. The seller's act of shipping goods constitutes an acceptance of the offer, but, since the goods are nonconforming, the grocery store can reject them under the Uniform Commercial Code and avail itself of the remedies available to a buyer when the seller breaches a sales contract. Under the U.C.C., a buyer who receives nonconforming goods has a choice of rejecting them or accepting them. If the buyer chooses to accept the nonconforming goods, she may recover damages from the seller resulting from the breach, but only if she gives notice to the seller within a reasonable time after she discovers or should have discovered the breach. (A) is incorrect because the grocery store need not accept the milk. If the buyer chooses to reject the goods under the rule stated above, the rejection must be accomplished within a reasonable time after their delivery, and the seller must be notified of the rejection. Thus, the grocery store has the option of rejecting the milk within a reasonable time after its delivery. (C) is incorrect. When a buyer orders goods from a seller, and the seller complies with the order and ships goods, a contract has been formed under the U.C.C. The seller is liable for breach of contract if it ships nonconforming goods, unless it specifically states that it is shipping them as an accommodation, in which case it has made a counteroffer. In this case, the shipment constitutes an acceptance rather than a counteroffer, because there was no notice that this nonconforming tender was shipped only as an accommodation. (D) is incorrect because the dairy's nonconforming shipment was not a counteroffer. As discussed above, the shipment here constitutes an acceptance rather than a counteroffer, because there was no notice that this nonconforming tender was shipped only as an accommodation. In addition, if the grocery store rejects the nonconforming goods but has possession of the goods at the time of rejection, it need only hold them for a reasonable time for the dairy to remove them. If the dairy did not have an agent or office at the place of rejection, the grocery store would be obligated to sell the milk, which is perishable, for the account of the dairy. Because the dairy has an office in the same city as the grocery store, the grocery store need not sell the milk for the dairy's account. The grocery store has no responsibility to reship the milk to the dairy, even at the dairy's expense, if it decides not to accept delivery.

Answer to Question 7

(C) The investor owns the painting. While it is true that the buyer had a valid option contract with the collector, she did not effectively accept the collector's offer to sell the painting when she dropped the check into the mailbox on September 8. The majority view is that acceptance of an option is effective only when received by the offeror, so the usual "mailbox rule" does not apply to make the acceptance effective on dispatch. This means that the buyer did not effectively accept the option within the stated period, *i.e.*, by September 8. When the collector sold the painting to the investor on September 9, this indirectly revoked his offer to the buyer. Because the option period had expired by then, the collector was free to revoke his offer to the buyer at that time, so the investor owns the painting. (A) is incorrect because, as discussed above, the buyer does not own the painting because acceptance of an option is effective only when received by the offeror, and here the collector would not have received the buyer's acceptance until it was too late. (B) is incorrect because the consideration exchanged by the offeree (the buyer) for the offeror's (the collector's) promise not to revoke need not be "adequate"—generally, consideration of any value is sufficient to support an option. (D) is incorrect. While this choice accurately sets forth the Statute of Frauds rule for the sale of goods, the outcome of the dispute here does not turn on this issue. Perhaps if the collector had changed his mind about selling the painting to the investor, he could assert that the Statute of Frauds required the agreement to be in writing to be enforceable. However, the facts do not present that situation.

Answer to Question 8

(D) The daughter will lose because there is no consideration to support the promise. Promises to make gifts in the future are unenforceable even if they are in writing and are intended by the promisor to be enforceable. Hence, (C) is incorrect. A promise to make a gift does not involve a bargained-for exchange, and the requirement of consideration is not fulfilled. (A) is incorrect. This answer states the principle of promissory estoppel. Under the doctrine of promissory estoppel, where there is substantial detrimental reliance by a party on a promise of the promisor, the promise will be enforceable even absent consideration. It is unlikely that the daughter's visiting her mother occasionally and bringing small gifts would constitute substantial detrimental reliance. Absent consideration or a substitute, the mother's original promise would not be enforceable, and her daughter would be unsuccessful in her suit against the executor. (B) is incorrect because the emotional support given to the mother by her daughter was not bargained-for consideration. It was voluntarily given before there was any promise to leave property by will, and therefore does not make the promise enforceable. In order to be part of the bargain, the element of consideration must be part of the bargained-for exchange. Thus, if the mother had said to her daughter, "If you will give me emotional support, I will leave you half my estate," the emotional support thereafter given by the daughter would have been bargained for by the mother in exchange for part of her estate. Because the daughter gave her support gratuitously before the promise, the mother's promise did not induce the legal detriment, and was therefore not supported by consideration.

Answer to Question 9

(C) The estate's best defense is that there is no consideration for the promise. The key to analyzing this question is the aunt's statement telling her niece that she should go to college and stating that the aunt would leave her niece $10,000 upon the aunt's death. These are two separate statements: "You should go to college," and "I will leave you $10,000." There is no causal connection between the two. The statement contains only a relative's advice as to going to college, with a separate promise to make a gift, unsupported by consideration, of $10,000. It is unlike the questions where the relative says, "If you go to college, I will pay your tuition." In those questions, there is a bargain which is not present here. (A) would not be the best defense because, if this were an issue of offer and acceptance, the niece could argue that the offer was the statement by her aunt and the acceptance was the action. In other words, the niece could argue that her aunt's statement had the meaning, "If you go to college, I will leave you $10,000." By going to college, the niece could argue that she accepted the offer, and thereby became entitled to the money. Of all the defenses offered in the choices to this question, (A) is not the most effective argument against the niece. (B) is incorrect because the promise does not have to be in writing unless the Statute of Frauds requires that it be in writing. This scenario does not fall into one of the categories under the Statute of Frauds. The most likely provision to be applicable would be the one-year provision. Here, the aunt simply said that her niece should go to college and that she would leave her $10,000. Each of these tasks could be performed within one year of the time the discussion took place. In fact, the better argument is that no contract existed at all between the parties, making the Statute of Frauds inapplicable, because the aunt's suggestion that her niece attend college was completely separate from her promise to make a gift of $10,000 upon her death. (D) is incorrect. Assuming that a contract was made, a contract with a minor is voidable at the minor's option, not the other way around. Thus, the minor may affirm or disaffirm a contract within a reasonable time after she reaches majority. A suit on the contract by the niece would constitute an affirmance of the contract, if there is one.

Answer to Question 10

(D) The producer's reply likely would be a rejection and counteroffer. This question deals with the "battle of the forms" provision of the U.C.C., and is a ***recurring favorite MBE question***. Under section 2-207 of the U.C.C., an acceptance containing additional or different terms is effective unless: (i) the offeree makes his acceptance conditional on assent by the offeror to the additional terms; (ii) the offeror objects to the additional or different terms in a timely fashion; or (iii) the new terms materially alter the economic risks and benefits or impair an otherwise available remedy. In this fact pattern, because the producer made his purported acceptance conditional on the distributor's assent to the 10% discount, his communication would be a rejection and a counteroffer. Hence, (D) is correct and (A), (B), and (C) are incorrect.

Answer to Question 11

(C) The creditor will prevail. The mother made a gratuitous promise to the creditor; she received no consideration for it (she did not ask for anything in return for her promise). The creditor's reliance in allowing the statute of limitations to lapse was not exchanged for the promise. However, even without consideration, under section 90 of the Restatement (Second) of Contracts, the creditor could enforce the mother's promise because he reasonably and foreseeably relied on the promise in declining to sue the debtor within the limitations period. (A) is incorrect because, although the statute of limitations has run on the debtor's debt, the creditor is not suing the debtor on his promise, but rather the mother on hers. (B) is incorrect because, while it is true that the mother received no consideration for her promise, the promise is enforceable under promissory estoppel principles. (D) is incorrect because there is no "main purpose" exception to the statute of limitations. The main purpose rule is an exception to the Statute of Frauds; however, that is not an issue here because the mother's promise was in writing.

Answer to Question 12

(C) The wholesaler will prevail if the proprietor had reason to know of the mistake. Where one party makes a unilateral mistake about a basic assumption on which the contract is based, and the other party knew or had reason to know of the mistake, the mistaken party will be allowed to rescind the contract. In this case, there is a substantial disparity between the contract price of $4 per shirt and the market value of the shirts at wholesale, which seems to be $8 a shirt. If the proprietor, because of the disparity in price, was or should have been aware that the wholesaler had made a mistake, the wholesaler will be able to rescind the contract and therefore will prevail. Hence, choice (D) is incorrect. (A) also is incorrect. This is a case where the wholesaler made a unilateral mistake in quoting the wrong price to the proprietor. Making a unilateral mistake alone, however, is not sufficient to allow the mistaken party to rescind the contract. A contract can be rescinded for unilateral mistake only when the other party knew of the mistake or when the mistake was so obvious that the other party should have known that the first party made a mistake. (B) is incorrect because there is no mutual mistake. Mutual mistake occurs when both parties to a contract are mistaken about a basic assumption on which the contract is made. Unilateral mistake occurs when there is a mistake by only one of the two parties as to a basic assumption upon which the contract is made. The facts of this question present a typical case of unilateral mistake, evidenced by the wholesaler's quoting the wrong price for the shirts. There is no mistake on the part of the proprietor, and the wholesaler will be able to rescind the contract only if it can be shown that the proprietor knew or should have known of the wholesaler's mistake.

Answer to Question 13

(A) The modification is enforceable because it was made in good faith. Article 2 of the U.C.C. applies because coal is a movable good. Under section 2-209 of the U.C.C., consideration is not required for an enforceable modification; however, any modification will be subject to the general Code requirement of good faith and fair dealing, which requires honesty in fact and conformity with reasonable commercial standards. It appears that the coal company was being honest in informing the agent of the clerical error and that both parties made the modification freely. There is no indication that the modified price is commercially unreasonable, despite the required assumption that the disparity was not sufficient to indicate any mistake to the agent. (B) is incorrect because it is not true that the law will only support modifications of otherwise unconscionable contracts. (C) is incorrect because U.C.C. Article 2 abolishes the preexisting duty rule and the requirement of additional consideration to support a modification. (D) is incorrect because Article 2 does not require changed circumstances in order to support a valid modification. All that is required is good faith.

Answer to Question 14

(B) The manufacturer has a cause of action for breach of contract. Because the contract was in excess of $500, the Statute of Frauds must be satisfied under U.C.C. section 2-201. Because both the ski-shop operator and the manufacturer are merchants, a memorandum of the terms of the sale sent by the manufacturer to the ski-shop operator satisfies the Statute of Frauds unless the ski-shop operator objects within 10 days, which she did not do. (A) is incorrect because identifying the goods to the contract and tendering the goods does not satisfy the Statute of Frauds. (C) is incorrect because, while the price makes the Statute of Frauds applicable, it is satisfied by the memorandum written by the manufacturer to the ski-shop operator, which was never rejected. (D) is incorrect because neither payment for nor acceptance of goods is necessary to make a contract enforceable, which it is here because the Statute of Frauds was satisfied by the memorandum sent by the manufacturer to the ski-shop operator.

Answer to Question 15

(B) The association may reject the softballs and sue for damages. Softballs obviously are movable goods; therefore, Article 2 of the U.C.C. applies. According to section 2-206(1)(b), an order for "prompt shipment" may be accepted by shipment of ***either*** conforming or nonconforming goods, and a contract is created upon such shipment. This alters the traditional rule that a shipment of nonconforming goods was a counteroffer which the buyer accepted upon taking delivery. The association may reject the nonconforming shipment [U.C.C. §2-601] and sue for damages. It may also, if it wishes, accept the shipment [U.C.C. §2-601], notify the seller of the breach [U.C.C. §2-607(3)], pay the contract price [U.C.C. §2-607(1)], and seek damages even after accepting the nonconforming goods [U.C.C. §2-714]. (A) is incorrect because, while a contract was indeed formed by shipment under U.C.C. section 2-206(1)(b), the association is not required to accept shipment, but may reject it. [U.C.C. §2-601] (C) is incorrect because the shipment constitutes an acceptance, not a counteroffer, as described above. Additionally, even where a buyer rightfully rejects a nonconforming tender, the buyer is under no obligation to reship prior to receipt of reasonable instructions from the seller. [U.C.C. §2-603] (D) is incorrect because, as discussed above, the shipment constitutes an acceptance, not a counteroffer.

Answer to Question 16

(C) The supplier will recover $260. Dishes are movable goods, and so Article 2 of the U.C.C. applies. Under Article 2, when goods fail in any respect to conform to the contract, the buyer may accept the goods [U.C.C. §2-601] and pay the contract price for the goods accepted [U.C.C. §2-607]. However, the buyer has a right to offset its damages. When a seller fails to deliver goods as promised, the buyer may "cover" under U.C.C. section 2-712 by making a reasonable purchase of substitute goods, and then may recover as damages the difference between the contract price and the "cover" price. Here, the difference between the contract price and the cover price is $40 (2,000 plates × $.02). (A) is incorrect because the U.C.C. permits a buyer to accept a nonconforming or partial delivery without waiving the right to sue for damages; thus, there is no need for an express reservation of rights at the time the goods are accepted. (B) is incorrect because the correct measure of damages is not based on the reasonable value of the goods accepted, but rather on the contract price. [*See* U.C.C. §206-7(1)] (D) is incorrect because the U.C.C. requires that the buyer pay for any goods accepted. [U.C.C. §2-607] The common law rule, which discharges the buyer's obligation to pay if there has been material breach, is displaced by U.C.C. section 2-607.

Answer to Question 17

(D) ***This is a favorite MBE question.*** The airline will prevail because the supplier's rights had not vested at the time of the modification. The rights of the third-party beneficiary do not vest until: (i) it manifests assent in a manner invited or requested by the parties; (ii) it learns of the contract and detrimentally relies on it; or (iii) it brings a lawsuit to enforce its rights. Until a third party's rights have vested, a modification of the contract can take place without the consent of the third party. The proper analysis is that the supplier's rights have not vested. Even if the supplier was aware of the contract, and even if the supplier was pleased with it, the supplier had not assented to the contract in any manner, had not detrimentally relied, and had not brought suit on the contract before it was modified. Therefore, the supplier's rights had not vested, and the contracting parties were free to modify the contract. Moreover, notwithstanding the oral modification clause, while the oral modification will be enforceable between the food company and the airline only if an exception to the Statute of Frauds applies (*e.g.*, the parties admit the modification or perform the contract as modified), it is doubtful that a court would allow the supplier to use the Statute to prevent the parties from admitting their modification. Thus, the modification is valid, and (A) is incorrect. (B) is wrong because the supplier's rights had not vested. (C) is a true statement, but (D) is a better answer, because it states the specific reason that the supplier's rights had not vested.

Answer to Question 18

(C) The banker will prevail because he could not acquire the house. In general, the parol evidence rule bars oral evidence contradicting a written agreement which was intended to be a full and exclusive embodiment of the parties' agreement. However, one exception to this general rule provides that parol evidence is admissible to show a condition precedent to the existence of a contract. Here, the contract between the banker and the dealer for the sale and purchase of the rug was only to be effective if the banker acquired the house he wanted. This condition precedent may be shown by the banker despite the fact that it was not reduced to writing. (A) is incorrect. This contract must be in writing because it is for the sale of goods of more than $500 in value. However, there is a written agreement here and the question is whether the written agreement precludes proof of the oral agreement. Under the parol evidence rule, a written agreement can prevent proof of an oral agreement even if the agreement does not have to be in writing. (B) is incorrect because a condition precedent to a written agreement's enforceability may be shown by parol evidence. (D) is incorrect because specific performance is not the issue here; whether the contract is enforceable at all is the issue. If this contract is enforceable, specific performance may be available because the rug might be considered unique.

Answer to Question 19

(C) The property owner will win because the contractor breached. When the contractor notified the property owner on March 1 that he would not perform his obligations on a binding contract unless he was given more money, he committed an anticipatory breach. That breach gave the property owner the right both to terminate the contract and to engage a new contractor to complete the work. The property owner was not required to give notice to the contractor to exercise that right, which is why choice (A) is incorrect. (B) is incorrect because, when the contractor notified the property owner on March 1 that he would not perform his obligations on a binding contract unless he was given more money, he committed an anticipatory breach. That breach gave the property owner the right to terminate the contract and engage a new contractor to complete the work, without giving notice to the contractor. The contractor had no right to perform the contract once he had breached it; therefore, the fact that he showed up ready to perform the work on the day required by the contract is irrelevant. (D) is incorrect because the price at which the property owner was able to obtain a replacement contractor has no bearing on whether the property owner had the right to terminate the contractual rights of the original contractor. Indeed, after the contractor's breach, he could have chosen not to have the dock repaired at all, or if the lowest bid was from someone who would only do the work for more than $80,000, he could have accepted that bid and charged the contractor for the difference between the contract price and the cost of the cover.

Answer to Question 20

(B) ***This is a favorite MBE question.*** The best advice is not to file suit because the golf pro's e-mail does not constitute an anticipatory repudiation. Language may constitute ***an expression of doubt*** as to one's ability to perform under the contract without being an outright refusal. ***This will not be an anticipatory repudiation, but a prospective inability to perform.*** If there is an anticipatory repudiation, then the nonbreaching party can (i) sue for damages, (ii) contract with a third party, or (iii) do nothing. If the fact pattern language amounts to a prospective inability to perform, the innocent party may suspend performance until he receives adequate assurances that performance will be forthcoming. Here, the golf pro's e-mail does not constitute an anticipatory repudiation because he merely states that he "may not" get to the club by April 1. Thus, (B) is correct, and (D) is incorrect. (A) is an incorrect statement of law because a repudiation can be by any means: oral, written, or by actions. An e-mail message clearly stating an intent not to perform would be sufficient. (C) is also incorrect because the golf pro's actions constitute a prospective inability to perform, which allows the club to suspend performance to the golf pro and demand assurances; it does not result in an immediate breach.

Answer to Question 21

(C) The storm delay would best support the manufacturer's case. The storm may have made delivery on time impossible, which may excuse performance under either the doctrine of impracticability of performance or the doctrine of impossibility of performance. These defenses can be used not only to excuse performance totally, but also to excuse the delay in performance. (A) is incorrect because an oral agreement made prior to a written agreement on the same subject will not be admissible to alter the written agreement under the parol evidence rule. Therefore, the oral agreement does not modify the terms of the written contract and this contention will not help the manufacturer's case. (B) is incorrect. The fact that goods are specially made creates an exception to the Statute of Frauds, but it does not excuse the obligation to tender conforming goods in the correct quantity at or before the time specified for delivery. The perfect tender rule is incorporated into every contract for the sale of goods except where the contract specifies different terms or where there is an explicit installment contract. (D) is incorrect. If the buyer became insolvent, the manufacturer could, under the U.C.C., require that the buyer pay cash upon delivery or give assurances of payment. Here, however, the manufacturer has not requested that payments be made in cash or that the buyer give assurances. Moreover, the buyer only suffered a decrease in his credit rating; he is not insolvent. Therefore, the manufacturer would have had no basis for making either request. The manufacturer is not excused from performance by the buyer's decreased credit rating.

Answer to Question 22

(D) The broker can recover the money from the physician. Because the patient did not receive notice of either assignment and paid the physician in good faith, neither assignee will be successful in a suit against her. The physician is contractually obligated to repay the broker's advances, and the broker can recover the $25,000 from the physician. The assignment to the daughter was a gift, not supported by consideration. The daughter therefore cannot sue the physician for the amount of the assignment. (A) and (B) are incorrect because the patient did not receive notice of either assignment and paid the physician in good faith; hence, neither the broker nor the daughter will be successful in a suit against her. (C) is incorrect because the assignment to the daughter was a gift, not supported by consideration. The daughter therefore cannot sue the physician for the amount of the assignment.

Answer to Question 23

(C) The painter may recover the reasonable value of his services less the farmer's damages. Unless there is an expressed condition that would reasonably be understood to provide for forfeiture of payment unless there is full performance, a breaching party may seek restitution damages for the fair value of any benefit conferred, the reasonable value of services provided. As a nonbreaching party, the farmer has the choice of remedies. The farmer may enforce the benefit of this bargain and elect to pay the painter the contract price ($6,000) minus the cost to have the final barn painted. Alternately, the farmer may rely on the material breach as a reason to set aside the bargain, in which case the farmer need only pay the painter the net benefit received, *i.e.*, the reasonable value of the painter's services in painting the two barns, less any damages incurred due to the painter's failure to perform. (A) is incorrect because paying the painter nothing would result in unjust enrichment of the farmer. While the terms of the contract are no longer enforceable, the painter is entitled to payment based on substantial performance. The farmer is entitled to an allowance for hiring someone else to complete painting the third barn. Therefore, the measure of recovery is the promised price minus any amount it will cost the farmer to have the third barn painted as the painter promised to do. (B) is incorrect. This answer has elements of the correct answer except that it does not contemplate the harm the farmer may have suffered from the painter's refusal to paint the third barn. In establishing the value for restitution, the court must consider not only the benefit conferred (in this case from painting two barns), but also the injury resulting from the breach of the contract. (D) is incorrect because the increase of value, if any, is not relevant to value of service provided. The painter is entitled to payment based on the reasonable value of the service provided in restitution for the fair value of any benefit conferred.

Answer to Question 24

(C) The contractor should recover $20,000. The primary objective of contract damages is to put the nonbreaching party in the same position that he would have been in had the contract been performed. The normal measure of damages is expectation damages. The contractor has a legally enforceable right to have the work within the subcontractor contract performed for $200,000. Because the contractor paid the subcontractor $100,000 and needed to spend $120,000 to have the work completed by a third party, the contractor has spent $220,000. This establishes the contractor's right to seek $20,000 from the subcontractor for its breach. (A) is incorrect because the breaching party may seek payment in restitution, measured by the fair value of the benefit conferred, the reasonable value of services provided, adjusted to reflect the injury (the contractor's damages) caused by the breach. (B) is incorrect because a breaching party will only prevail where the nonbreaching party seeks to keep a fair value of the benefit conferred without paying and therefore is unjustly enriched. Here, the contractor suffered $20,000 in damages due to the breach, the excess cost over the contracted price. The subcontractor's costs are immaterial. (D) is incorrect. To provide no remedy to either party on the theory stated in (D) is to make the contractor pay a total of $220,000 for the performance that was promised by the subcontractor for $200,000. The primary objective of contract damages is to put the nonbreaching party in the same position that he would have been in had the contract been performed. Therefore, this theory fails.

Answer to Question 25

(C) The customer should recover $40,000 minus the retailer's lost profit. The correct measure of damages is the lost profits of the retailer. That amount should be deducted from the deposit and the balance returned. The U.C.C. authorizes four different measures of damages when a buyer defaults after putting down a deposit. First, the code allows the deposit to serve as liquidated damages if the contract so provides, within certain limits. However, this rule is inapplicable in this case because a liquidated damages clause was not included in the contract. Second, the code provides in section 2-718(2) that when a deposit is given and there is no liquidated damages provision, the seller may keep 20% of the contract price or $500, whichever is less. In this case, the $500 limitation would control. However, if actual damages are more, as they are in this case, the seller may collect actual damages rather than the statutory amount. In section 2-708, the code provides two measures of actual damages when the buyer defaults. The first is the traditional expectancy measure of damages, resale price minus contract price. In a case such as this, there are no damages under this measure because the boat was resold for the contract price. The second alternative under section 2-708 applies here. When the seller is a dealer and the traditional measure of damages is inadequate to put him in as good a position as he would be in if the sale went through, then the measure of damages is lost profit. Here, since the dealer could have ordered as many boats as there were buyers, he actually lost his profit on this sale. (A) is incorrect because even a defaulting party has the right to recover a portion of the deposit back in restitution if the amount of the deposit exceeds the contract damages to which the non-defaulting party is entitled. (B) is incorrect. While it is true that the retailer would have made profits on two boat sales instead of one if the customer had not defaulted, it did make the profit on the second sale, and cannot collect this from the customer. The lost profit on the first sale amounts to $29,500, less than the $40,000 advance. Therefore, the customer is entitled to $10,500, the difference between the amount of advance and the profit actually lost. (D) is incorrect because, as discussed above, actual damages allowed under U.C.C. section 2-708 exceed the $500 allowed under U.C.C. section 2-718(2), so the higher amount of damages would be awarded.

Criminal Law

Questions and Analytical Answers

barbri®

Criminal Law

1. Ⓐ Ⓑ Ⓒ Ⓓ
2. Ⓐ Ⓑ Ⓒ Ⓓ
3. Ⓐ Ⓑ Ⓒ Ⓓ
4. Ⓐ Ⓑ Ⓒ Ⓓ
5. Ⓐ Ⓑ Ⓒ Ⓓ

6. Ⓐ Ⓑ Ⓒ Ⓓ
7. Ⓐ Ⓑ Ⓒ Ⓓ
8. Ⓐ Ⓑ Ⓒ Ⓓ
9. Ⓐ Ⓑ Ⓒ Ⓓ
10. Ⓐ Ⓑ Ⓒ Ⓓ

11. Ⓐ Ⓑ Ⓒ Ⓓ
12. Ⓐ Ⓑ Ⓒ Ⓓ
13. Ⓐ Ⓑ Ⓒ Ⓓ
14. Ⓐ Ⓑ Ⓒ Ⓓ
15. Ⓐ Ⓑ Ⓒ Ⓓ

16. Ⓐ Ⓑ Ⓒ Ⓓ
17. Ⓐ Ⓑ Ⓒ Ⓓ
18. Ⓐ Ⓑ Ⓒ Ⓓ
19. Ⓐ Ⓑ Ⓒ Ⓓ
20. Ⓐ Ⓑ Ⓒ Ⓓ

21. Ⓐ Ⓑ Ⓒ Ⓓ
22. Ⓐ Ⓑ Ⓒ Ⓓ
23. Ⓐ Ⓑ Ⓒ Ⓓ
24. Ⓐ Ⓑ Ⓒ Ⓓ
25. Ⓐ Ⓑ Ⓒ Ⓓ

Question 1

To punish a gambler who owed him money, a bookie purchased from a demolitions expert a small explosive device that he planned to place under the driver's seat of the gambler's automobile. The demolitions expert assured the bookie that the explosive would be strong enough to cause severe damage to the legs and ankles of anyone sitting in the front seat of the car, but would under no circumstances be strong enough to kill. The device would go off when the ignition was turned on. On Sunday night, the bookie planted the device in the gambler's car. On Monday, the gambler was sick and did not go to work. That afternoon, the gambler's 15-year-old son came home from school and saw his father's car in the driveway. The son took an extra set of keys from the house to take the car for a joyride, even though the gambler had forbidden his son to drive the car without permission. When the 15-year-old turned on the ignition, the explosive device went off and the boy died instantly.

If the bookie is charged with the murder of the gambler's son, he will probably be found:

(A) Guilty, because the bookie's act caused the son's death.

(B) Guilty, because he intended to cause serious bodily harm to the gambler.

(C) Not guilty, because he did not intend to cause the death of any person.

(D) Not guilty, because it was not foreseeable that the son would attempt to drive the car.

Question 2

During a heated argument, a man punched his female coworker in the stomach after learning that she had been awarded "Employee of the Month." Angered, the woman responded by stabbing the man with a letter opener in the heart, killing him instantly.

The police arrested the woman. After receiving her *Miranda* rights, she confessed to killing her coworker, but stated that she had not previously held any grudge against him. When asked why she killed him, she stated, "He just made me so mad. I went from calm to furious in about 10 seconds, and I saw red when he said that I was a terrible employee and that he deserved the reward instead of me." The district attorney charges the woman for homicide.

If the jury believes the woman's statement, she is most likely to be found:

(A) Guilty of murder.

(B) Guilty of voluntary manslaughter.

(C) Guilty of involuntary manslaughter.

(D) Not guilty of a homicide crime.

Question 3

A heavily armed robber took two hostages at a bank when the police arrived. Witnesses told the police that the robber was a white male of average build wearing a bright yellow scarf around his neck, but they were otherwise vague as to his description. As the standoff continued, the robber made one hostage put on the bright yellow scarf that the robber had been wearing. The robber then pushed the other hostage out of a small unguarded back door, followed her through it with his bag of money, and ran away. The lights were still on in the bank and a police sharpshooter saw a white male of average build, wearing a bright yellow scarf, standing with his back to the window. The sharpshooter fired and the bullet killed the man instantly.

The robber is arrested and prosecuted for felony murder of the hostage shot by the police. The jurisdiction does not follow the "agency theory" of liability.

The robber should be:

(A) Acquitted, because the robbery had ended and the robber had escaped by the time that the hostage was killed.

(B) Acquitted, because the robber did not kill the hostage and is not responsible for the acts of the police.

(C) Convicted, because the robber caused the death of the hostage, who was killed during the course of a felony.

(D) Convicted, because putting the hostage in a position of danger shows intent to kill.

Question 4

A robber attempted to rob a liquor store with an accomplice. A police officer arrived at the scene and deliberately shot and killed the robber's accomplice, who was guarding the door. Meanwhile, the store owner pulled out a gun and shot at the robber but missed. The robber then killed the store owner in self-defense before he could fire a second shot.

The robber is guilty of felony murder for the death of:

(A) The store owner and the accomplice.

(B) The store owner only.

(C) The accomplice only.

(D) Neither the store owner nor the accomplice.

Question 5

A father who was paralyzed in an accident and unable to work refused to accept financial support from relatives or the government to help him care for his family. When one of his children became seriously ill and needed medical attention, the father refused to allow the child to receive medical care at the local public health clinic because of his feelings regarding the acceptance of charity. The child subsequently died of his illness.

What crime has the father most likely committed?

(A) Murder.

(B) Voluntary manslaughter.

(C) Involuntary manslaughter.

(D) No crime.

Question 6

A man asked a coworker who was a wine collector to lend him a bottle of expensive wine to put in his liquor cabinet, because he was inviting his mother over for dinner and wanted to impress her. The coworker permitted the man to take a bottle of wine worth $700 to his apartment for the dinner as long as he returned it the next morning. Instead of inviting his mother, the man instead invited his girlfriend over for a romantic dinner, at which they drank the bottle of wine. The next day the man told his coworker that he had been mugged on his way home and that the muggers made off with the wine. Suspicious, the coworker found the empty wine bottle in the man's trash from his apartment.

If the man is charged with theft in a common-law jurisdiction, he is most likely to be convicted of:

(A) Larceny by trick.

(B) Larceny.

(C) Embezzlement.

(D) No crime.

Question 7

A cashier at a bookstore who accepted a $50 bill as payment from a customer placed the bill underneath all of the $20 bills in the cash register and took it home with her at closing time. At the cashier's second job as a truck driver, she drove her tractor to a trucking terminal and attached a trailer filled with wine. At the first truck stop, the cashier entered the trailer, took a bottle of wine from a case and drank it.

In a common law jurisdiction, the cashier is guilty of:

(A) Larceny for the money and embezzlement for the wine.

(B) Embezzlement for the money and larceny for the wine.

(C) Larceny for both the money and the wine.

(D) Embezzlement for both the money and the wine.

Question 8

A shopper at a flea market noticed a vase and asked a nearby person how much it cost. The person replied, "One hundred dollars." The shopper paid him the money and took the vase. The person, who was not the owner of the vase but merely a bystander, absconded with the $100.

What crime has the bystander committed with respect to the $100?

(A) Embezzlement.

(B) Larceny by trick.

(C) Larceny.

(D) Obtaining property by false pretenses.

Question 9

A small business owner lived on the second floor of a small convenience store/gas station that he owned. One night he refused to sell a customer a six-pack of beer after hours, saying he could not violate state law. The customer became enraged and deliberately drove his car into one of the gasoline pumps, severing it from its base. The ensuing explosion caused a ball of fire to go from the underground gasoline tank into the building. The building burned to the ground and the owner was killed.

In a common law jurisdiction, if the customer is charged with murder and arson, he should be:

(A) Convicted of both offenses.

(B) Convicted of involuntary manslaughter and acquitted of arson.

(C) Convicted of arson and involuntary manslaughter.

(D) Acquitted of both offenses.

Question 10

A drug addict entered a pawnshop with a starter pistol that could not fire real bullets, intending to rob it so he could buy drugs. However, once inside the pawnshop, the addict was too afraid to do anything and turned to leave. He bumped into another customer who was coming in as he was going out, and the pistol fell from his coat pocket. The shopkeeper saw it and realized what the addict had intended. She grabbed a pistol from behind the counter and yelled to the addict to stop. However, the addict picked up his pistol and started to run out the door. The shopkeeper fired her gun and the bullet struck and killed the other customer who had just come into the shop.

The addict is charged with burglary, which is defined in this jurisdiction as "breaking and entering of any building for the purpose of committing a felony."

His best defense would be that:

(A) His pistol was inoperative.

(B) The pawnshop was open for business.

(C) He had abandoned his plan to commit the robbery.

(D) As a drug addict, he was incapable of forming the requisite intent.

Question 11

A man intending to kill his friend armed himself with a pistol and crouched behind some bushes overlooking a path on which his friend frequently jogged. On this morning, however, the man saw the friend jogging on another path about a half mile away. The man was not aware of the range of the pistol so he fired five shots at the friend. None of the five shots came anywhere close to the friend because he was well out of range.

The man is:

(A) Guilty of attempted murder, because he was not aware of the limited range of his pistol.

(B) Guilty of attempted murder, if a reasonable person would not have been aware of the limited range of his pistol.

(C) Not guilty of attempted murder, or any lesser included offense, because, under the circumstances, it was impossible for him to kill his friend.

(D) Not guilty of attempted murder, but guilty of assault.

Question 12

Three men agreed to rob a restaurant in a nearby town and bought pistols, ski masks, and gloves for that purpose. Prior to entering the restaurant, the man who was to be the lookout had a change of heart and wanted to call off the robbery. The other two men refused so the lookout threw down his gun and went to the nearby bus station to catch a bus back to his home. The remaining two men went into the restaurant and robbed it and its patrons. A patrol car happened by as they were leaving, and one of the men seized one of the customers as a hostage. In the exchange of gunfire with the police, a police officer and the hostage were killed. Both men escaped initially, but one of them was later captured and charged with robbery and murder. However, because of illegal police conduct in connection with his arrest and subsequent confession, all evidence connecting him with the charged crimes was suppressed and the charges dismissed.

If the lookout is also arrested and charged with murder, which of the following is his strongest defense?

(A) He did not have the requisite mental state to be convicted of murder.

(B) He did not physically participate in the events that led to the killings of the police officer and the hostage.

(C) He had withdrawn from the conspiracy before the two others began the robbery that led to the killings.

(D) He cannot be prosecuted for a crime as to which the principals have not been convicted.

Question 13

An irate woman seeking vengeance against an appliance store owner for selling her a defective television set went to the store armed with two pistols. Just as she was about to enter the store, she spotted a young mother walking by with a baby carriage, The woman pointed one of the pistols at the mother and one at the carriage, saying, "I hate the owner of this store! Take this gun, go into his store, and do the job or the kid gets it!" The mother began pleading for her baby's life, but the woman cocked the pistol pointing at the carriage and began counting. The distraught mother took the other pistol and "did the job."

Criminal charges are filed against the mother. At trial, she asserts duress as a defense.

She will be found guilty if "the job" she did on the store owner was:

(A) "Pistol whipping" the owner.

(B) Robbing the owner at gunpoint.

(C) Fatally wounding the owner with the pistol.

(D) Kidnapping the owner at gunpoint.

Question 14

A police officer patrolling at 2:00 a.m. saw a figure leap over a hedge in front of a condominium. Although it was dark, the officer could see that he was carrying a briefcase in one hand and a gun in the other. Just then, someone limped out of the building and pointed at the figure, yelling, "He shot me!" The officer then twice commanded the figure to stop and fired three warning shots in the air. The person kept running, so the officer fired a fourth shot, bringing the person down. The person was later identified as a robber.

If the officer is charged with battery, he should be found:

(A) Not guilty, because he had a right to use deadly force to stop a getaway.

(B) Not guilty, because a police officer cannot commit a crime while acting within the scope of his duty.

(C) Guilty, because a police officer does not have the right to use deadly force to prevent a getaway.

(D) Guilty, because he did not see the robber steal anything.

Question 15

Suspecting that a husband had slain his wife, police detectives persuaded one of the husband's colleagues at work to remove a drinking glass from the husband's office so that it could be used for fingerprint comparisons with a knife found near the body. The fingerprints matched. The prosecutor announced that he would present comparisons and evidence to the grand jury. The husband's lawyer immediately filed a motion to suppress the evidence of the fingerprint comparisons so as to bar its consideration by the grand jury, contending that the evidence was illegally acquired.

The motion should be:

(A) Granted, because, if there was no probable cause, the grand jury should not consider the evidence.

(B) Granted, because the employee was acting as a police agent and his seizure of the glass without a warrant was unconstitutional.

(C) Denied, because motions based on the exclusionary rule are premature in grand jury proceedings.

(D) Denied, because the glass was removed from the husband's possession by a private citizen and not a police officer.

Question 16

A driver was stopped by the police after running a red light. Her roommate was also in the car. Because the driver did not have a driver's license, the officer lawfully placed her under arrest and took her to the police station. At the time of the arrest, the officer searched the passenger compartment of the car. He opened up a shopping bag sitting on the floor of the back seat and found that it contained a newly purchased bathing suit. The officer asked the driver if she had made any other purchases that day, and she responded that the additional purchases were in the trunk. The officer then searched the trunk of the car, where he found additional clothes purchased at the store along with a bag of marijuana that the roommates had purchased that morning from a neighbor.

The two roommates were prosecuted for possession of marijuana. At her trial, the driver's attorney moved to suppress the marijuana because it was discovered in an illegal search, and the motion was granted. Then the other roommate who was the passenger in the car was tried for possession of the marijuana.

Should her motion to suppress the marijuana be granted?

(A) Yes, because the marijuana was the fruit of an illegal search.

(B) Yes, because the judge had suppressed this evidence at the driver's trial.

(C) No, because she has no standing to object to an illegal search.

(D) No, if she admits that she owns the marijuana.

Question 17

Police received an anonymous tip that a woman was growing marijuana in her backyard, which was surrounded by a 15-foot-high, solid wooden fence. The police officer who investigated was unable to view the yard from the street, so he used a police helicopter to fly over the woman's house. The police officer identified a large patch of marijuana plants growing right next to the house and used this observation to obtain a search warrant. The woman is prosecuted for possession of marijuana and moves to suppress use of the marijuana in evidence.

The court should:

(A) Grant the motion, because the only purpose of the officer's flight was to observe the yard.

(B) Grant the motion, because the woman had a reasonable expectation of privacy in the curtilage around her house and the police did not have a warrant.

(C) Deny the motion, because a warrant is not required for a search of a residential yard.

(D) Deny the motion, because the woman had no reasonable expectation of privacy from aerial observation.

Question 18

A police officer detected a car exceeding the speed limit and ordered it to stop. The officer approached the car and ordered the driver to exit the car and place his hands on the roof of the car. When the driver exited the car, the officer observed a firearm in a shoulder holster. The driver admitted that he had no permit for the weapon. He then ordered a passenger in the front seat to get out of the car and place his hands on the roof. As the passenger exited the car, he dropped a package of crack cocaine on the ground.

The driver has been charged with illegal possession of a firearm, and the passenger has been charged with illegal possession of a controlled substance. The driver filed a motion to suppress the gun and the passenger filed a motion to suppress the package of crack cocaine.

The court should:

(A) Grant the driver's motion to suppress and deny the passenger's motion to suppress.

(B) Grant the passenger's motion to suppress and deny the driver's motion to suppress.

(C) Grant both motions to suppress.

(D) Deny both motions to suppress.

Question 19

While on walking patrol, a police officer noticed that a light was on in a machine shop. Curious, the officer tried to look through a window of the shop, but it had been painted on the inside so that only a strip about three inches wide at the top, eight feet above street level, was still transparent. The officer stood on a trash can, and saw, through the strip of unpainted window, that the shop owner's son was inside with another man, snorting white powder into his nose through a rolled up tube of paper from the surface of a small mirror. Recognizing from his experience and training that the son was snorting cocaine, the officer knocked at the front door and the son let him in. The officer immediately arrested the son and the other man. In the back room of the shop through whose window he had peered, the officer found and seized several grams of cocaine, a razor blade, and a mirror.

In the son's subsequent prosecution for possession of cocaine, the son seeks to bar introduction of the cocaine, mirror, and razor blade into evidence.

His motion will probably be:

(A) Granted, because the officer could not have known that the son was snorting cocaine absent a chemical test of the substance.

(B) Granted, because the officer violated the son's reasonable expectation of privacy.

(C) Denied, because the search was incident to a valid arrest.

(D) Denied, because the son consented to the officer's entry into the shop.

Question 20

The sheriff's department received an anonymous tip that a farmer was growing marijuana on his rural property. Investigators flew low over the farmer's property in a small plane belonging to the sheriff's department and took aerial photos of the property. Once developed, the photos indicated that the area in the center of the farmer's fields contained marijuana plants. That afternoon, four officers went to the perimeter of the farmer's property. Using wire cutters, they cut their way through the farmer's barbed wire fence and walked to the center of the field and found the marijuana plants. The officers then obtained a warrant to search the farmer's house. On arrival, they produced the search warrant and searched the farmer's house, finding large quantities of marijuana packaged and ready for sale.

The marijuana was seized and the farmer was charged with numerous drug offenses. At trial, the prosecution seeks to introduce into evidence the marijuana seized from the house. The farmer's attorney moves to suppress.

Should the marijuana seized from the farmer's house be suppressed?

(A) Yes, because it is the fruit of the poisonous tree, since the officers did not have a warrant when they entered the farmer's property through the fence.

(B) Yes, because the police had no right to rely on anonymous information to search the farmer's property.

(C) No, because the police had probable cause to obtain a warrant.

(D) No, because the open fields doctrine applies.

Question 21

Several students at a public high school told a teacher that a fellow student was selling illegal drugs to other students at the school. The accused student was called into the principal's office and informed of the accusations. The student denied everything, but the principal grabbed the student's purse, which was on top of his desk, and opened it. He removed five small transparent plastic bags, each of which contained a white powder, and immediately called the police. The police arrested the student and conducted tests confirming that the white powder was cocaine.

The student was charged with possession of a controlled substance with intent to sell. At her trial, the state sought to introduce the bags and their contents into evidence. The student's attorney moved to suppress the evidence.

The motion should be:

(A) Granted, because there was adequate time to obtain a warrant.

(B) Granted, because the principal lacked probable cause.

(C) Denied, because the principal had a reasonable suspicion that the student was selling drugs.

(D) Denied, because a principal, acting in loco parentis, has the right to search students whenever he chooses to do so.

Question 22

A police officer who stopped a driver for speeding noticed that the driver resembled the description of a hit-and-run driver who had struck and killed a nine-year-old boy two days before. The officer examined the driver's car and found recent dents. The driver was arrested for the hit-and-run offense and read his *Miranda* rights. However, the officer failed to inform him that the child struck in the hit-and-run accident had subsequently died. On the way to the police station in the squad car, the driver blurted out, "You got me. I was the hit-and-run driver. I just hope the kid is okay." The officer still failed to inform him that the child had died. At the station house, the arresting officer said to the driver, "Look, you've already confessed. How about writing it down?" The driver replied, "I don't think I should write or sign anything without a lawyer, but I'll talk." He again admitted that he was the hit-and-run driver. The officer made a tape recording of his confession.

In addition to speeding, the driver has been charged with leaving the scene of an accident and involuntary manslaughter. At the driver's trial, the prosecution seeks to admit both the first confession (in the squad car) and the second confession (in the station house). The driver's attorney moves to suppress both confessions.

How should the court rule on the motion?

(A) Granted as to the first confession; denied as to the second.

(B) Granted as to the second confession; denied as to the first.

(C) Granted for both confessions.

(D) Denied for both confessions.

Question 23

A police officer outside a mall heard gunshots coming from the indoor dining area. He rushed into the dining area and saw a woman standing there with an assault rifle lying on the ground beside her. Several patrons were scattered prostrate about the dining area, some obviously suffering from gunshot wounds. The officer said, "What the hell happened here?" The woman replied in a dazed manner, "I just wiped out the lunch crowd."

The woman was subsequently charged with several murders and attempted murders. At trial, testimony indicated that none of the surviving customers saw or heard anything that would shed light on how they were injured. The prosecution offers the testimony of the police officer, who will relate what he observed, including the woman's statement. Counsel for the woman objects to admission of any statements made by her to the police officer.

The court should rule for:

(A) The state, since the woman was not in custody when she made the statement to the officer.

(B) The state, because the need for the information is great, and there are guarantees of its reliability equivalent to recognized exceptions to the hearsay rule.

(C) The woman, because the officer did not advise her of her constitutional rights before questioning her.

(D) The woman, because the prejudicial effect of such evidence far outweighs its probative value.

Question 24

A suspect was arrested on a charge of bank robbery. After formal charges had been filed, the suspect was scheduled for a lineup identification procedure. The suspect's attorney was notified of the lineup and arrived at the station prior to the scheduled lineup. He was directed to wait in the hallway outside the lineup room. When the suspect was escorted into the lineup room, the officer acknowledged the attorney but did not motion for him to follow them into the lineup room. The attorney remained seated in the hallway. Inside the lineup room, the six members of the lineup, including the suspect, stood on one side of the one-way mirror in full view of the witnesses gathered on the other side in the viewing area. The lineup members stepped forward one by one for a closer inspection. After the first two lineup members had been presented, an officer realized that the suspect's attorney was not present and immediately escorted him to the viewing area. The attorney arrived in time to witness the presentation of the suspect and the remaining three members of the lineup. Two witnesses then identified the suspect as the robber.

At trial, if the defense objects to the introduction of the lineup evidence, the objection should be:

(A) Overruled, because the attorney's absence from the lineup procedure was the product of a good faith mistake.

(B) Overruled, because the attorney was present when the suspect was presented in the lineup for identification by the witnesses.

(C) Granted, because the right to have counsel present at a post-charge lineup includes the right to have counsel present for the entire lineup.

(D) Granted, unless the witnesses are unavailable at trial.

Question 25

Two men were arrested while riding in a stolen automobile. They were taken to the police station, booked, and fingerprinted. They were then taken to an interrogation room. As the detective started to give them their *Miranda* warnings, one of the men said, "Forget it. As soon as you check for outstanding warrants, you'll find out that I escaped from prison. Since I am going back anyway, it's a farce to deny that we stole that car." The other man said nothing, and the first man proceeded to write and sign a full confession.

The man who remained silent pled not guilty to the charge of grand theft auto. At his trial the prosecutor seeks to introduce evidence to show that he did not deny that he stole the automobile when the other man told the police in front of him that he was a party to the theft.

The court should hold that this evidence is:

(A) Proper, because silence in this situation is indicative of guilt and is an implied admission.

(B) Proper, because the man who confessed had voluntarily waived his right to remain silent.

(C) Improper, because an accomplice's evidence is inherently unreliable and unduly prejudicial.

(D) Improper, because under this circumstance, the man who remained silent had no duty or responsibility to deny the allegation.

STOP

Answer to Question 1

(B) The bookie is guilty because his act, which caused the death of the gambler's son, was committed with an intent to cause serious bodily harm. At common law, murder was the killing of a human being with malice aforethought. The mental state of malice aforethought could be established with any one of the following states of mind: (i) intent to kill; (ii) intent to cause serious bodily harm; (iii) reckless indifference to an unjustifiably high risk to human life ("depraved heart"); or (iv) the intent to commit a dangerous felony ("felony murder"). In this question, the bookie clearly intended to cause serious bodily harm to the gambler. Under the doctrine of transferred intent, if the actor intended to kill or cause serious bodily harm to one person and caused the death of another person, malice aforethought as to the unintended victim was established. Thus, under the doctrine, the bookie's intent to harm the gambler will be transferred to the gambler's son, and the bookie will be guilty of the murder of the gambler's son. (A) is not as good an answer as (B). It is true that the bookie's act caused the gambler's son's death and that cause must be established to hold the bookie responsible for murder. However, it will take more than "cause" to hold the bookie criminally liable; there must also be malice aforethought. Therefore, (A) is too broad a statement. (C) is wrong because, at common law, a person could be guilty of murder even if he did not intend to cause a death; intent to cause serious bodily harm, depraved heart, or felony murder are sufficient intent for malice aforethought. (D) is not a very good answer. The unforeseeability that the gambler's son would drive the car or get killed would not, in and of itself, be a defense. The unforeseeable result would at best be a factor in deciding whether the bookie's act was the criminal proximate cause of the death, but the facts in the question clearly establish proximate cause.

Answer to Question 2

(B) The woman would most likely be found guilty of voluntary manslaughter in light of the provoking event. Adequate provocation will reduce a killing to voluntary manslaughter if the defendant was both reasonably provoked and actually provoked. Although the woman would have to offer evidence that a punch in the stomach and taunting would cause an ordinary person to be provoked, her statement in conjunction with the facts makes this the best answer. (A) is incorrect. At common law, murder was the unlawful killing of a human being with malice aforethought. Malice aforethought could be established with any one of the following states of mind: (i) intent to kill; (ii) intent to cause serious bodily harm; (iii) the depraved heart killing (a reckless indifference to an unjustifiably high risk to human life); or (iv) the commission of a felony. While at least an intent to cause serious harm may be present here, the provocation will reduce the homicide to voluntary manslaughter. (C) is incorrect because involuntary manslaughter is a killing that results from criminal negligence, which theory these facts do not support. (D) is incorrect because, as discussed above, the woman would likely be guilty of voluntary manslaughter.

Answer to Question 3

(C) The robber will be found guilty of felony murder because a victim was killed during his commission of the crime of bank robbery, and it was foreseeable that one of the hostages would be killed. (A) is incorrect because, although the robber had escaped, the robbery had not ended. The police were still surrounding the bank, believing that the bank robber was still inside. A felon will not avoid prosecution for felony murder unless the death occurred after the felony ended and the felon had reached a place of temporary safety; that has not occurred here. (B) and (D) are incorrect because, under the felony murder doctrine, it is not necessary for the robber to kill the victim, nor is it necessary to show intent to kill. All that is necessary is that a foreseeable victim be killed during the commission of a felony. Note, however, that if the jurisdiction followed the "agency theory" of felony murder, the robber might be able to escape criminal liability for the death.

Answer to Question 4

(B) The robber is guilty of felony murder of the store owner only. This choice represents an exception to the general rule that almost any death occurring in the course of a felony is felony murder. In the majority of jurisdictions, the robber would not be held guilty of felony murder for a justifiable killing of a co-felon by a police officer. The *Redline* view (the majority position) holds that the killing of a felon by a police officer to prevent the felon's escape cannot be the basis for felony murder. Thus, (A) and (C) are incorrect. (C) and (D) are incorrect because a person has no right of self-defense when he is the aggressor, and especially if he is engaged in a felony. The store owner, who was the victim of this felony, had the right to use at least the threat of force against the robber. Because the death occurred in the course of the felony, and the robber had no right of self-defense, he is guilty of felony murder, as well as deliberate premeditated murder.

Answer to Question 5

(C) The father has committed involuntary manslaughter. A father has a duty to provide the necessities for his child. His failure to do so has caused the child's death. Such an omission is criminal, so (D) is incorrect. (A) is incorrect because malice, required for murder, does not appear to be present under the facts, so the father could only be charged with manslaughter. (B) is not correct because this is not a heat of passion killing, which would be voluntary manslaughter. Criminal negligence, a form of involuntary manslaughter, is an unintended killing caused by the negligence of another. Criminal negligence requires a greater deviation from the reasonable person standard than is required for civil liability, but less negligence than the reckless disregard for human life required for malice. Certainly a parent's failure to provide medical treatment for a critically ill child is criminal negligence. Note that intent is not an element of involuntary manslaughter.

Answer to Question 6

(A) The man can be convicted of larceny by trick. The owner of the wine gave possession of the bottle of wine to the man, but clearly did not give up ownership, because possession was transferred on the coworker's explicit promise to return it the next day. Therefore, a theft crime of some sort was committed, but that crime is not pure common law larceny because there was no trespassory taking. If the man obtained possession of the wine by fraud or misrepresentation, then he is guilty of larceny by trick. Because it is fairly clear that it was the man's intent to drink the wine all along, the possession was obtained by fraud and the crime is larceny by trick, not embezzlement (the crime which would have occurred if he obtained rightful possession). Therefore, (D) is incorrect. (B) is incorrect because this is not a true trespassory taking; possession, even though obtained by fraud, was given. (C) is incorrect because, although the coworker had possession of the wine (which would normally indicate embezzlement), he obtained that possession by fraud (which indicates larceny by trick).

Answer to Question 7

(C) The cashier is guilty of larceny in both cases. The cashier is guilty of larceny in the case of the money, even though she originally had possession of the $50 bill when she first received it from the customer. If she had converted it at that time, she would have been guilty of embezzlement because the money never reached the possession of her employer. However, when she placed the bill in the cash register, the employer then obtained possession of the bill, and the cashier's rights over the money were reduced to custody. When she took the bill from the cash register at the end of the day, she committed a trespassory taking from her employer's possession and therefore committed larceny. (B) and (D) are therefore incorrect. The cashier is also guilty of larceny in the case of the wine. Here, she clearly was in possession of the entire trailer. However, when she entered the trailer and took one wine bottle, she broke bulk and merely had control of the wine bottle. When she removed that bottle from its place in the trailer with the intention of depriving its owner of the wine permanently, she committed larceny; hence, (A) and (D) are incorrect.

Answer to Question 8

(D) The bystander has obtained property by false pretenses. In the crime of false pretenses, the defendant obtains title to the property by means of a false representation of a material present or past fact that causes the victim to pass title to his property to the defendant, who knows his representations to be false and intends thereby to defraud the victim. Under the circumstances, by replying that the price of the vase was $100, the bystander implied that he was its owner or was authorized to sell it, which he was not. This false representation induced the victim to pass title to his money to the bystander, who knew the representation to be false. Therefore, he is guilty of obtaining money by false pretenses. (A) is incorrect because the bystander took title, not mere possession. Therefore, the crime is false pretenses, not embezzlement. The physical transfer of that cash without any limitations on its use was a transfer of title to the money. Therefore, the crime is the obtaining of money by false pretenses. (B) is incorrect because larceny by trick occurs when the defendant obtains possession of another's property by lying or trickery. Here, the bystander obtained title to, rather than mere possession of, the money, and is therefore not guilty of larceny by trick. (C) is incorrect because the bystander obtained title to the money from the shopper when the shopper handed it to him. Therefore, there was no trespassory taking necessary for larceny.

Answer to Question 9

(A) The customer should be convicted of both offenses. Arson is the ***malicious*** burning of the dwelling of another. The malice required for arson requires either the intent to burn the dwelling of another, or an act done under such circumstances that there is obviously a plain and strong likelihood of such a burning (a wanton and reckless disregard for the safety of others through a wanton and reckless disregard for their habitation). Here, the customer's act of driving the car into a gasoline pump was an act done under circumstances that there was a plain and strong likelihood of such a burning. Because the business owner lived above the gas station, his dwelling was burned. The customer should also be convicted of murder. Murder is a criminal homicide committed with malice aforethought. Conduct that involves a wanton and willful disregard of an unreasonable human risk and that results in the death of another creates malice even though there is no intent to kill or do great bodily injury. The reckless conduct must involve a very high degree of risk to human life, and the risk must be unjustifiable under the circumstances. Driving a car into a gasoline pump would be such a high degree of risk and would be unjustifiable. This would be second degree murder. Hence, (A) is correct and (D) is incorrect. (B) and (C) are incorrect. Involuntary manslaughter is an unintentional homicide, without malice, which is neither justified nor excused. Thus, if a homicide is murder, it cannot be involuntary manslaughter. Here, because there is malice based on the customer's act involving the unreasonable risk to human life, he cannot be convicted of involuntary manslaughter. (B) is also incorrect because the customer can be convicted of arson, as discussed above.

Answer to Question 10

(B) Because this statute requires that the defendant "break and enter," the addict's best defense is that, because the pawnshop was open to the public, he had not "broken" in but entered with the implied consent of the pawnshop owner. (A) is wrong because it is immaterial to the crime of robbery (the underlying felony in this burglary) that the robber was incapable of carrying out his threat of harm, as long as the victim reasonably believed that he was. (C) is not the best answer because the statute requires only that the defendant enter the building with the intent to commit a felony. The fact that the intent was abandoned after entry would not make the defendant not guilty of burglary. (D) is wrong because there is nothing in the facts indicating that the addict was incapable of realizing what he was doing, and being a drug addict in and of itself does not show that the defendant is incapable of forming an intent to commit a crime.

Answer to Question 11

(A) The man is guilty of attempted murder. To be guilty of attempted murder, the man must first have intended to kill his friend and take steps going beyond mere preparation to carry out that intent. Both of these elements are satisfied by the fact pattern. The only fact which could negate that intent is his knowledge that the gun did not have the range to cause bullets to hit his friend. He would be guilty of attempted murder under those circumstances. The factual impossibility of committing the substantive crime is not a defense to attempt. (B) is incorrect because the standard of knowledge concerning the range of the pistol, which is required to negate the crime of attempted murder in these circumstances, is subjective knowledge of the defendant, not the knowledge of a reasonable person. (C) is incorrect because the impossibility presented in this case is a factual impossibility because of the range of the gun. That will not be a defense to the crime unless the defendant knew of the impossibility so that he could not have had the intent to kill when he fired the five shots. (D) is incorrect. Because the man possessed the intent to kill, not merely to harm, the crime is attempted murder, not assault.

Answer to Question 12

(C) The lookout will not be guilty of murder if he withdrew from the conspiracy before the robbery and killings took place. At common law, each person who took part in the planning of a crime was criminally liable for the crime of conspiracy and for each offense committed in furtherance of the conspiracy. However, if one of the conspirators "withdrew" from the criminal effort before the substantive crimes occurred, he was not liable for the subsequent crimes. To successfully withdraw, the actor must notify all members of the conspiracy that he has withdrawn; this must be done in time for them to have an opportunity to abandon the planned crimes. The facts in the question clearly indicate that he had withdrawn. (A) is not as good an answer as (C) because, if the lookout had not withdrawn, he would be guilty of murder under a felony murder theory. His ***strongest*** argument is that he withdrew. (B) is wrong because it is no defense to a charge of murder that the actor did not physically participate. The lookout would be guilty if he had not withdrawn, even without physical participation. (D) is wrong because, if the theory of the prosecutor's murder charge was that the lookout was a conspirator and is liable for all crimes committed in furtherance of the conspiracy, it would make no difference whether the other conspirators are being prosecuted. (***All*** persons must be ***acquitted*** for this defense to be effective.)

Answer to Question 13

(C) The mother will be found guilty if she fatally wounded the owner with the pistol. The defense of duress requires the commission of an otherwise criminal act under the threat of imminent infliction of death or great bodily harm. Duress is a defense to all crimes ***except homicide***. Note, though, that under certain circumstances it may reduce the homicide from murder to manslaughter. The crimes in (A), (B), and (D) would be offenses for which the mother could assert the defense of duress. However, even under duress, she would be found guilty of the homicide in choice (C).

Answer to Question 14

(A) The officer should be found not guilty of battery. Police officers are generally entitled to use whatever force is reasonably required, including deadly force, to apprehend or prevent the escape of a dangerous felon. Here, the robber was a dangerous felon who was attempting to escape. (B) is an incorrect statement of law, there is no blanket immunity. (C) is wrong because an officer may use deadly force to prevent a getaway if the felon poses a significant threat of death or serious bodily injury to others. (D) is wrong because it is irrelevant whether the officer saw the robber steal anything. He saw the weapon and the wounded victim, and thus had probable cause to believe that the robber was dangerous.

Answer to Question 15

(C) The motion should be denied. The issue in this question is not whether the seizure of the glass was valid, but whether it is an appropriate time to raise this issue. The exclusionary rule does not apply in grand jury proceedings. According to *United States v. Calandra* (1974), illegally seized evidence is admissible in grand jury proceedings. A pretrial motion to suppress is the appropriate vehicle to test the constitutionality of the seizure. The grand jury is not the appropriate forum. (A) is incorrect because the function of the grand jury is to consider evidence to determine whether there is probable cause to indict. It is not the function of the judge to take this matter away from the grand jury. A pretrial motion is the appropriate vehicle to challenge probable cause. (B) is incorrect because this choice goes to the legality of the seizure, which is not the issue in this question. The issue in this question is not whether the seizure of the glass was valid, but whether it is the appropriate time to raise the legality of the seizure. (D) is incorrect because it reaches the right result for the wrong reason. This choice goes to the legality of the seizure, which is not the issue in this question, as discussed in the explanation to (B).

Answer to Question 16

(C) The roommate's motion should be denied. Even though the search was illegal, a passenger in the automobile has no standing to object to the search. The driver was the owner of the car, and she was the victim of this search. Thus, she has standing to object to the search. The passenger has no such standing, even though the tainted evidence may be used against her. Thus, (A) is incorrect. (B) is incorrect because the judge's actions at the previous trial are irrelevant here, because the basis for suppressing the evidence is totally different. (D) is incorrect because the issue of admitting evidence from a search is separate and unconnected to any admission of ownership of the seized evidence.

Answer to Question 17

(D) The court should deny the woman's motion. The law of search and seizure is grounded in reasonable expectations of privacy. While a backyard surrounded by a fence is entitled to the same expectation of privacy from surface inspection as a home, there is no reasonable expectation of privacy from aerial inspection because the yard has no roof. Therefore, the helicopter flyover was not an unreasonable search, and evidence obtained by it can be used for purposes of obtaining a search warrant. (A) is incorrect. It is true that the purpose of the flight was to observe the yard. The issue, however, is whether the owner of the yard has a reasonable expectation that his yard will not be observed from the air. He does not. (B) is incorrect because, while the yard of a residential home is a curtilage and is entitled to an expectation of privacy from surface intrusion as a home, it does not have the same expectation of privacy from aerial surveillance because a yard, unlike a home, is open to the sky. (C) is incorrect; a warrant is required for a surface inspection of a residential yard because it is the curtilage around a home.

Answer to Question 18

(D) The court should deny both motions to suppress. Under *Pennsylvania v. Mimms* (1977), an officer at a routine traffic stop has the right to order the driver to exit the car. Thus, (A) and (C) are incorrect. Under *Maryland v. Wilson* (1997), the officer has the right to order a passenger to exit the vehicle when making a routine traffic stop. (B) and (C) are therefore incorrect.

Answer to Question 19

(B) The son's motion should be granted. The son has a reasonable expectation of privacy, as evidenced by the obscuring of the window so that passersby could not see into the shop. Hence, the officer's search would have to be based on a valid warrant or qualify under one of the exceptions to the warrant requirement. Climbing onto the trash cans and peering through a narrow opening of a window eight feet above the pavement would be considered a violation of the son's Fourth Amendment rights, and not a "plain view" of criminal activity. Because the seizure of the cocaine, mirror, and razor were based on the illegal search, the evidence could not be used by the state. (A) is wrong because absolute certainty of illegal activity is not required for a valid search. A reasonable belief is required. (C) is wrong because the arrest itself is probably invalid, and in any event a search of the next room would not be an area within the immediate control of the defendant. (D) is wrong because consent to enter the shop is not consent to search the back room.

Answer to Question 20

(C) The marijuana should not be suppressed. The search of the farmer's house, which led to the seizure of the marijuana, was based on probable cause and a valid warrant. Therefore, the evidence will not be suppressed. The United States Supreme Court has held that a person does not have a "reasonable expectation of privacy" in any land or field not a part of the curtilage. Thus, there is no Fourth Amendment protection in such areas. Therefore, the police did not violate the Fourth Amendment when they took pictures or when they cut through the fence and entered the field. All evidence obtained through those activities could be the basis for a warrant to search the farmer's house, and a search of a home based on a valid warrant will be considered reasonable under the Fourth Amendment. (A) is wrong because "open fields," even if they are fenced in, are not protected by the Fourth Amendment, and so a warrant to enter the lands was not necessary. The police may have committed a tort or perhaps violated the state criminal code when they cut the fence and entered onto the land, but the Fourth Amendment was not violated. (B) is wrong because the police could rely on anonymous information when deciding to investigate the farmer. The search of the house, which led to the marijuana, was based on a warrant and facts observed by the police. (D) is not as good an answer as (C) even though it is true that the open fields doctrine applies to the fields that the officers entered. Here, the motion to suppress relates to the marijuana taken from the house; for that, a warrant is required.

Answer to Question 21

(C) The motion should be denied. Reasonable grounds for a search are a sufficient basis to justify searches by public school officials. Neither a warrant nor probable cause is required. Thus, even though the principal did not have ***probable*** cause to believe that the drugs were in the student's purse, the principal did have sufficient ***reasonable*** grounds to search her purse. Therefore, (A) and (B) are incorrect. (D) is incorrect because it is an overbroad statement of the rights of public school officials.

Answer to Question 22

(D) The driver's motion to suppress both confessions will be denied because the facts do not indicate a violation of his constitutional rights. Under basic principles of evidence, the state can introduce evidence of a confession on the part of the defendant in a criminal case. Such evidence would be considered an admission by a party. The defendant can have the confession suppressed if the confession resulted from a violation of the defendant's constitutional rights. On the facts presented in this question, the defendant might attempt to argue that: (i) *Miranda* was not complied with; (ii) the confession was ***involuntary;*** or (iii) the confession was the direct result of an illegal arrest. All three arguments will fail with respect to both confessions. Regarding the ***first confession,*** the driver's constitutional rights were not violated. (i) *Miranda* warnings are required prior to in-custody interrogation. Here, the defendant was not being interrogated; the facts state that he "blurted out" the confession. In addition, the warnings were, in fact, given. There is no requirement under *Miranda* that the police inform the defendant of the possible charges that may be brought. (ii) The confession was voluntary. There is nothing in the facts to suggest coercion; rather, the facts state he "blurted out" the statement. (iii) The arrest was lawful; under the facts, the police had probable cause to arrest the driver. Regarding the ***second confession***, (i) while the *Miranda* analysis is not as clear-cut, in all likelihood *Miranda* has not been violated. The warnings were given at the time of the arrest and, as this confession occurred within a short period of time in a conversation with the arresting officer, it is extremely unlikely that the court would require a second set of warnings. As to (ii), again the question contains no facts that suggest an involuntary confession, and (iii) shows that the police had probable cause to make the arrest. The driver may also claim that his right to have counsel present has been violated because he mentioned the need for an attorney. However, a request for counsel, accompanied by a willingness to speak without counsel, is a valid waiver of the right to have counsel present during an interrogation. Thus, the confession does not violate the driver's constitutional rights, and (A), (B), and (C) are incorrect.

Answer to Question 23

(A) The court should rule for the state. If a person questioned by the police has not been deprived of her freedom of action in any significant way, she is not in custody and need not be advised of her constitutional rights. Thus, the rule of *Miranda* does not preclude evidentiary use of the woman's statement to the police officer. The fact that the woman was dazed does not change the admissibility of her statement. If she had been holding the assault rifle when the officer arrived, he probably would have had probable cause to suspect she had committed the offense, and at that time he would have had to read her the *Miranda* warnings. However, because the weapon was lying on the floor, the officer had no reason to suspect the woman of the crime. (B) is not the best answer because the problem is not the hearsay rule, because the woman's statement is clearly an admission. (C) is wrong because, as stated above, the woman need not be advised of her rights unless she had been taken into custody. (D) is wrong because the probative value of a confession is seldom outweighed by any unfair prejudicial effect. ***Answer choices that suggest this are almost always wrong***.

Answer to Question 24

(C) The objection should be granted. A post-charge lineup is a critical stage of the prosecution at which a defendant has the right to counsel. Once the government has initiated adversary judicial criminal proceedings, the presence of counsel is a prerequisite to the conduct of a line-up. This right attaches as soon as the accused is within sight of a potential identification witness. Here, the attorney was not present in the room until after the lineup had commenced. (A) is incorrect because the requirement that counsel be present during a post-charge lineup has never turned on a showing of government bad faith, or even government error. The government has an affirmative obligation to ensure counsel's presence at a post-charge lineup. (B) is incorrect because the fact that the attorney was present when the suspect was asked to step forward does not remedy the constitutional violation. The accused is entitled to have counsel present at all times during the lineup procedure when the accused is visible to the witnesses. Because the suspect was visible at all times during the lineup, not just when he stepped forward for closer viewing, he was entitled to counsel at all times during the lineup procedure. (D) is incorrect. It is true that, if the witnesses are unavailable at trial, their "prior identification" testimony would be inadmissible under the Federal Rules of Evidence. However, the evidence is inadmissible regardless because of a violation of the right to counsel.

Answer to Question 25

(D) The court should hold that this evidence is improper because the man who remained silent had no duty to deny the allegation here. A defendant in custody has no duty to speak at all, and the exercise of this constitutional right cannot be used against a defendant to show probable guilt. Thus, (A) is incorrect. (B) is immaterial, because the question only refers to the silent defendant's conduct and not the confessing defendant's statement. (C) suffers from the same problem, in addition to being a misstatement of the law.

Evidence

Questions and Analytical Answers

barbri®

Evidence

1. Ⓐ Ⓑ Ⓒ Ⓓ
2. Ⓐ Ⓑ Ⓒ Ⓓ
3. Ⓐ Ⓑ Ⓒ Ⓓ
4. Ⓐ Ⓑ Ⓒ Ⓓ
5. Ⓐ Ⓑ Ⓒ Ⓓ

6. Ⓐ Ⓑ Ⓒ Ⓓ
7. Ⓐ Ⓑ Ⓒ Ⓓ
8. Ⓐ Ⓑ Ⓒ Ⓓ
9. Ⓐ Ⓑ Ⓒ Ⓓ
10. Ⓐ Ⓑ Ⓒ Ⓓ

11. Ⓐ Ⓑ Ⓒ Ⓓ
12. Ⓐ Ⓑ Ⓒ Ⓓ
13. Ⓐ Ⓑ Ⓒ Ⓓ
14. Ⓐ Ⓑ Ⓒ Ⓓ
15. Ⓐ Ⓑ Ⓒ Ⓓ

16. Ⓐ Ⓑ Ⓒ Ⓓ
17. Ⓐ Ⓑ Ⓒ Ⓓ
18. Ⓐ Ⓑ Ⓒ Ⓓ
19. Ⓐ Ⓑ Ⓒ Ⓓ
20. Ⓐ Ⓑ Ⓒ Ⓓ

21. Ⓐ Ⓑ Ⓒ Ⓓ
22. Ⓐ Ⓑ Ⓒ Ⓓ
23. Ⓐ Ⓑ Ⓒ Ⓓ
24. Ⓐ Ⓑ Ⓒ Ⓓ
25. Ⓐ Ⓑ Ⓒ Ⓓ

Question 1

An airline passenger nearly killed in a crash is suing the airline for personal injuries. To prove the extent of his injuries, the passenger offers a videotape taken by a local news station immediately after the crash that shows serious burns covering much of the passenger's face. The airline moves to exclude the videotape on grounds that its probative value is substantially outweighed by the danger of unfair prejudice.

In making his ruling, it is ***inappropriate*** for the judge to consider that:

(A) The videotape will make it more likely that the passenger will win the suit.

(B) There are other methods of proving the passenger's damages.

(C) The videotape can be restricted to its proper purpose by instructing the jury to disregard any possible emotional appeal.

(D) The videotape will encourage the jury to decide the suit on an emotional basis.

Question 2

A plaintiff is suing members of the police department after receiving a near-fatal beating in jail. The plaintiff sues in federal court for violation of federal civil rights laws.

Which of the following items of evidence will the court be likely to admit despite timely objections by the opposing attorney?

(A) Testimony by a witness for the plaintiff, who was locked up in an adjoining cell, that the plaintiff was in fact beaten by the defendant police officers, objected to on grounds that calling this witness constitutes an unfair surprise.

(B) Testimony by an expert witness who will affirm the testimony of a previous expert that the injuries suffered by the plaintiff were inconsistent with injuries likely from the alleged police beating, objected to on grounds that it will unnecessarily present cumulative evidence.

(C) Introduction of the bloodstained shirt that the plaintiff wore on the night of the beating, objected to on grounds that it will create a danger of unfair prejudice.

(D) Testimony by a police officer that, because the plaintiff was arrested in a bar frequented by gay people, the officers feared that he might have AIDS, and consequently would not have beaten him for fear of being infected, objected to on grounds that it may confuse the issues or mislead the jury.

Question 3

A defendant is being prosecuted in federal court for illegally transporting persons across state lines for immoral purposes. The prosecutor alleges that her route was from New York to Tampa. The court takes judicial notice of the fact that it is impossible to get from New York to Tampa without crossing a state line.

The effect of the court's action is that:

(A) The fact judicially noticed is conclusively established.

(B) The burden of persuasion is shifted to the defendant.

(C) The burden of proof is shifted to the defendant.

(D) The prosecutor's burden of producing evidence on this point is satisfied.

Question 4

A defendant charged with murder admitted to the killing but claimed that he shot the victim in self-defense as she attacked him with a knife. At trial, the investigating officer testified about the scene of the crime and the condition of the victim at the time of death. The prosecutor showed the officer a photograph of the scene of the crime taken by the police photographer and asked the officer whether the photograph accurately depicted what he had observed at the scene. The officer testified that it did. The photograph showed the deceased lying in a pool of blood with both her hands cut off.

The court should rule that the photograph is:

(A) Inadmissible, because it does not tend to prove or disprove that the defendant acted in self-defense.

(B) Inadmissible, because it has not been properly authenticated.

(C) Admissible, unless the court determines that its probative value is substantially outweighed by the danger of unfair prejudice.

(D) Admissible, because it is relevant to the issue of self-defense.

Question 5

In a property dispute, a granddaughter claims that her grandfather gave her a deed to his home just before he died. The grandfather's son claims that the property is rightfully his by a previously executed will. At issue is the authenticity and content of the deed. The granddaughter begins to testify as to the content of the deed, but the son's attorney objects.

The court should rule that the testimony is:

(A) Inadmissible, because only the original deed itself is admissible to prove its contents.

(B) Inadmissible, unless the court is satisfied that the granddaughter is accurately testifying as to its contents.

(C) Admissible, if the judge is satisfied that the deed is unavailable.

(D) Admissible, if the deed is recorded, because the court can take judicial notice of the recorded deed.

Question 6

A defendant is on trial for first degree murder and the prosecution wants to introduce a recorded telephone call by the victim to the police just before she was killed. Distraught, the victim failed to identify herself during the call. A witness is called to testify that the voice recorded was that of victim's.

Under which of the following circumstances would the trial court likely sustain an appropriate objection by the defense counsel to admission of the tape recording into evidence?

(A) The witness had spoken with the victim numerous times, but had never heard her speak over the telephone.

(B) The witness had spoken with the victim over the telephone many times, but had never met her in person.

(C) The witness had heard the victim's voice in several recorded telephone conversations between the victim and the victim's father, and the victim's father had told the witness that it was the victim with whom he was speaking.

(D) The witness had been present with the victim when she made the call to the police, but had heard only the victim's half of the conversation.

Question 7

A defendant on trial for robbery took the stand in his own defense and testified that the robber was his neighbor. The jury acquitted the defendant based on this testimony. The neighbor was then indicted and brought to trial for the robbery. At that trial the prosecution called the defendant from the first trial to the stand, expecting him to incriminate the neighbor. Surprisingly, the defendant testified: "My neighbor didn't have anything to do with that robbery, but I know who did! I committed the robbery myself." When asked about the testimony he gave at his own trial, the defendant refused to answer, invoking his privilege against self-incrimination.

Finding her case in shambles, the prosecutor calls a juror from the first trial to the stand as a witness, who is prepared to testify that the defendant said at the first trial that the neighbor committed the robbery.

On objection by the defense, the court should rule that the juror's testimony is:

(A) Admissible to impeach the first defendant's credibility as a witness, but not as substantive evidence of the neighbor's guilt.

(B) Admissible to impeach the first defendant's credibility as a witness, and as substantive evidence of the neighbor's guilt.

(C) Inadmissible, because former jurors are not competent to testify concerning cases upon which they sat as jurors.

(D) Inadmissible, because a transcript of the first defendant's testimony at his robbery trial is the best evidence.

Question 8

A defendant charged with criminal battery testified on his own behalf at trial and asserted that he acted in self-defense.

Which of the following offered for impeaching the defendant's credibility is most likely to be barred, if objected to by the defendant?

(A) A public record showing that the defendant had been convicted of the felony of aggravated battery two years ago.

(B) A public record showing that the defendant had been convicted of the misdemeanor of filing a false police report eight years ago.

(C) Testimony from a competent witness that the defendant regularly cheats at cards.

(D) Testimony from a competent witness that, in the opinion of the witness, the defendant is a habitual liar.

Question 9

A defendant charged with auto theft under a theory of accomplice liability testified at trial on his own behalf that although he was in the car when the police apprehended the driver, he was unaware that the car was stolen.

On cross-examination, the prosecutor asks the defendant whether he lied on an employment application three years ago when he falsely claimed to hold a college degree.

If the judge allows the question, it will be because:

(A) The evidence may tend to establish that the defendant is a dishonest person and therefore may have committed the crime charged.

(B) The prosecutor has a right to inquire about prior bad acts during cross-examination.

(C) The evidence is relevant to the issue of the credibility of the witness and the court determines that its value is not outweighed by other considerations.

(D) The evidence may tend to establish the intent of the defendant to commit auto theft.

GO ON TO THE NEXT PAGE

Question 10

In a wrongful death action after a car accident involving a drunk driver, the family of the decedent sued the driver's employer for allowing its employee to drink too much at a company party.

When the company's attorney asked the driver-employee on the stand how many drinks she had, she testified that she had four drinks. The company's attorney now wants to question her about her deposition testimony, in which she said that she had two drinks.

Is this permissible?

(A) No, because it is hearsay not within any exception.

(B) No, because the company cannot impeach its own witness.

(C) Yes, but only if it is being offered to help the driver refresh her memory.

(D) Yes, because it can be offered as substantive evidence, even if it results in impeaching the driver's testimony at trial.

Question 11

At the defendant's trial for a brutal assault, in which the victim identified the defendant as her assailant, the defense calls a witness who will testify that he has worked with the defendant for 20 years and that all of his business associates regard the defendant as an honest person.

If the prosecution objects to the witness's testimony, the court should rule for:

(A) The defendant, because the testimony is relevant to show the defendant's character for truth and veracity.

(B) The defendant, because the testimony demonstrates the defendant's good character, which is inconsistent with the particular crime charged.

(C) The prosecution, because the testimony presents no evidence of any relevant character trait.

(D) The prosecution, because the testimony is hearsay not within any exception.

Question 12

The defendant, a used car salesman, is on trial for criminal fraud, charged with selling used cars with major mechanical problems while representing to buyers that the cars were mechanically sound. The defendant claims that she had no knowledge the cars were not fit for sale. At trial, the prosecution offers evidence to show that, eight months prior, the defendant was fired from a different used car lot for knowingly selling defective automobiles with major mechanical problems.

The evidence will most likely be:

(A) Admitted as evidence tending to show the defendant's criminal character.

(B) Admitted as evidence of the defendant's criminal intent.

(C) Excluded, because the previous incident did not result in a conviction.

(D) Excluded, because it is evidence of another crime tending to show the defendant's bad character.

Question 13

At a defendant's trial for rape and murder of a victim, two witnesses each testified to hearing a duck call while they were walking in the wildlife preserve before discovering the body of the victim with an arrow in her back. The prosecution then calls a third witness to the stand to testify that a year earlier, she was walking in the wildlife preserve when the defendant accosted and sexually assaulted her. Afterwards, he told her that she would have a 30-second head start before he would blow a duck call and come after her with his bow and arrow. She then fled the defendant, he blew the duck call, pursued her, and shot an arrow that narrowly missed her, enabling her to escape.

The defense counsel's objection to the third witness's testimony should be:

(A) Sustained, because her testimony is more prejudicial than probative.

(B) Sustained, because evidence of prior misconduct is not admissible to show the defendant's propensity to commit the specific crime with which he is charged.

(C) Overruled, because the testimony tends to establish that the defendant was the killer.

(D) Overruled, because the testimony tends to establish that the defendant is a violent man.

Question 14

A defendant is on trial for a murder that occurred during a robbery at the victim's home. A witness helped the police artist compose an accurate depiction of the defendant. The witness was unavailable at the time of trial and the prosecutor offers the sketch into evidence.

The sketch is:

(A) Inadmissible, under the best evidence rule.

(B) Inadmissible, as hearsay not within any exception.

(C) Admissible, as a record by a public employee.

(D) Admissible, as prior identification.

Question 15

The plaintiff is suing the defendant for serious, life-threatening injuries she suffered when the defendant's car collided with the plaintiff's at a busy intersection. At trial, the plaintiff testified that the light was green when she entered the intersection. She was not cross-examined. She also testified that she lost consciousness after the collision but awoke to find a witness comforting her as she lay on the ground. The plaintiff calls the witness to testify that, when she awoke, she said "Help, I'm dying! Why did [the defendant] enter the intersection when the light was green for me?"

The witness's testimony concerning the plaintiff's statement is:

(A) Inadmissible because it is hearsay not within any exception.

(B) Inadmissible because a party is not permitted to introduce her own out-of-court statement which is consistent with her testimony on the witness stand.

(C) Admissible as an excited utterance.

(D) Admissible as a statement under belief of impending death.

Question 16

The issue at trial is whether the sun was shining in a particular city on a particular day at 11 a.m. A witness testified that he was lying beside his wife on the beach in that city at 11 a.m. that day and she said to him, "Now that the sun is out, I'll be able to get my great tan!"

The statement is:

(A) Inadmissible as hearsay.

(B) Inadmissible because the witness does not have first-hand knowledge.

(C) Admissible only if the witness's wife is unavailable.

(D) Admissible whether or not the witness's wife is unavailable.

Question 17

A pedestrian is suing a driver after being run over by the driver. At trial, a copy of a hospital record is offered into evidence. The record indicates that hospital personnel took the pedestrian's statement 30 minutes after the accident, and includes the following statement: "The pedestrian's leg was run over by a car driven by the driver who ran a red light while the pedestrian was in the crosswalk." The driver's counsel objects to the admission of the portion of the record following the word "car."

That portion of the record is:

(A) Admissible even though hearsay within hearsay, because there is an applicable exception to each level of hearsay.

(B) Admissible as a business record relating to the plaintiff's medical treatment.

(C) Inadmissible as hearsay not within any exception.

(D) Inadmissible because of the physician-patient privilege.

Question 18

At a trial in which a pedestrian is suing a driver, a hospital record was admitted into evidence that included the following statement: "The pedestrian's leg was run over by a car driven by a driver who blew through a red light while the pedestrian was lawfully crossing in a crosswalk."

The driver's attorney now wishes to admit the other portion of the hospital record, which says, "The pedestrian stepped off the curb without first carefully looking both ways for traffic."

The court should:

(A) Admit the statement because the defendant is permitted to introduce hearsay to complete the evidence on a subject if the plaintiff has successfully introduced hearsay evidence on the same subject.

(B) Exclude it because it is hearsay.

(C) Exclude it because it is self-serving.

(D) Admit the statement as a past recollection recorded.

Question 19

A music fan sued a well-known groupie of a rock band, alleging that she was assaulted by the groupie during a melee at a concert. The fan's attorney calls the custodian of records for the hospital that treated her. He wishes to introduce a portion of the record by the emergency room physician reporting that the fan said she was assaulted by the groupie.

Assuming the custodian testifies that the record is an original, kept in the ordinary course of hospital business, that portion of the hospital record is:

(A) Admissible as hearsay within the exception for records of regularly conducted activity.

(B) Admissible as a statement made for the purpose of medical diagnosis or treatment.

(C) Inadmissible, unless the doctor who made the record is present at trial and available for cross-examination.

(D) Inadmissible as hearsay not within any exception.

Question 20

A driver and his passenger who were involved in an accident with another car consulted with a lawyer to represent them in a suit against the other driver. In attendance at the initial consultation were the lawyer, the paralegal, the driver, and the passenger. Soon thereafter, the passenger sought independent counsel and sued the driver on a cross-complaint. Prior to trial, the paralegal left the lawyer's employ. At trial, the driver's lawyer calls his former employee, the paralegal, to take the stand. The lawyer wishes to elicit testimony from her regarding the passenger's conversation with the lawyer at the initial consultation.

The testimony is:

(A) Admissible, because there was never an attorney-client privilege.

(B) Admissible, because the paralegal is not bound by the privilege after she left the lawyer's employ.

(C) Inadmissible, because of the attorney-client privilege.

(D) Admissible as an admission.

Question 21

A wife is on trial for murdering her husband. At trial, the prosecution entered into evidence the fact that the wife fired the gun which killed her husband. The wife testified in her defense that her husband was threatening her with a knife when she picked up the gun and shot him.

The prosecutor did not cross-examine her, but reserved the right to question her later in the case. In rebuttal, the prosecution calls one of the officers who responded to the wife's 911 call right after the shooting. The officer will testify that the wife said, "I accidentally dropped my gun on the floor and it went off, killing my husband."

The officer's testimony is:

(A) Admissible as an excited utterance.

(B) Admissible to impeach the wife and as evidence that she did not act in self-defense.

(C) Inadmissible, because of the wife's privilege against self-incrimination.

(D) Inadmissible to impeach the wife, because the prosecutor did not call her attention to her statement to the officer on cross-examination.

Question 22

A passenger injured in a car accident is suing the owner of a bar for allegedly allowing the driver to become intoxicated. The passenger wants to show that, after the accident, the bar owner visited him in the hospital and offered to pay all of the passenger's medical expenses, stating, "That's the least I can do after letting your driver leave the bar so drunk last night."

The statement that the driver was drunk when he left the bar on the night of the accident is:

(A) Admissible as an admission by the bar owner that the driver was drunk when he left the bar.

(B) Admissible as a factual admission made in connection with an offer of compromise.

(C) Inadmissible, as hearsay not within any exception.

(D) Inadmissible, as a statement made in connection with an offer to pay medical expenses.

Question 23

The son of a famous author who has not been seen in two years brings an action against an insurance company to compel payment of the proceeds of the author's insurance policy, for which the son is the sole beneficiary.

The son introduced evidence that, on the day the author disappeared, a plane left from the city where she lived and was lost while traveling over the ocean. The manifest of the airline was introduced showing that a passenger with a name similar to hers was aboard the airliner. The son wants to testify that his mother told him that she was going to be on that plane and, to preserve her privacy, was going to travel under the name that matches the name in the manifest.

Is the son's testimony admissible?

(A) Yes, because it is a relevant indication of state of mind.

(B) Yes, provided that there is corroborative evidence in addition to the son's mere statement.

(C) No, because it is hearsay not within any exception.

(D) No, because it is not relevant.

Question 24

A husband and wife were charged with transporting stolen goods over state lines, a federal offense. At the husband's trial, the wife voluntarily took the stand for the prosecution. She is prepared to testify that they consulted a lawyer after the charges were filed and, in the presence of the lawyer and his secretary, the husband said to his wife, "Dear, we really did know those TVs were hot. After all, we bought them for $10 each!"

On objection by the husband's attorney, the trial judge should:

(A) Exclude the testimony because of the attorney-client privilege.

(B) Exclude the testimony because of the marital privilege.

(C) Allow the testimony.

(D) Exclude the testimony because of both the attorney-client privilege and the marital privilege.

Question 25

A camper sued the manufacturer of thermal underwear, alleging that while he was attempting to stomp out a fire, the camper's underwear caught fire and burned in a melting fashion up to his waist because it was defective, and that, a half hour later, he suffered a heart attack as a result of the burns he suffered.

A physician hearing the camper testify to the events that occurred is called by the camper and asked whether the camper's heart attack could have resulted from the burns.

His opinion is:

(A) Admissible as a response to a hypothetical question.

(B) Admissible, because the physician's expertise enables him to judge the credibility of the camper's testimony.

(C) Inadmissible, because a hypothetical question may not be based on prior testimony.

(D) Inadmissible, because an expert's opinion may not be based solely on information provided by lay persons.

STOP

Answer to Question 1

(A) The judge may not consider whether the videotape will make it more likely that the passenger will win. This question involves the use of the probative value/prejudicial impact balancing test contained in Federal Rule of Evidence 403. Under this test, relevant evidence is admissible unless its prejudicial impact substantially outweighs its probative value. Since the question asks which argument is ***least*** appropriate for the trial judge to consider, turn the question around and ask which of the choices are ***appropriate*** to consider when balancing the probative value and prejudicial impact of an item of evidence. The key to answering this question is to recognize that the only kind of prejudice that can properly be balanced under this test is ***unfair*** prejudice. The fact that evidence, if admitted, will help one party and hurt another party could be considered prejudicial in the most general sense, but it does not make the evidence unfairly prejudicial within the meaning of the balancing test. Thus, (A) is the correct answer. In determining whether the videotape, which shows serious burns over the passenger's face, should be excluded, it would be inappropriate for the trial judge to consider the argument that the videotape will make it more likely that the passenger will win the suit. That would not render the evidence ***unfairly prejudicial***. Unlike (A), all the other choices contain arguments that would be appropriate to consider when applying the probative value/prejudicial impact balancing test. It is appropriate to consider whether the videotape would cause jurors to decide the suit on an emotional basis; that is the essence of unfair prejudice. Thus, (C) is incorrect. (D) is incorrect because it is likewise appropriate to consider whether an instruction to the jury to disregard any possible emotional appeal would be effective. (B) is incorrect because it is also appropriate to consider whether there are other means available to the passenger to prove damages that would bear on how necessary (*i.e.,* how probative) the videotape would be to prove damages. If other evidence is available to prove damages, especially evidence less emotionally charged than the videotape, a judge should consider that fact in determining whether the prejudicial impact of the videotape substantially outweighs its probative value.

Answer to Question 2

(A) The court will most likely admit the testimony by the witness from the adjoining cell. Under Federal Rule of Evidence 403, a trial judge has broad discretion to exclude relevant evidence if its probative value is substantially outweighed by the danger of unfair prejudice, confusion of the issues, or misleading the jury, by considerations of undue delay, waste of time, or needless presentation of cumulative evidence. Although some states list unfair surprise as an additional basis for exclusion, the Federal Rules do not, reasoning that surprise can be prevented by discovery and pretrial conference, or mitigated by granting a continuance. From the foregoing principles, if the witness in (A) is in fact a surprise witness, this will not suffice as a basis to exclude this otherwise relevant evidence under the Federal Rules, which govern this action. At most, the court should grant a continuance. In all of the other situations, while the evidence is arguably admissible, the circumstances present the judge with a basis under the Federal Rules for exclusion. The testimony in (B) may be excluded because the testimony of the second expert will not add anything to the testimony already given by the first expert. Thus, allowing this testimony will simply waste time and repeat evidence already presented. Pursuant to Rule 403, this constitutes a permissible ground of exclusion. Regarding (C), the bloodstained shirt might be deemed to be inflammatory and capable of producing an unfairly prejudicial effect on the jury. As such, it is within the realm of the judge's discretionary power of exclusion. Regarding (D), the testimony of the police officer is relevant because it tends to render more probably untrue the allegation of a police beating than it would have been without this testimony. However, the plaintiff's sexual orientation and whether he has AIDS are not issues in the case, and the statement referring to them might well cause confusion of the issues or tend to mislead the jury. Thus, the testimony of the police officer is subject to exclusion under the Federal Rules.

Answer to Question 3

(D) The court's action satisfies the prosecutor's burden of producing evidence on this point. This question involves the effect of taking judicial notice of a fact. Judicial notice allows a party to "prove" a fact by the court's recognizing that the fact is a matter of common knowledge within the jurisdiction or is able to be quickly determined by resorting to sources whose accuracy cannot reasonably be questioned. [Fed. R. Evid. 201(b)] Since judicial notice functions are a substitute for more formal evidence (*i.e.,* testimonial evidence), it has the same effect as more formal evidence. If the prosecutor had presented competent testimonial evidence to establish that it is impossible to get from New York to Tampa without crossing a state line, the prosecutor's burden of producing evidence on that point would have been satisfied. Thus, the prosecutor's burden of production is likewise satisfied if the point is established through judicial notice. (A) is incorrect because this is a criminal case. (A) would be correct if this were a civil case because, in civil cases, a fact judicially noticed is conclusively established, and thus binding on the jury. However, in criminal cases, a judicially noticed fact is not binding on the jury; the jury is ***permitted*** to find facts that have been judicially noticed, but never is ***required*** to do so. [Fed. R. Evid. 201(g)] If a jury were required to find specific facts in a criminal case, even facts that had been judicially noticed, the defendant's right to trial by jury would be undermined. (B) and (C) are also incorrect. Since this is a criminal case, the burden of establishing the defendant's guilt always stays with the prosecution. If the interstate nature of the New York-Tampa route were established through more formal evidence, the burden of establishing the defendant's guilt would stay with the prosecution. The prosecution would not be relieved of this burden if judicial notice, rather than more formal evidence, were used to establish the interstate nature of the route. (These choices were questionable from the outset because they draw a distinction between "burden of persuasion" and "burden of proof," two concepts that are often treated as interchangeable.)

Answer to Question 4

(C) The photograph should be admissible unless unfairly prejudicial under Rule 403. This question raises basic issues pertaining to the definition of relevance and the admissibility of relevant evidence. Federal Rule 401 defines relevant evidence as evidence having ***any*** tendency to make the existence of a consequential fact ***more probable or less probable*** than it would be without the evidence. Whether the defendant acted in self-defense is a consequential fact; he admitted killing the victim but claims he shot her in self-defense as she was attacking him. The photograph, showing the victim in a pool of blood with her hands cut off, makes the fact of self-defense less probable than it would be without the evidence. For this reason (A) is clearly incorrect. At first glance, (D) appears correct. (D) asserts that the photograph is admissible because it is relevant. Relevant evidence, however, is not necessarily admissible. If the probative value of evidence is substantially outweighed by ***its prejudicial impact***, the evidence is inadmissible even though relevant. [Fed. R. Evid. 403] A gruesome photograph, such as is involved here, is the kind of evidence that is sometimes excluded, notwithstanding its relevance, because of its potentially prejudicial impact. Thus, (C) is the correct answer; the photograph is admissible unless the court determines that its probative value is substantially outweighed by potential prejudice. (B) is incorrect because the photograph was properly authenticated. The photograph is demonstrative evidence, used to illustrate the police officer's testimony. The basic requirement for the authentication of demonstrative evidence is to establish that the evidence is ***a fair representation*** of what it purports to show. Here, the evidence is properly authenticated by the investigating officer's testimony that the photograph was an accurate representation of what he had observed at the murder scene.

Answer to Question 5

(C) The court should rule that the testimony is admissible if the deed is unavailable. When a proponent is attempting to prove the contents of a document, the best evidence rule applies and the original must be accounted for in order to introduce secondary evidence as to its contents. Hence, (A) is incorrect. (D) is wrong because the court may take judicial notice of court records, but the proponent of a recorded document must produce the document or record she desires introduced into evidence. A court has no power to take judicial notice of public records. (B) makes no sense because the court has no way of making such a determination.

Answer to Question 6

(C) The objection would likely be sustained where the witness was relying on the father's identification of the victim's voice. This is the only answer where the witness's knowledge of the victim's voice is based upon hearsay and not personal experience. (A) and (B) are wrong because whether the witness had heard the victim in person or over the phone goes to the weight rather than the admissibility of the evidence. (D) is wrong because if the witness heard the conversation recorded, even if only the victim's half, she would obviously authenticate it.

Answer to Question 7

(B) The juror's testimony is admissible to impeach the first defendant's credibility and as substantive evidence of the neighbor's guilt. As long as the witness is given an opportunity to explain or deny the statement, extrinsic proof of a prior inconsistent statement is admissible to impeach the witness's testimony. If the prior inconsistent statement was made under oath at a prior trial, hearing, or other proceeding, it is admissible nonhearsay; *i.e.*, it is admissible as substantive evidence. In this case, the prior inconsistent statement was made under oath at the first defendant's trial and thus is admissible for its substance as well as for impeachment. (A) is incorrect because, as discussed above, the juror's testimony is admissible as substantive evidence of the neighbor's guilt. (C) is incorrect because jurors are incompetent to testify only (i) before the jury on which they are sitting, and (ii) in post-verdict proceedings as to certain matters occurring during jury deliberations. Since the juror is not testifying before the jury on which she was sitting and is not testifying about jury deliberations, she is a competent witness. (D) is incorrect because the best evidence rule does not apply to this situation. The juror is not being called to prove the terms of a writing or to testify about knowledge she gained from reading a writing. The facts she is testifying to exist independently of any writing; thus, the best evidence rule does not apply.

Answer to Question 8

(C) The defendant's cheating at card games is most likely to be barred. This question involves the use of three different forms of evidence (reputation or opinion testimony, evidence of specific conduct, and prior criminal record) to impeach the testimony of a witness by showing that the witness has a propensity to be dishonest. Because the question asks which item of evidence is least likely to be admissible to impeach the defendant's testimony, turn the question around and ask which of the items of evidence would be ***admissible*** to impeach the defendant's testimony. The evidence in (B) is a public record of the defendant's misdemeanor conviction for filing a false police report eight years ago. Although only a misdemeanor, this conviction is admissible under

Federal Rule 609(a)(2) because it is for a crime involving dishonesty. It does not matter that the conviction is eight years old, because Rule 609(b)'s limitation on the admissibility of criminal convictions applies only if ***10 years*** have passed since the conviction or the end of the convict's incarceration. Nor does it matter that the prejudicial impact of the criminal offense involving ***dishonesty*** is offered to impeach a witness's testimony. Thus, the evidence in (B) would be admissible and so (B) is wrong. The evidence in (D) is testimony from a competent witness that, in the opinion of the witness, the defendant is a habitual liar. Federal Rule 608(a) allows such testimony, as long as the witness is competent (*i.e.,* able to base the opinion on personal knowledge). The testimony clearly relates to the defendant's character for truthfulness or lack of truthfulness. Thus, the evidence in (D) is wrong. The evidence in (A), a public record of the defendant's felony conviction for aggravated battery two years ago, is possibly admissible. Federal Rule 609(a)(1) permits evidence of a witness's past conviction for a serious crime (one punishable by death or imprisonment of more than one year) to be used to impeach the witness's testimony. Such evidence, however, is subject to a probative value/prejudicial impact balancing test. It is possible that evidence of the defendant's felony conviction would not be admissible because of the prejudicial impact it might have on his defense, particularly since the crime for which he was convicted (aggravated battery) is virtually identical to the crime with which he is now charged. However, evidence of a criminal conviction for committing a felony, particularly a recent conviction, has traditionally been freely admitted to impeach the testimony of a witness. Thus, the evidence in (A) might be admitted. The evidence in (C), testimony from a competent witness that the defendant regularly cheats at cards, is almost certainly ***inadmissible.*** This is evidence (here, the testimony from the witness) to prove specific conduct of another witness (the defendant) bearing on his character for dishonesty. Specific acts of the defendant's dishonesty may be brought out on cross-examination, but not through the use of extrinsic evidence. Thus, (C) is correct because it is a better answer than (A); it is the least likely to be admissible for the purpose of impeaching the defendant's credibility.

Answer to Question 9

(C) The judge will allow the evidence if it is relevant and its value is not outweighed by other considerations. Under Federal Rule 608, the trial court is given the ***discretion*** to allow counsel to inquire, during cross-examination, about specific instances of bad conduct on the part of the witness which show a lack of credibility. Therefore, (C) is a more accurate answer than (B). (A) is wrong; specific instances of previous bad conduct on the part of the accused are not admissible to prove the accused is the type of person who may have committed the crime. (D) is wrong; it is true that the prosecutor can prove previous bad acts to establish intent, but the prior behavior must show more about the defendant's intent at the time of the crime than this behavior does, because not all prior bad acts can be inquired about during cross-examination.

Answer to Question 10

(D) The deposition testimony is admissible. This question raises important issues concerning hearsay evidence and impeachment evidence. The driver has made an out-of-court statement (at her deposition) that she had had two drinks on the night of the accident. At trial, she testifies that she had had four drinks that night. Is her prior inconsistent statement admissible? (A) says no, because it is hearsay not within any exception. This answer is incorrect for two reasons: (i) If the deposition testimony is being offered merely to ***impeach*** the driver's credibility, then, by definition, it is not hearsay evidence. To constitute hearsay, an out-of-court statement must be offered into evidence ***to prove the truth of the matter asserted*** in the statement. [Fed. R. Evid. 801(c)] When a prior inconsistent statement is used to impeach, the truth or falsity of the statement is immaterial; what is important is that the witness has spoken inconsistently. (ii) Even if the deposition testimony is being offered for the purpose of establishing its truth, it still would not constitute hearsay evidence. Rule 801(d)(1)(A) excludes certain prior inconsistent statements altogether from the definition of hearsay evidence. If the declarant (the driver) testifies and is subject to cross-examination concerning her prior inconsistent statement, the prior statement is considered nonhearsay if it was given under oath, subject to the penalty of perjury, at a deposition. The driver's statement was made under oath at a deposition, subject to the penalty of perjury, and thus qualifies as a nonhearsay statement. (B) incorrectly states that the driver's deposition testimony cannot be used because the company (the driver's employer) cannot impeach its own witness. Rule 607 explicitly allows ***any party*** to attack the credibility of ***any witness***, even if the witness has been called by the party now attempting to impeach her. This reflects the modern view that often a party must call as witnesses persons who are hostile, or who at least have no allegiance to that party. The older view, that a party cannot impeach its own witness because of a perceived shared identity between party and witness, has been discarded. (C) incorrectly states that the driver's deposition testimony is admissible only if it is being offered to help the driver refresh her memory. As previously discussed, the driver's deposition testimony is admissible ***either*** to impeach her in-court testimony ***or*** to establish the truth of her deposition testimony (that she had only two drinks on the night of the accident). (D) correctly states these two purposes that can be served by admitting the evidence.

Answer to Question 11

(C) The court should rule for the prosecution on relevancy grounds. This question involves the admissibility of "propensity" evidence—evidence that a person has a propensity to act in a certain way because of a character trait the person possesses. Although this type of character evidence is generally inadmissible, an exception to the rule is that a criminal defendant is permitted to introduce evidence that he possesses a character that is ***inconsistent*** with the crime charged. [Fed. R. Evid. 404(a)(1)] For example, a criminal defendant accused of murder is allowed to present evidence that he is a nonviolent person; a criminal defendant accused of fraud is allowed to present evidence that he is an honest person. The defendant is charged with two crimes of violence (rape and felonious assault). The defendant's witness is prepared to testify to the defendant's reputation for honesty. However, possession of the character trait of honesty is not inconsistent with the commission of a violent crime. Honest people can and do commit violent crimes. Thus, the witness's testimony does not pertain to a relevant character trait, and so it is inadmissible. For this reason, (C) is correct and (A) and (B) are incorrect. Although phrased slightly differently, both (A) and (B) assert that the character trait of honesty is inconsistent with the commission of a violent crime, and is thus relevant, but as stated, that assertion is incorrect. Note that (A) would be correct if the defendant had testified and his character as to veracity had been attacked. In that case, the witness's testimony would be admissible to rehabilitate a witness (the defendant) whose testimony had been impeached. [Fed. R. Evid. 608(a)] But there is no indication that the defendant has testified as a witness or that, if he has, his character for truth and veracity has been attacked. Thus, (A) is a tempting answer but clearly wrong. (D) is incorrect because reputation evidence to prove character ***is*** admissible under a hearsay exception. [Fed. R. Evid. 803(21)] If the witness's proposed testimony pertained to a relevant character trait, the hearsay rule would pose no barrier to its admission.

Answer to Question 12

(B) The evidence will most likely be admitted as evidence of intent. Evidence of past crimes or misconduct may not be admitted to show the accused's criminal character or her disposition to commit the present crime. However, such evidence is admissible to show the accused's knowledge or to show lack of mistake. This evidence, then, may be admitted to show the defendant's intent to commit criminal fraud. Thus, (D) is wrong. (A) is wrong because, as stated, the evidence cannot be admitted to show her criminal character. (C) is wrong because a conviction is not necessary; merely substantial evidence is needed of the past crime of misconduct.

Answer to Question 13

(C) The objection should be overruled because the testimony tends to establish that the defendant was the person who murdered the victim. Evidence of other crimes or misconduct by the accused is admissible if those acts are relevant to some issue other than the defendant's character or disposition to commit the crime charged. [Fed. R. Evid. 404(b)] Evidence of misconduct that connects this defendant to the crime is admissible. Similarly, evidence that the accused committed prior criminal acts that are so distinctive as to operate as a "signature" may be introduced to prove that the accused committed the act in question. Here, the third witness's testimony connects the defendant to the crime because the distinctiveness of the location, weapon used, and duck call operates as a sufficient "signature" to identify the defendant as the man who raped and murdered the victim. Note also that, under Rule 413, evidence of a defendant's prior acts of sexual assault are admissible in a criminal case alleging sexual assault, independent of the requirements of Rule 404(b). (A) is incorrect. Rule 403 gives a judge broad discretion to exclude relevant evidence if its probative value is ***substantially*** outweighed by the danger of ***unfair*** prejudice and her testimony is highly probative. Therefore, her testimony cannot be excluded on unfair prejudice grounds. (B) is incorrect because evidence of the defendant's assault of the third witness is being offered to prove identity, not the defendant's propensity to commit rape and murder. When a person is charged with one crime, extrinsic evidence of his other crimes or misconduct is inadmissible if such evidence is offered solely to establish a criminal disposition. [Fed. R. Evid. 404(b)] However, if these acts are relevant to some other issue (*e.g.,* to show motive, opportunity, or identity), they are admissible. While the third witness's testimony cannot be used to show the defendant's propensity to commit rape and murder, it can be used, as here, to establish the identity of the killer. (D) is incorrect because, as discussed above, while the third witness's testimony may not be used to establish the defendant's criminal character, it may be used to prove some other relevant issue. Here, the third witness's testimony is used to establish that the defendant raped and murdered the victim, by giving evidence of a prior act bearing the same "signature."

Answer to Question 14

(B) The sketch is inadmissible on hearsay grounds. Under Rule 801 of the Federal Rules, prior identification can be admissible, and the sketch could be deemed a prior identification. However, to be admissible, the witness must be there to testify at trial and be subject to cross-examination. The witness in this case is unavailable; hence, this exception does not apply. (D) is therefore incorrect. (A) applies to documentary evidence and has no relevance to this question. (C) is likewise not applicable, because this exception applies only to information within the ***personal knowledge*** of the public employee. In this case, the public employee gained the knowledge from the hearsay statements of an absent witness.

Answer to Question 15

(C) The witness's testimony is admissible as an excited utterance. For a statement to be admissible as an excited utterance, it must relate to a startling event and be made while the declarant was under the stress of excitement caused by that event. These conditions are met in this fact pattern. The statement was made immediately after the plaintiff regained consciousness after the accident, and appears to have been made while the plaintiff was under the excitement caused by the accident. Moreover, the other choices can clearly be eliminated. (A) is incorrect because, while the statement is clearly hearsay, it reasonably could come within the excited utterance exception under Federal Rule 803(2). For a statement to be admissible as an excited utterance, it must relate to a startling event and be made while the declarant was under the stress of excitement caused by that event. These conditions are fulfilled in this fact pattern. The statement was made immediately after the plaintiff gained consciousness after the accident, and appears to be made while the plaintiff was under the excitement caused by the accident. (B) is incorrect because the statement is too broad. A party is permitted to introduce her own consistent out-of-court statement as long as that statement is relevant and is not inadmissible hearsay. In this case, the statement is clearly relevant and could reasonably come within the excited utterance exception to the hearsay rule under Federal Rule 803(2). (D) is incorrect. ***The apparent dying declaration is a favorite trick on the MBE. Remember that if the victim does not die, she must be unavailable to testify before the dying declaration is admissible on those grounds.*** Although the statement of the plaintiff was made at a time when she believed that her death was imminent and related to what would have been the cause of death, her statement is not admissible under Federal Rule 804(b)(4). That exception, while not requiring that the declarant actually die of the cause described in the statement, does require that the declarant be unavailable. In this case, the declarant is actually testifying and therefore not unavailable.

Answer to Question 16

(D) The statement is admissible whether or not the witness's wife is unavailable. The statement by the witness's wife is hearsay, an out-of-court statement offered to prove the truth of the matter stated, that the sun was out at a specific time. However, it is admissible as a present sense impression under Federal Rule 803(1) because she was observing the condition of the sun at the time that she made the statement. Unavailability is not required for this exception. Therefore, (A) and (C) are incorrect. (B) is incorrect on the law and the facts. The present sense impression exception to the hearsay rule, which is applicable in this case, only requires that the witness actually hear the declarant make the statement at the time that the declarant is observing the event. It does not require that the witness also observe the event. Moreover, as a factual matter, although it is not legally relevant, the witness would have first-hand knowledge of the event described because he was on the beach, too.

Answer to Question 17

(C) That portion of the record is inadmissible. The business records exception to the hearsay rule, under Federal Rule 803(6), admits into evidence those records kept in the course of the regular conduct of business. Therefore, the statement about the pedestrian's medical condition would be admissible. The record itself is kept in the ordinary course of the hospital's business of treating patients, and the pedestrian's statement about his medical condition, while not made by someone with a duty to keep a record, is admissible both as a statement of present physical condition under Federal Rule 803(3), and as a statement made for purposes of medical treatment under Federal Rule 803(4). However, the pedestrian's statement about the manner in which the driver drove the car does not pertain to his medical treatment and comes within no other exception to the hearsay rule, and therefore is inadmissible. Hence, (B) is incorrect. (A) is incorrect because the hearsay within the hearsay is not admissible. The admitting officer could not have known the facts stated in the record unless the pedestrian (or someone else) told him. Federal Rule 803 provides that this statement is admissible if each level of the hearsay—here (i) the pedestrian's statement to the admitting officer, and (ii) the admitting officer's statement in the record—comes within a hearsay exception. The record itself (level (ii)) is admissible under the business records exception to the hearsay rule, Rule 803(6); this is a record kept in the regular conduct of business. However, the portion of the pedestrian's statement (level (i)) in question does not come within any hearsay exception. The first part of the statement would qualify as both a statement of present physical condition under Rule 803(3) and as a statement made for purposes of medical diagnosis under Rule 803(4). However, the portion in question does not involve any information admissible within those two exceptions. Likewise, this statement was made too long after the accident to be a present sense impression or an excited utterance. Since no hearsay exception applies, the portion of the statement in question is inadmissible. (D) is incorrect because the physician-client privilege is waived by the patient when he introduces his medical record at trial.

Answer to Question 18

(A) The court should admit the statement. Federal Rule 106 provides that, when a statement or part of a statement is introduced, the adverse party may introduce any other statement or part of the statement which ought, in fairness, to be considered contemporaneously with it. (B) is incorrect because Federal Rule 106 applies even if both statements are inadmissible hearsay. (C) is incorrect. The fact that evidence is self-serving is often just another way of saying that it is hearsay. However, the rule stated in Rule 106 applies even when the remaining part of the document contains inadmissible hearsay. (D) is incorrect because the statement in the hospital record bears none of the required indicia for a past recollection recorded. There is no indication that the pedestrian's memory has failed or that the report was made under his direction to accurately reflect his memory of the incident. Moreover, the statement is admissible under Federal Rule 106 because it ought, in fairness, be considered to counterbalance the evidence already improperly admitted, even if it is hearsay.

Answer to Question 19

(D) That portion of the record is inadmissible. The statement is an assertive out-of-court statement by the music fan which does not qualify under any exception to the hearsay rule. For a business record to be admissible as an exception to the hearsay rule, the declarant must either have personal knowledge of the fact stated or must have received the information from someone with personal knowledge who transmitted it in the ordinary course of business. In this case, the music fan's statement does not qualify for the business record exception because she did not transmit it in the ordinary course of business. It likewise does not qualify as a statement made for the purpose of medical diagnosis or treatment. The statement is not offered to describe the injuries which the music fan suffered so that she could be treated for them, but rather to identify the assailant. The exception for statements made for the purpose of medical treatment under Federal Rule 803(4) is inapplicable here. Therefore, (A) and (B) are incorrect. (C) is incorrect because the presence of the doctor is irrelevant under the business record exception. That exception does not require the presence of the author of the record, only a custodian of the record.

Answer to Question 20

(D) The testimony is admissible. Since this is the passenger's statement, it is the statement of a party-opponent and can be admitted by the driver's lawyer as an admission. The attorney-client privilege is inapplicable in this case because the clients who jointly consulted the attorney are now suing each other, and there is no confidentiality between them in statements they made to the attorney in the presence of each other. (A) is incorrect because an attorney-client privilege exists in any lawsuit between the passenger and driver on one side and anyone else on the other. A lawsuit against the driver of the other car is one where the privilege would exist. This is true despite the presence of the paralegal, an assistant, at the meeting. However, the conversations were not confidential as far as the driver and the passenger are concerned, and the attorney-client privilege does not apply with respect to statements made at the joint conference in a lawsuit by either client against the other. Therefore, (C) is incorrect. (B) is incorrect. While it correctly states that the evidence is admissible, it states the wrong reason as to why. If there were an attorney-client privilege, a person whose presence does not destroy the privilege is bound by the privilege even if she leaves the employ of the attorney.

Answer to Question 21

(B) The officer's testimony is admissible. Since the wife is a party, any statement she makes can be offered against her as an admission. Admissions are not hearsay and therefore need not qualify for an exception to the hearsay rule. The statement is admissible substantively because it contradicts, and therefore tends to disprove, the self-defense theory. It is likewise a prior inconsistent statement which can be used to impeach the wife's credibility as a witness. Since the wife is still available to be recalled as a witness to explain the prior statement, the extrinsic evidence is admissible for impeachment purposes under Rule 613(b). (A) is incorrect because the statement made in this case was made to a police officer when he arrived at the house some time after the shooting. Moreover, the form of the statement shows it to be the product of reflection, rather than an unthinking response to an exciting event. (C) is incorrect because as a general rule the privilege against self-incrimination only permits an individual to refuse to give an answer to a question because it might tend to incriminate her; it does not require that an answer already given be held inadmissible later when offered in evidence. The exception is when an individual is held in custody and interrogated by the police without being given *Miranda* warnings and without waiving *Miranda* rights. However, *Miranda* warnings are not required when a statement is volunteered and not the product of interrogation, as here. (D) is incorrect because the wife is available to be recalled. Federal Rule 613(b) only requires that an impeached witness have the opportunity to explain a prior inconsistent statement. While this opportunity most often occurs during cross-examination, before extrinsic evidence of the prior inconsistent statement has been given, the opportunity may be given by recalling the witness after the prior inconsistent statement has been admitted into evidence.

Answer to Question 22

(A) The statement is admissible as an admission. This question involves an offer to pay medical expenses [Federal Rule 409], not an offer to settle a dispute [Federal Rule 408]. Although the line between these two types of offers is sometimes fuzzy, the facts in this case clearly indicate that no settlement offer was made. The defendant/bar owner offered to pay all of the passenger's medical expenses, but there is no indication of an offer to settle the entire claim that the passenger ultimately brought against him. The timing of the offer (the day after the accident, before any demand has been communicated to the defendant) and its informality (being made orally by a nonattorney to a hospitalized victim) bolster the conclusion that this case involves an offer to pay medical expenses, not an offer to settle the case. Thus, (B), which states that an offer of compromise has been made, is wrong. Moreover, even if this case were misinterpreted as involving a settlement offer, (B) would still be wrong because statements made in connection with settlement offers are inadmissible for reasons of public policy. (D) is wrong because statements made in connection with an offer to pay medical expenses, unlike statements made in connection with a settlement offer, ***are admissible***. An offer to pay medical expenses is essentially a unilateral and unconditional humanitarian gesture. Thus, negotiation and discussion are tangential to the offer itself. Consequently, there is little reason to protect from disclosure such statements as the defendant's careless admission ("letting your driver leave the bar drunk last night") even though it was accompanied by an offer to pay the passenger's medical expenses. (C) is wrong because the defendant's statement is a party admission, an out-of-court statement by a party being offered against that party, and an admission is not a hearsay statement. [Fed. R. Evid. 801(d)(2)] Moreover, even if an admission were incorrectly identified as a hearsay statement, it would nonetheless be treated as an exception to the hearsay rule and would be admissible. Thus, (A) is the correct answer. The defendant's statement is an admission. Because it is highly probative and not unfairly prejudicial, it would be admissible.

Answer to Question 23

(A) The testimony is admissible as evidence of state of mind. A declaration of intent to do something in the future is admissible as circumstantial evidence tending to show that the intent was carried out. This falls under the "present mental state" exception to the hearsay rule, and so (C) is incorrect. (B) is incorrect because at issue is the ***admissibility*** of the testimony, not its sufficiency to support a finding that the author perished on the plane. Thus, corroborative evidence is not needed. (D) is incorrect because the testimony of the author's son is relevant; it tends to make more probable the fact that the author was on the ill-fated plane and, consequently, that she is dead. Thus, the testimony of the son is admissible as circumstantial evidence that the author carried out her declared intent to travel on the plane under an assumed name.

Answer to Question 24

(A) The testimony is inadmissible because of the attorney-client privilege. The husband's communication was made to a lawyer for the purpose of legal advice at a time when he was in need of such advice. The other parties present were his wife and the lawyer's secretary, neither of whom destroys the expectation of confidentiality which is necessary to the attorney-client privilege. Therefore, the attorney-client privilege applies, and the evidence will be excluded. On the other hand, the testimony will not be excluded because of the marital privilege. The marital privilege at issue here requires a private conversation between husband and wife. The presence of two other parties destroys that necessary privacy. Therefore, the marital privilege does not apply and (B) is incorrect. (C) is incorrect; the testimony is inadmissible because of the attorney-client privilege. (D) is incorrect because the testimony will not be excluded because of the marital privilege. It will be excluded only because of the attorney-client privilege.

Answer to Question 25

(A) The expert's opinion is admissible. An expert need not have personal knowledge of the facts on which the expert bases an opinion. Under Federal Rule 703, the expert may base an opinion upon facts or data perceived by or made known to the expert at or before the hearing. Federal Rule 705 permits the expert to give the opinion without prior disclosure of the underlying facts or data, although the opposing attorney can inquire into the basis of the opinion on cross-examination. Here, the witness is volunteering the facts on which the opinion is based by answering a hypothetical question. The expert may give an opinion in response to a hypothetical question, as long as the facts assumed in that question can be found by the trier of fact based upon admissible evidence. Since the underlying facts have been introduced in evidence, this opinion is admissible. (B) is incorrect because the expert's function is not to judge the credibility of the witness, but rather to assume those facts and use his or her expertise to make a judgment based on those facts. (C) is incorrect because Federal Rule 703 permits an expert to testify concerning facts made known at the hearing. By listening to the plaintiff's testimony, this expert obtained sufficient knowledge of the facts on which to base an opinion. (D) is incorrect because there is no requirement that the information on which an expert opinion is based be anything other than information supplied by lay persons, as long as the expert can then apply to those facts the expert's expertise in the field to give an opinion on relevant evidence.

Real Property

Questions and Analytical Answers

Real Property

1. Ⓐ Ⓑ Ⓒ Ⓓ
2. Ⓐ Ⓑ Ⓒ Ⓓ
3. Ⓐ Ⓑ Ⓒ Ⓓ
4. Ⓐ Ⓑ Ⓒ Ⓓ
5. Ⓐ Ⓑ Ⓒ Ⓓ

6. Ⓐ Ⓑ Ⓒ Ⓓ
7. Ⓐ Ⓑ Ⓒ Ⓓ
8. Ⓐ Ⓑ Ⓒ Ⓓ
9. Ⓐ Ⓑ Ⓒ Ⓓ
10. Ⓐ Ⓑ Ⓒ Ⓓ

11. Ⓐ Ⓑ Ⓒ Ⓓ
12. Ⓐ Ⓑ Ⓒ Ⓓ
13. Ⓐ Ⓑ Ⓒ Ⓓ
14. Ⓐ Ⓑ Ⓒ Ⓓ
15. Ⓐ Ⓑ Ⓒ Ⓓ

16. Ⓐ Ⓑ Ⓒ Ⓓ
17. Ⓐ Ⓑ Ⓒ Ⓓ
18. Ⓐ Ⓑ Ⓒ Ⓓ
19. Ⓐ Ⓑ Ⓒ Ⓓ
20. Ⓐ Ⓑ Ⓒ Ⓓ

21. Ⓐ Ⓑ Ⓒ Ⓓ
22. Ⓐ Ⓑ Ⓒ Ⓓ
23. Ⓐ Ⓑ Ⓒ Ⓓ
24. Ⓐ Ⓑ Ⓒ Ⓓ
25. Ⓐ Ⓑ Ⓒ Ⓓ

Question 1

An elderly grandfather who wanted to ensure that his property would remain in the family after his death included the following clause in his will: "I give my house in the city to my son, but if he ever tries to sell it while he is alive, I want it taken away from him and given to my grandson." The grandfather's will was properly executed.

When the grandfather later died, what interests did the son and grandson take in the property?

(A) The son took a fee simple.

(B) The grandson took a fee simple.

(C) The son took a fee simple subject to an executory interest, and the grandson took an executory interest.

(D) The son took a fee simple determinable, and the grandson took a contingent remainder.

Question 2

The owner of land conveyed it "to my best friend, and upon her death to my daughter." The best friend took possession of the land and lived there for four years. She then conveyed "my interest in the land" to her longtime neighbor. Since the neighbor took up residence on the land, he has been sent two county property tax bills which he has refused to pay. The county is now threatening to force a sale of the property to satisfy the tax lien. The daughter filed an appropriate suit, asking the court to evict the neighbor from the land and to compel him to pay the taxes for his period of occupancy.

The court should rule that:

(A) The neighbor has a life estate in the land and he must pay the taxes on the property.

(B) The neighbor has a life estate in the land for the period of the friend's life and the neighbor does not have to pay the taxes on the property because taxes are the responsibility of the holder of the future interest.

(C) The neighbor has a life estate in the land for the period of the friend's life and the neighbor must pay the taxes on the property.

(D) The daughter owns the land, because the friend could not convey her interest to her neighbor since the daughter held the future interest.

Question 3

A woman owned 400 acres of land, half of which was densely wooded and the other half of which was almost entirely occupied by a large gravel pit which had not been in operation for a few years. A small house located on the edge of the pit was in very poor condition and had been vacant for many years. The woman transferred the 400 acres to her son for life, with the remainder going to a local charity on the son's death. Now the son wants to resume gravel production and expand the pit by tearing down the house. He also wants to cut the trees on the wooded half and sell them for profit. The local charity, holder of the remainder, sues to enjoin the son from doing any of these things.

How will the court likely rule?

(A) The charity can stop both the gravel mining and the tree cutting and can block the destruction of the house.

(B) The charity can stop neither the gravel mining nor the tree cutting but can block the destruction of the house.

(C) The charity can stop the tree cutting but not the gravel mining or the destruction of the house.

(D) The charity can stop the gravel mining and the tree cutting but not the destruction of the house because it is dangerous and unfit for use.

Question 4

An anti-smoking advocate sold his farm to a friend, a heavy smoker. In his deed to the friend he inserted the following language:

> To [the friend] and her heirs, provided, however, that if she smokes on this property while I'm alive, then the local anti-smoking league shall have the right to enter and retake my property for their ownership in fee simple.

The friend quit smoking and took possession of the property, but several years later she relapsed and was caught by the seller smoking on the property. She was told that the anti-smoking league would be notified and was resigned to losing the farm. However, when she notified the anti-smoking league board, they just laughed at her and have made no attempt to enter and claim her farm.

Has she lost the farm?

(A) No, because the league had a right of entry and they have not exercised this right; title did not go to them automatically with the breach of the condition.

(B) No, because the gift over to the league is invalid as violating the Rule Against Perpetuities, since it could be longer than lives in being plus 21 years before someone smoked on the property.

(C) Yes, because the league received an executory interest which cut short the fee simple granted to the friend on the happening of the designated event.

(D) Yes, because the friend's fee simple on a condition subsequent was terminated by the happening of the condition.

Question 5

The owner of a parcel of land in fee simple executed a will leaving the property to her sister for life, with remainder to the children of the owner's daughter. At the time of the execution of the will, the daughter had two children, Sam and Donna. Shortly after the will was executed, Sam was killed in a skiing accident, leaving his wife, Wanda, as his only heir. Two years later, the owner's daughter had a third child, Debbi. A year later, the owner of the land died. Shortly after the owner's death, Donna died in a plane crash, leaving all of her estate to her husband, Harold. Two years after the owner's death, her daughter had a fourth child, Steve. One year later, the owner's sister died. Sixteen months after that, the daughter's final child Sid was born.

Now who owns the property?

(A) Wanda, Debbi, Steve, Harold, and Sid in equal shares.

(B) Debbi, Harold, Steve, and Sid in equal shares.

(C) Harold, Steve, and Sid in equal shares.

(D) Debbi, Harold, and Steve in equal shares.

Question 6

The owner of land conveyed it to a husband and wife by a deed that created a co-tenancy in equal shares with right of survivorship. The husband then conveyed "my undivided, one-half interest in the land" to a friend. The husband then died. There is no statute directly applicable to this situation in the jurisdiction.

In an action between the wife and the friend, in which both claim sole title to the land, the wife will prevail only if:

(A) The co-tenancy created in the husband and the wife was a tenancy by the entirety.

(B) The wife was once the sole owner of the land.

(C) The husband and the wife owned the land as tenants in common.

(D) The wife had knowledge of the conveyance prior to the husband's death.

Question 7

A husband and wife held land as joint tenants with right of survivorship. On the marriage of their daughter, the husband and wife conveyed a 10% interest to her. Two years later, the husband, without the wife's knowledge, conveyed another 10% interest to the daughter's spouse.

Which of the following best describes how the land is now owned?

(A) The husband and wife hold an 80% interest as joint tenants, and the daughter and her spouse each hold a 10% interest as tenants in common.

(B) The husband and wife hold an 80% interest as joint tenants, and the daughter and her spouse a 20% interest as joint tenants.

(C) The husband has a 40% interest, the wife has a 40% interest, the daughter has a 10% interest, and her spouse has a 10% interest, all as tenants in common.

(D) The husband has a 35% interest, the wife has a 45% interest, the daughter's spouse has a 10% interest, and the daughter has a 10% interest, all as tenants in common.

Question 8

A couple living in a jurisdiction that did not recognize common law marriages held themselves out as husband and wife even though they were never married. When the couple purchased a home, the deed identified the grantees as "husband and wife, as tenants by the entirety." Both signed the note and deed of trust as husband and wife. Because the couple maintained separate bank accounts for convenience, the man made the monthly payments on the house while the woman paid for household expenses.

Two years later, the man was involved in a near-fatal automobile accident and was hospitalized for several months. During this period, the woman made the monthly house payments from her own checking account. When the man was discharged from the hospital he abandoned the woman and entered a monastery. The woman continued to make the monthly house payments and after six months brought an action for partition of the property.

Her request for partition should be:

(A) Granted, because the estate created by the deed was not a tenancy by the entirety.

(B) Granted, because the tenancy by the entirety was severed when the man abandoned the woman.

(C) Denied, because the man had made most of the mortgage payments from his separate property.

(D) Denied, because a tenant by the entirety has no right to partition.

Question 9

The elderly owner of a small furnished vacation cottage who had not used it for several years decided to rent it out to vacationers. His first tenants, a newlywed couple, agreed to pay $400 for a month stay, although the owner apologized that he had not been able to clean the cottage before renting it because he had not been there for several years. When they arrived at the cottage, the wife started carrying the luggage up the wooden steps of the house and one of the steps collapsed, seriously injuring her. On inspection it was revealed that the steps had rotted. Although no one had been aware of the defect, a reasonable inspection would have disclosed it.

Is the owner liable to the wife for her injuries?

(A) No, because the owner neither knew nor had reason to know that the steps were rotted.

(B) No, because the owner told the tenants that he had not been to the house for several years and so was not aware of its current condition, and the wife could have discovered the defect if she had made a reasonable inspection.

(C) Yes, because a landlord warrants that premises are free of latent defects.

(D) Yes, because the lease is for one month and the house is furnished.

Question 10

A tenant entered into a two-year apartment lease with a landlord on July 1. Rent was specified in the lease to be $850 per month, payable on the first of each month.

On June 15, near the end of the two-year term, the landlord asked the tenant if he wanted to renew the lease for an additional term. The tenant said he would like to think about it, and the landlord agreed, but added that the rent for the new lease would be $975 per month. The landlord heard nothing from the tenant. On July 10, the landlord found that the tenant was still in the apartment and told him that he was imposing a new tenancy on the tenant for the period allowed by the law under these circumstances.

What tenancy can be imposed, and at what rent?

(A) The landlord can impose a new periodic tenancy of month-to-month and the rent will be $850 per month.

(B) The landlord can impose a new periodic tenancy of month-to-month and the rent will be $975 per month.

(C) The landlord can impose a new periodic tenancy of year-to-year and the rent will be $850 per month.

(D) The landlord can impose a new periodic tenancy of year-to-year and the rent will be $975 per month.

Question 11

The owner of a house purchased a new home but decided to keep his old residence for a few months until the real estate market improved. He rented it to a tenant with the understanding that the tenant might have to move out in a few months if the house was sold. The tenant paid the owner the agreed rent of $100 per week every Friday.

During the next few months, the owner's business suffered serious setbacks so he decided to sell his new home and move back into his old one. He informed the tenant that he would have to vacate the old home, but the tenant refused to vacate and tendered the $100 rental payment the following Friday, which the owner refused to accept.

The owner immediately filed suit to eject the tenant. The jurisdiction requires that a statutory written notice be served on any tenant whose term is for less than month-to-month or is not for a fixed term at least three days prior to commencement of eviction proceedings. No written notice of any kind was given to the tenant.

The owner is most likely to gain immediate possession of his home by arguing that the tenant is:

(A) A tenant from month to month.

(B) A tenant at sufferance.

(C) A licensee.

(D) A trespasser ab initio.

Question 12

A woman owned two adjacent parcels. The east parcel fronts on a poor unpaved public road, while the west parcel fronts on a major highway. Fifteen years ago, the woman conveyed the east parcel to her son "together with a right-of-way 25 feet wide over the east side of the west parcel to the highway." At that time, the east parcel was improved with a 10-unit motel.

Ten years ago, the woman died. Her will devised the west parcel "to my son for life, remainder to my daughter."

Five years ago, the son executed a deed purporting to convey the east and west parcels to his friend in fee simple. The friend then enlarged the motel to 12 units.

Six months ago, the son died and the daughter took possession of the west parcel. She brought an appropriate action to enjoin the friend from using the right-of-way.

Who should prevail?

(A) The daughter, because merger extinguished the easement.

(B) The daughter, because the friend has overburdened the easement.

(C) The friend, because he has an easement by necessity.

(D) The friend, because he has the easement granted by the woman to her son.

Question 13

A man and a woman who owned two adjacent properties executed and recorded reciprocal easements to five-foot strips of land on the border of their properties for the purpose of constructing a 10-foot-wide common driveway to their street, on which each of them had only five feet of frontage. After the driveway had been constructed, the town constructed a new road abutting the woman's property in the rear. The woman constructed a new driveway to that new street, and soon thereafter ceased using the common driveway. One year later, the woman sold the property to a buyer, who used the new driveway for four years and did not use the old one. The man then commenced using the entire 10 feet of the old driveway by parking his cars on both sides, and the buyer commenced an action to prevent the man's use of the five feet of the driveway on the buyer's land. The period for acquiring title by adverse possession in the jurisdiction is five years.

In that suit:

(A) The buyer will prevail because nonuse is insufficient to cause abandonment of the easement.

(B) The buyer will prevail because he is a bona fide purchaser.

(C) The man will prevail because the easement was abandoned by the woman and the buyer through their use of only the new driveway.

(D) The man will prevail because the period required for adverse possession is five years.

Question 14

A woman who owned a parcel of land had direct access to the main road by an unpaved driveway. However, she decided that it would be more convenient to use a paved driveway on an adjoining parcel, so she began doing so. The man who owned the adjoining parcel also used the driveway, but he did not discover that the woman was using the driveway until two years later. At that time, he wrote a letter to the woman protesting the use of the driveway, but the woman continued to use the road. After she had used the road for a total of 20 years, she filed an action for declaratory judgment, claiming a prescriptive right to use the driveway on the west parcel. The time limit necessary to obtain an easement by prescription in this jurisdiction is 20 years.

Which of the following is the most accurate statement with regard to the woman's use of the driveway now?

(A) The woman could not acquire a prescriptive easement in the west parcel because her original use was wholly trespassory and without any claim of right.

(B) The prescriptive period began to run when the woman first began using the driveway because the woman was in open and notorious possession, despite the fact that the man did not know of it.

(C) The prescriptive period began to run when the woman first began using the driveway despite the fact that, at that time, she was sharing her use with the man.

(D) The prescriptive period did not begin to run until two years after the woman began using the driveway, at the time her use of the driveway was contested.

Question 15

An owner of two abutting lots on a street deeded the north parcel to a buyer and inserted in the deed the following language: "Grantee, his heirs and assigns shall not plant any shrubbery within 10 feet of the boundary line." The buyer recorded. The buyer later deeded the north parcel to a friend and did not include the language about the shrubbery in the deed. The friend planted a row of shrubbery within five feet of the common boundary.

If the owner sues the buyer's friend to require him to remove the shrubbery:

(A) The owner will prevail because there is a covenant running with the land.

(B) The owner will prevail because the deed from the buyer to the friend carried with it an implied promise not to plant shrubbery within 10 feet of the common boundary of the two parcels.

(C) The friend will prevail because the deed from the buyer to the friend created only a personal contract between them.

(D) The friend will prevail because there was no writing signed by the buyer, the friend's predecessor in title.

Question 16

Several decades ago, a square tract of 640 acres was subdivided into lots, streets were constructed, and utilities were installed. As the developer sold off each of the lots, each lot's deed contained a restriction limiting the lots to residential use only. The deeds were all recorded. Over the years, houses were constructed on all of the lots. The property to the south, east, and west of the subdivision was initially forest, but gradually the city expanded to surround the development. Unfortunately, the city expansion was mostly industrial and some commercial property, but no residential property. The subdivision is now bounded on all sides by many industries that operate 24 hours a day. The combination of noise, dirt, fumes, and other pollution has made many of the houses in the subdivision unfit for residential use, yet each deed still stipulates "residential use only."

Can the restriction be voided?

(A) Yes, the restriction can be voided on all lots in the subdivision since changed conditions have made the houses unusable as residences.

(B) Yes, the restriction can be voided under these circumstances, but only as to the lots that have actually been rendered unfit for residential purposes.

(C) No, the restriction cannot be voided because in this circumstance the proper remedy is the tort action of nuisance.

(D) No, the restriction cannot be voided unless every single lot is so seriously affected by the pollution that the houses are unfit for residential use.

Question 17

A buyer contracted to purchase from a seller a corner lot with a house. The contract gave the street address of the property as 235 East Madison Street and additionally gave the following metes and bounds: "East 80 feet along Madison Street, then south 80 feet along Jensen Street, then east 80 feet, then north 80 feet." A casual inspection of the lot and a careful reading of the metes and bounds description would make it clear that the third call should have read "west 80 feet" instead of "east 80 feet."

Prior to the closing date, the seller died, and when the buyer appeared on the closing day with a certified check in the amount of the purchase price, the seller's personal representative refused to convey the parcel or to accept the money from the buyer. The representative claimed that the buyer had no rights in the parcel because the contract description was so defective as to call into question what was to be conveyed.

If the buyer sues the seller's estate for specific performance, the likely result is:

(A) The buyer wins, because the fourth call prevails over the third call in a legal description.

(B) The buyer wins, because equity will not allow a forfeiture based on a technicality.

(C) The buyer loses, because metes and bounds is an improper way to legally describe land.

(D) The buyer loses, because street names do not provide an adequate legal description of land.

Question 18

A first-time home buyer financed the purchase of a house with a $100,000 mortgage she took out with a bank. The mortgage was recorded. A few years later she borrowed $5,000 from a finance company to pay for a foreign trip, using her house as security. The finance company recorded its mortgage on the property. One year after that, she borrowed $40,000 from an equity company to pay for an addition on the house. The equity company did not record the mortgage it took on the property. Shortly thereafter, she lost her job and was unable to make payments on either the finance company's or the equity company's mortgages, but she was able to make payments on the bank's mortgage. The finance company filed foreclosure of its mortgage, and a purchaser bought the property at the foreclosure sale.

What is the purchaser's obligation regarding the bank's mortgage and the equity company's mortgage?

(A) The purchaser takes the property subject to both mortgages.

(B) The purchaser takes the property subject to neither mortgage.

(C) The purchaser takes the property subject to the equity company's mortgage, but not subject to the bank's mortgage.

(D) The purchaser takes the property subject to the bank's mortgage, but not subject to the equity company's mortgage.

Question 19

A seller agreed to sell a tract of land by an enforceable written contract to a buyer for an agreed price. At the time and place designated for closing, the seller tendered the deed to the land, but the buyer refused to complete the transaction because of a secured note on the land, saying that the contract required the seller to supply a deed free of encumbrances. The seller responded that she intended to pay the secured loan, which was substantially less than the contract price, with the proceeds of the sale of the land. The seller offered to put the proceeds of the sale in escrow for that purpose, for which the buyer could pick the escrow agent. The buyer refused the seller's proposal. The seller then brought suit against the buyer for specific performance of the land sale contract.

The seller's best argument in support of her claim for relief is:

(A) Under the doctrine of equitable conversion, title has already passed to the buyer and the only issue is how the purchase price is to be allocated.

(B) As the seller of real estate, the seller had an implied right to use the proceeds to clear the title being conveyed.

(C) Since the seller partially performed, the agreement is specifically enforceable.

(D) A secured note does not remain attached to property, but rather remains attached to the borrower.

Question 20

An owner conveyed his property to a buyer, who put the deed in his suitcase and took off for a five-month tour of the world. The owner, knowing that the buyer had left the country, sold the property to a speculator for $5,000, although the speculator had heard the buyer say he had bought the property. The speculator promptly recorded the deed. When the buyer returned from his trip, he recorded his deed to the property. Two weeks after the buyer recorded, the speculator conveyed the property to an investor for $15,000. The investor knew nothing about the buyer's deed and the investor promptly recorded the deed from the speculator. A month later, the investor conveyed the property to a developer for $17,000. The developer knew that the buyer held a deed to the property but paid the investor the $17,000 anyway. Instead of recording, however, the developer immediately filed an appropriate action against the buyer and against the investor to determine ownership of the property.

The property is situated in a jurisdiction containing the following statute: "Any conveyance of an interest in land, other than a lease for less than one year, shall not be valid against any subsequent developer for value, without notice, whose conveyance is first recorded."

The court will rule that:

(A) The buyer has superior rights to those of both the investor and the developer.

(B) The investor has superior rights to those of both the buyer and the developer.

(C) The developer has superior rights to those of both the buyer and the investor.

(D) The developer has superior rights to those of the investor, but the buyer has superior rights to those of the developer.

Question 21

A buyer purchased an old house, financing his purchase by taking out a mortgage on the property with a bank, which the bank recorded. Shortly after moving in, the buyer realized that new windows would have to be installed, so he purchased some custom-made windows, easily removable for cleaning, from a retail dealer, who agreed on an installment payment plan, with the windows as security. The old windows were removed and placed in the basement of the house.

After three payments to the bank on the mortgage and two payments to the retailer on the windows, the buyer lost his job and ceased making payments to both the bank and the retailer. The buyer has left town, and the retailer plans to remove the windows from the house. The bank files suit to prevent the retailer from removing the windows.

How should the court rule?

(A) The retailer may remove the windows, because the old windows are available for the bank to use in restoring the house to its original condition.

(B) The retailer may remove the windows, because the windows are designed to be removable.

(C) The retailer may not remove the windows, because windows are an integral part of the house.

(D) The retailer may not remove the windows, because the bank's lien is senior to the retailer's.

Question 22

A buyer purchased a tract home in a new development, putting up 20% of the purchase price as a down payment and financing the rest through a mortgage with a bank. The mortgage contained a due-on-sale clause. After three years, the buyer put her house on the market, continuing to make all mortgage payments promptly. The buyer eventually sold the house to a third party, who took subject to the mortgage. After the third party took possession, the bank received no further mortgage payments from either the buyer or the third party.

In most states, which of the following best describes the remedy or remedies available to the bank?

(A) The bank may foreclose on the land, but may not sue either the buyer or the third party on the underlying debt.

(B) The bank may foreclose on the land, or it may sue the buyer on the underlying debt.

(C) The bank may foreclose on the land, or it may sue the third party on the underlying debt.

(D) The bank may foreclose on the land, or it may elect to sue either the buyer or the third party on the underlying debt.

GO ON TO THE NEXT PAGE

Question 23

A father gave his daughter marketable title to a five-acre parcel of undeveloped land that adjoined 200 acres of uninhabited forest owned by a neighbor. When she visited her property with her father, he mistakenly pointed out the boundary line. She subsequently staked out the boundaries and built a log fence along what she thought was the boundary line. Approximately an acre of the neighbor's land was inside her fence. The daughter built a cabin and lived in it for 30 years until she had to sell the property for medical reasons.

The daughter entered into a contract to sell the land. In accordance with the contract, the purchaser had a survey of the land done, which revealed the boundary discrepancy in the legal description. The purchaser contacted the neighbor, who said he knew nothing of the matter and did not consent to the daughter's placement of the fence on his property. The purchaser then refused to proceed with the purchase. The jurisdiction in which the parcel was located had a 20-year period of occupation to satisfy the requirements of adverse possession.

If the daughter sues for specific performance of the land sale contract, she will:

(A) Prevail, because the daughter satisfied all elements required to make out adverse possession of the portion of the neighbor's property within her fence.

(B) Prevail, because the land sale contract was unaffected by the minor discrepancy in the legal description.

(C) Not prevail, because the daughter's title to the land is not marketable.

(D) Not prevail, because the daughter's fencing in of the neighbor's property was not hostile, even if the neighbor had no knowledge of her actions.

Question 24

Twenty-five years ago, a nephew received a deed to a farm as a gift from his aunt. The aunt's deed was properly executed and delivered, and the nephew recorded. He moved onto the farm and farmed it until his death five years later. In his will, the nephew devised the farm to his son for life with the remainder to his grandson, who was a child at that time. The son did not have the slightest desire to even visit the farm, so shortly thereafter a neighbor who owned the adjacent land offered to buy the farm. The son transferred all his rights in the farm to the neighbor by quitclaim deed. The neighbor had a full-time job and only wanted the land to live in the farmhouse. The neighbor remained in possession of the farm for five years, and then took a job in a distant city for five years. After five years, the neighbor returned to the farmhouse. Shortly thereafter, the son died, leaving his son (the grandson) as his only heir. The neighbor was aware that the grandson loved farming and would want to take over the property in a few years, so the neighbor built and moved into a home on his own land. After 10 more years of schooling, the grandson finally moved to the farm.

Shortly thereafter, the grandson discovered that the aunt who made the initial transfer to her nephew had not in fact been the fee simple owner of the farm. The true owner of the property, according to the records, was the aunt's half-sister who died 20 years ago, leaving her daughter as her only heir. The grandson brought an action to quiet title to the farm. The statutory period for adverse possession in the jurisdiction is seven years.

The grandson should:

(A) Lose, and the neighbor will take clear title to the farmhouse and the entire farm by virtue of his adverse possession for over 10 years.

(B) Lose, and the neighbor will take clear title to the farmhouse but not to the rest of the farm that was not actually possessed by him.

(C) Win, because he had the farm for over 10 years after his father died, more than the seven-year statutory period for adverse possession.

(D) Lose, and the daughter is the fee simple owner of the farm.

Question 25

A manufacturer owned property on which were located a manufacturing building and a storage building. Both of these buildings were located on the east side of the manufacturer's land. A developer owning land on that side began constructing the foundation of an office building on the property, excavating up to the edge of the lot bordering the manufacturer's property. Late one night, the manufacturer's storage warehouse collapsed and his manufacturing building suffered severe structural damage when the ground shifted. An engineering survey, which both parties stipulate is correct, determined that the collapse would not have occurred had the weight of the supplies in the manufacturer's storage building not put so much downward pressure on the manufacturer's land.

In a suit by the manufacturer against the developer for the damage to the land and the buildings:

(A) The developer will only be liable if it is shown that the developer was negligent in excavating the developer's land.

(B) The developer will be strictly liable for all damage to the manufacturer's property.

(C) The developer will be strictly liable for damage to the manufacturer's land, but will only be liable for damage to the buildings if the developer was negligent.

(D) The developer will be liable for damages to the manufacturer's land if the developer was negligent, but will not be liable for damage to the manufacturer's buildings even if the excavation was done negligently.

STOP

Answer to Question 1

(A) The son received a fee simple in the property. The grandfather attempted to give his son a fee simple, but placed a restraint on alienation. Direct restraints on alienation of a fee simple are void. The grant is simply read as if it had been "O to A in fee simple." The grandson gets nothing. Thus, (A) is correct. (B) is incorrect because the grandson could not have gotten a fee simple in this devise even if there had not been the problem of restraints on alienation. He would, even by the terms of the will, take only if the son tried to sell the property. (C) is wrong because of the rule prohibiting restraints on alienation of a fee simple. Absent the rule on restraints, these would be the interests taken by the son and grandson. (D) is incorrect because the form of the language does not support a fee simple determinable in the son (no "so long as" type of language), and the grandson could not have a remainder because a remainder can never follow a fee simple.

Answer to Question 2

(C) The neighbor has a life estate for the life of the friend and must pay taxes. When the best friend transferred her life estate to the neighbor, he took an estate that will terminate when the best friend dies. That is all that the best friend owned and all that she could convey. In addition, the rule is that the life tenant is responsible for paying taxes on the property (had there been a mortgage, the life tenant would have had to pay the interest on the mortgage but not the principal). (A) is incorrect. While it is true that the neighbor had a life estate and he does have to pay taxes, this is not a full answer since it does not recognize that his life estate is not an ordinary one; it is one measured by the best friend's life, not his own. (B) is incorrect. The neighbor does have a life estate measured by the best friend's life, but he must pay the taxes. Taxes are not a responsibility of the holder of the future interest, but are an obligation of the life tenant. (D) is incorrect. A life tenant can transfer the life estate to anyone, and the holder of the future interest has no say in the matter. Of course, if the new tenant abuses the property, the holder of the future interest has the ability to sue to stop waste, but cannot stop the transfer itself.

Answer to Question 3

(C) The charity can stop only the tree cutting. The charity would be suing the life tenant on a theory of waste. Both the gravel mining and the tree cutting could be voluntary waste. Generally, a life tenant can only maintain the property and not sell off any of the natural resources, such as trees and gravel. But there is an exception for existing exploitation of these resources. Since the gravel mine was operating prior to the son's taking of the life estate, that preexisting use is protected and the son is not liable for continuing the mining of gravel. But the trees do not fall under this exception. Since the property had not been in use as a tree farm, the general rule applies and the cutting of the trees would be waste. The destruction of the house might be considered ameliorative waste—the destruction of improvements on the life estate that increase the value of the property (*i.e.*, they make the gravel mining more profitable). Generally, a life tenant cannot tear down improvements simply because the life tenant wants to make a more profitable use of the land. But an exception exists when changed conditions have made the destruction of the improvement reasonably necessary. Here, the house was on the edge of the pit, vacant because of its very poor condition. Changed conditions (the encroachment of the pit) have made the house reasonably unsuitable so the life tenant can tear it down. (A) is incorrect because the gravel mining cannot be stopped and the house can be destroyed. (B) is incorrect because the tree cutting can be stopped but the house can be destroyed. (D) is incorrect because the tree cutting is the only thing that can be stopped.

Answer to Question 4

(C) The friend has lost the farm as a result of the league's shifting executor interest. The draft language is very muddled. It grants a fee simple to the smoking friend and then purports to grant a "right of entry" to the anti-smoking league. This would be impossible, since a right of entry is the future interest retained by the grantor when the grantor gives a grantee a fee simple on a condition subsequent. A grantee cannot be given a right of entry. Here, if the condition operates, the property will go not to the grantor, but to another grantee. In this event, the friend must have gotten a fee simple subject to total divestment if the condition happened. No right of entry was retained by the grantor. Since the anti-smoking league will cut short the estate of the friend if the condition operates, they must have an executory interest. Thus, (C) is correct. The anti-smoking league could not have a remainder since remainders never follow a fee; the only other future interest in a grantee is an executory interest. (A) is incorrect. The anti-smoking league did not get a right of entry as this future interest is only available in a grantor. (B) is incorrect. The Rule Against Perpetuities does not apply to this grant since the smoking must occur during the owner's (the anti-smoking advocate's) lifetime for the condition to operate to vest title in the holder of the executory interest. (D) is incorrect. A fee simple on a condition subsequent is always accompanied by a right of entry in the grantor. Here, if the condition operates, it will shift title to the anti-smoking league, cutting short the fee simple in the friend.

Answer to Question 5

(D) Debbi, Harold, and Steve take. The gift-over to the daughter's children is a class gift. Sam predeceased the testator. Under the class gift rule of wills law, if a will makes a class gift and a class member predeceases the testator, that person drops out and the remaining members of the class will take. So Sam and, through him, Wanda are out. At the property owner's death, her daughter had Donna and Debbi, making their interests at that time vested remainders in fee simple subject to open to make room for any future children of the daughter. When Donna died, her vested remainder passed to Harold. When Steve was born, he joined Debbi and Harold, all three holding vested remainders in fee simple. When the owner's sister died, her life estate ended, giving the present possessory estate to the holders of the future interest—Debbi, Harold, and Steve. Why is Sid left out? Because of the class closing rule: Whenever any member of the class is entitled to a distribution, the class closes and the distribution is made then. Any later arrivals to the class lose out entirely. Since Debbi, Harold, and Steve are eligible for a distribution the moment the life tenant (the owner's sister) dies, they take, and Sid, not yet born, loses out. (A) is incorrect. Wanda does not take, since her claim comes through Sam, who predeceased the testator; Sid does not take, since he was born after a member of the class was entitled to a distribution. (B) is incorrect. Sid's birth came too late for him to be considered a member of the class, since others in the class were entitled to a distribution when the life tenant died. (C) is incorrect. Debbi should be included, and Sid should be left out, for the reasons noted above.

Exam Tip: For questions like this, when it is almost impossible to remember the many births, it is helpful to make a short chart:

Before the owner's (the testator's) death:

Sam born, Sam dies (gift lapses)

Donna born

Debbi born

After the owner's death, but before the death of the life tenant (her sister):

Donna dies, gift passes to Harold

Steve born

The sister dies

Notice that nothing that happens after the life tenant's death matters. Consulting the chart, you quickly see that Debbi, Harold, and Steve take.

Answer to Question 6

(A) The wife will prevail only if the co-tenancy was a tenancy by the entirety. The somewhat ambiguous description of the conveyance given in the problem could apply either to a joint tenancy with a right of survivorship or to a tenancy by the entirety. If the conveyance is a tenancy by the entirety, then further conveyance by the husband to the friend would not cause a severance and, on the husband's death, the wife would be the sole owner of the land. On the other hand, if it were initially a joint tenancy, the husband's conveyance would sever it, converging the estate of the wife and the friend into a tenancy in common. (Note that a tenancy by the entirety is always a marital estate.) (B) is irrelevant because the form of concurrent ownership, *i.e.*, tenancy by the entirety or joint tenancy, not the status of prior ownership, is determinative of the rights of the parties. (D) is also irrelevant because the form of concurrent ownership is controlling, regardless of knowledge or lack of knowledge of the subsequent conveyance to the friend. Under (C), the wife and the friend would each have an undivided ***one-half*** interest.

Answer to Question 7

(D) The respective interests are 35%, 45%, 10%, and 10%. When the husband and wife conveyed 10% to their daughter, each retained 45% as joint tenants with one another, and the daughter's 10% is, by severance, a tenancy in common. Since both the husband and wife joined in the conveyance to their daughter, their interests remain undisturbed as joint tenants. When the husband then conveyed 10% to the daughter's spouse, that conveyance severed the husband and wife's joint tenancy and left them as tenants in common. The daughter's spouse's 10% is, of course, also a tenancy in common. Since the husband's conveyance of 10% to the daughter's spouse was not joined by the wife, the 10% must come out of the husband's 45% interest. So when the dust settles, the husband is left with 35%, the wife has 45%, and the daughter and the daughter's spouse each have 10%, all as tenants in common. (A) is incorrect. The husband and wife could not have equal shares because the husband transferred 10% to the daughter's spouse solely. That 10% had to come out of his share, not the wife's. And the sale by the husband alone to the daughter's spouse severed the joint tenancy between the husband and wife, turning it into a tenancy in common. (B) is incorrect for the reason stated above. Additionally, the daughter and the daughter's spouse could in no way be joint tenants with each other since the four unities (time, title, interest, possession) were not satisfied as to their grants. (C) is incorrect because it does not recognize that the husband's sale of 10% to the daughter's spouse solely (without the wife's joining), means that this 10% can come only out of the husband's share, not the wife's. The husband can only have 35%; the wife must have 45%.

Answer to Question 8

(A) The woman's request for partition should be granted. A tenancy by the entirety can exist only between parties who are married to one another at the time of the grant. This requirement is absolute, and circumstances of living-like-married or saying-you-are-married will not suffice. Since the state did not recognize common law marriages and since there was no marriage ceremony, there was no tenancy by the entirety. If it is not a tenancy by the entirety, it can only be a joint tenancy or a tenancy in common. Since there is no language expressly making it a joint tenancy, it has to be a tenancy in common. Tenants in common, like joint tenants, always have the right to partition. Only tenants by the entirety do not have it. (B) is incorrect. The parties do not have a tenancy by the entirety. Even if they did, a tenancy by the entirety is severed only by death of one of the parties (which gives title to the survivor), a written agreement between the parties, divorce of the parties (which makes the parties tenants in common, with each owning an undivided half), or execution by ***a joint*** creditor (not an individual creditor of one of the parties). "Abandonment" by one of the parties, even if that party were a spouse, would not sever the tenancy by the entirety. (C) is incorrect. When determining the right to partition, only the nature of the co-tenancy, not the source of the funds for the purchase, is relevant. If it is a valid joint tenancy or a tenancy in common, partition is allowed. If it is a valid tenancy by the entirety, partition is not available. (D) is incorrect. It is true that a tenant by the entirety has no right of partition, but the fact that the parties were not married when the grant was made keeps this from being a tenancy by the entirety.

Answer to Question 9

(D) The owner is liable to the wife. Landlords are liable for latent defects even if they neither knew nor should have known of the defect if the lease is for a short term and the property is furnished. This is an exception to the general rule that a landlord is not liable for latent defects unless the landlord either knew or had reason to know of the defects. Thus, (A) is incorrect. (B) is wrong because there is no duty of the tenant to make an inspection of the property to detect latent defects, and the owner's lack of awareness of the condition will not excuse him when he leases a furnished dwelling for a short term. (C) is incorrect. Landlords do not impliedly warrant that premises are free of latent defects. A landlord will be liable only if, in the general situation, the landlord knew or had reason to know of the defect or, in the exception, the landlord rents furnished property for a short term.

Answer to Question 10

(B) The tenancy will be month-to-month at $975 per month. When a tenant wrongfully holds over after the expiration of a lease, the landlord has two choices: either treat the tenant as a trespasser and sue for damages and possession or impose a new periodic tenancy on the hold-over tenant. If the landlord chooses, as this landlord has done here, to impose the new periodic tenancy, most courts in residential situations would impose a month-to-month tenancy. While the rent (as well as other terms) of the new tenancy will generally be the same as the old tenancy, there is an exception when the landlord has told the tenant of a future higher rent and that notification came ***before*** the expiration of the old lease. In that event, the landlord can impose the higher rent in the new periodic tenancy. ***Exam Tip: The facts in this type of question may vary—be sure that the landlord told the tenant of the higher rent before the expiration of the old lease; otherwise, the old, lower rent applies.*** Since the landlord told the tenant that the tenant could stay on at $975 and this occurred on June 15, prior to the expiration of the two-year lease, then if the tenant held over and the landlord elected to hold the tenant to a new periodic tenancy, it would be at the higher rent. (A) is incorrect. While the new tenancy is month-to-month, the rent will be at $975, not $850. (C) is incorrect in both assertions. The landlord can impose a periodic tenancy of month-to-month and it will be at $975 per month, not $850. (D) is incorrect. While the rent will be $975, the new tenancy is month-to-month, not year-to-year.

Answer to Question 11

(C) The owner's best argument is that the tenant is a licensee. A license is a privilege to enter onto another's property. It may be revoked at any time merely by a manifestation of the licensor's intent to end it. (A) and (B) are wrong because a tenant at sufferance would be entitled to the statutory notice, and a month-to-month tenant would benefit from the common law right to a period of notice equal to the tenancy, *i.e.,* one month. (D) is wrong because the tenant is clearly not a trespasser ab initio since he entered onto the premises with permission.

Answer to Question 12

(D) The friend should prevail. The deed from the woman to her son granted the son an express easement. That easement was never terminated by merger and the friend, the owner of the motel property on the east parcel, still has a valid easement over the daughter's property, the west parcel. (A) is incorrect because, for there to be a merger which will extinguish an easement, each of the two parcels must be owned in exactly the same manner. In this case, the son owned the east parcel in fee simple but owned only a life estate in the servient estate, the west parcel. Therefore there was no merger of the two estates and the easement was not extinguished by the son's partial ownership of the servient estate. The friend likewise never owned the west parcel in fee simple because all that was owned by the son, his grantor, was a life estate in the west parcel. (B) is incorrect. The right of way over the west parcel at the time it was granted serviced a 10-unit motel. The expansion of the motel by an additional two units will cause a minimal increase of the use of the way and does not overburden it. (C) is incorrect because the friend does not have an easement by necessity. The east parcel fronts on a poorly paved public road. At the time the woman conveyed the east parcel to the friend's predecessor in title, the son, there was access to his property from a public way and there is no absolute necessity which would have created an easement by necessity. The friend therefore never received the property benefited by an easement by necessity.

Answer to Question 13

(A) The buyer will prevail. The easement in this case is an easement by grant. That easement was not used for five years, but there were neither acts which would have terminated that easement by adverse possession, nor was there a manifested intent to abandon. ***Exam Tip: Don't be fooled by very long periods of nonuse in the facts—make sure there is an act showing intent; otherwise, there can be no termination.*** Therefore, the easement was not terminated by mere nonuse, and the buyer will prevail as the successor to the easement granted to the woman. (B) is incorrect. While it correctly states that the buyer will prevail, his success does not depend on his status as a bona fide purchaser. The buyer holds the easement solely because it is appurtenant to the land which he purchased. His good faith in purchasing the land and paying value for it did not enlarge his rights. (C) is incorrect because nonuse alone does not terminate an easement. For the easement to be terminated by nonuse, it would have to be accompanied by an intention to abandon the easement, or the fee owner (the man) would have to exclude the buyer from using the easement in an open and notorious manner for the period necessary to acquire an easement by prescription. (D) is incorrect because the acts of the man in using a common driveway for over five years do not constitute the open and notorious blocking of the easement which is required to terminate an easement by adverse possession. When the man did start blocking the easement, the buyer took action to preserve his rights.

Answer to Question 14

(C) The woman's first use of the driveway started the prescriptive period running. There is no requirement of exclusive use for the woman to obtain an easement by prescription. Exclusivity is only required in cases of adverse possession. Adverse possession is not at issue here because the woman has not "possessed" any part of the west parcel, and does not require title to continue her use of the property, which is all she seeks. Therefore, (D) is incorrect. (A) is incorrect because the only way in which a prescriptive easement can be obtained is for a person to trespass on land and to continue to trespass for the statutory period. The fact that the use was wholly trespassory in fact gives the man the cause of action and starts the clock running on the statute of limitations. Whether the use was undertaken under a claim of right is wholly immaterial to the analysis. The statute of limitations runs whether or not the trespasser thinks the use is lawful. (B) is incorrect. This choice correctly states that the woman's conduct when she began using the driveway started the prescriptive period and correctly states that the man's lack of knowledge is irrelevant. It is incorrect because it does not correctly describe the conduct of the woman. She was not in open and notorious possession; she was merely using the man's driveway. The distinction is important because exclusive possession for the statutory period leads to title by adverse possession, while adverse use will only result in a prescriptive easement. The woman does not need to and could not live up to the more exacting standard of adverse possession in this case.

Answer to Question 15

(A) The owner will prevail because the covenant runs with the land. The covenant in the original deed from the owner to the buyer will be enforceable against the buyer's successor, the friend, only if the covenant runs with the land, either at law or as an equitable servitude. With the facts presented, the owner would prevail under either theory. This covenant was created by a signed writing. The buyer's acceptance and recording of the deed containing the covenant is the legal equivalent of his signature. Therefore, the covenant is enforceable between the original parties. Moreover, the covenant was intended to run with the land and bind the grantee's successors. The provision states that it binds the "grantee, his heirs and assigns." The covenant also clearly touches and concerns the land, since it controls the grantee's land use (for the benefit of the grantor's adjoining land). There is horizontal privity because the covenant was created in the deed from the owner to the buyer which also created the buyer's estate. Also, the friend is in vertical privity with the buyer, because the friend purchased from the buyer. Therefore, the covenant runs at law to the buyer's successor, the friend. The fact that the covenant was recorded in the friend's chain of title would also give him constructive notice of the covenant such that it could be enforced against him as an equitable servitude. Under either theory, the owner will prevail. (B) is incorrect because reliance on an "implied promise," which does not accurately reflect any recognized rule of law, is misplaced. This obligation is enforceable as a covenant running with the land. A successor to land subject to a covenant which runs with it would be bound by the covenant even if the original contracting party and the successor specifically disavowed the contractual obligation. (C) is incorrect. The covenant in the deed from the owner to the buyer did create an enforceable contract between the two. However, that mere contract became a covenant running with the land enforceable at law or as an equitable servitude against the buyer's successors in title, so the owner will prevail. (D) is incorrect because the covenant was created by a signed writing. While the Statute of Frauds normally requires a writing signed by the party to be charged for a contract relating to land to be enforceable, the buyer's acceptance and recording of the deed containing the covenant is the legal equivalent of his signature. Therefore, the covenant is clearly enforceable between the original parties, and as a covenant running with the land is also binding on their successors, including the friend.

Answer to Question 16

(D) The restriction cannot be voided. Restrictive covenants on all lots in a subdivision such as this can be voided only if changed conditions have made the property unusable for the specified use, and this means that each lot in the subdivision must be unusable. If some houses in the center of the subdivision are not affected by the pollution, then none of the restrictions can be voided; if all lots are affected, then all restrictions are voided. (A) is incorrect because it does not make clear that to void all the restrictions every house must be unsuitable for residential use. It simply says "houses," and does not recognize that it must be "all houses," as (D) does. (B) is incorrect. This is an all-or-nothing proposition. Either you void the restriction to all lots or you void it to none. Under no circumstances would you select from among the lots, voiding some but not others. (C) is incorrect. This situation may indeed give rise to tort liability in negligence, but that is not the only remedy. If homeowners want to sell out to nonresidential users, or engage in nonresidential use themselves, they must first get out from under the restriction in their deeds. This avenue exists independently from any right to sue in nuisance.

Answer to Question 17

(B) The buyer will win because equity does not like forfeitures based on technicalities. For the description of land in a land sale contract or deed to be adequate, it must accurately identify the property. As long as it is clear what property is the subject of the contract, the description is acceptable, even though it may contain errors. A court of equity may grant specific performance. The court will look at the description, together with the address of the land noted in the contract. These, taken together, make it clear that call three should have read "west" rather than "east," and that error will not prevent specific performance. (A) is incorrect because there is no such rule. (C) is incorrect because metes and bounds are the most common way land is described in land sale contracts and deeds. (D) is incorrect. A minority of states do not allow street addresses to be considered in determining whether a description of land is adequate. The majority, however, allow a court of equity to consider all available evidence in determining whether to grant specific performance. Since the street address here makes it clear that call three was "east" instead of "west" merely by accident, the court can grant relief.

Answer to Question 18

(D) The purchaser takes the property subject only to the bank's mortgage. A foreclosure sale wipes out all junior mortgages (those that came later in time than the mortgage that was foreclosed) but does not wipe out senior mortgages (those that came earlier). Since the bank's mortgage preceded the finance company's, it is senior and is not wiped out. The purchaser takes subject to this mortgage. Thus, (B) is wrong. Although the purchaser is not personally liable on this debt (he did not sign the note, only the original buyer did), he must pay the mortgage or face foreclosure by the bank. Since the equity company's mortgage came later than the finance company's, it is junior and is wiped out. Thus, (A) and (C) are wrong. If, after paying the cost of the foreclosure and paying off the finance company's mortgage, there is money left over from the sale, it will first go to paying off the equity company's mortgage. But regardless of whether the equity company's mortgage is paid off, the purchaser takes completely free of this obligation.

Answer to Question 19

(B) The seller had an implied right to use the proceeds to clear title. It is true that the seller is obligated to transfer a title free of encumbrances, and a mortgage qualifies as an encumbrance. It is also true, however, that a seller may use proceeds paid by the buyer at closing to pay off mortgages, and thus deliver clear title to the buyer. As long as the amount due from the buyer is enough to pay off the note, the seller has an implied right to do this, and the existence of the note under these circumstances does not breach the contract sale. (A) is incorrect. While equitable conversion does take place the moment the contract of sale is signed, and the effect of this is to give the buyer equitable title at that moment, legal title does not pass until the closing. A warranty by the seller that the deed given at closing will be free of encumbrances is unaffected by the doctrine of equitable conversion. (C) is wrong because the doctrine of part performance is used to take a sale out from under the Statute of Frauds, a situation not present here. If the seller promised a deed free of encumbrances, that is enforceable by the buyer even if the seller has performed or is ready to perform all other parts of the agreement. (D) is incorrect because it misstates the law. A secured note remains attached to the property, and does not remain with the borrower. If the purchaser fails to make payments on the note, the holder of the note can foreclose the mortgage and have the property sold to satisfy the note.

Answer to Question 20

(A) The court will rule that the buyer has superior rights. Under a race-notice statute, which is the statute applicable here, a subsequent purchaser will prevail only if that person took without notice of the earlier transfer and was the first to record. The investor did not know of the earlier transfer to the buyer, and the developer did know of it, but neither recorded before the buyer did. Since neither satisfied the requirements of the race-notice recording act, the previous purchaser, the buyer, prevails. (B) is incorrect. Since the investor did not record before the buyer did, he cannot have superior rights to the buyer. He may have taken without notice of the earlier sale, but in a race-notice jurisdiction that is not enough; he must also have been the first to record. (C) is incorrect. Not only did the developer take with notice that the buyer was the first to record—indeed, the facts show that the developer has never recorded. (D) is incorrect. The developer had notice of the earlier sale and the investor recorded before the developer, who has never recorded.

Exam Tip: On complex recording questions, the order of transfers and recordings is critical, so make a quick marginal chart of transactions:

1. Owner to buyer, no recording

2. Owner to speculator, speculator records & knows of buyer's deed

3. Buyer records

4. Speculator to investor, investor records

5. Investor to developer, no recording & developer knows of buyer's deed

Answer to Question 21

(D) The retailer may not remove the windows because they are fixtures and the bank's mortgage on the real property takes priority. Under the concept of fixtures, a chattel that has been annexed to real property is converted from personalty to realty. As an accessory to the real property, it is subject to any mortgage on the real property. In all common ownership cases (*i.e.,* those in which the person who brings the chattel onto the land owns both the chattel and the realty), whether an item that is not incorporated into a structure is a "fixture" (*i.e.,* part of the realty) depends upon the objective intention of the party who made the "annexation." This intention is determined by considering: (i) the nature of the article; (ii) the manner in which it is attached to the realty; (iii) the amount of damage that would be caused by its removal; and (iv) the adaptation of the item to the use of the realty. Under this analysis, the windows are fixtures. It should first be noted that the buyer is the fee simple owner of the house, rather than a tenant. The fact that the windows were easily removable (and therefore would cause minimal damage in the event of removal) would ordinarily indicate less of an intention to permanently improve the freehold, but here the facts indicate that they were easily removable to make it easier to clean them. Another important factor indicating that the windows are fixtures is that they cannot readily be used at any other house unless the window sills happen to correspond to those of the buyer's house. They were custom-made specifically for that house and, therefore, they were specially adapted to the use of the realty. They serve both functional and aesthetic purposes, they are an integral part of the house, and are necessary and appropriate to the use of the premises. Thus, in view of factors (i) and (iv) above, and considering the buyer's fee simple ownership and long-term plans for the house, they should be deemed fixtures.

The fact that the windows are fixtures does not resolve the dispute between the retailer and the bank, however. Under Article 9 of the Uniform Commercial Code, a seller of a chattel that will become a fixture can grant a security interest in the chattel for a portion of the purchase price and protect his interest by making a "fixture filing" even though the real property has a mortgage. Under U.C.C. section 9-313(4), a seller who provides a purchase money security interest in an affixed chattel will prevail (to the extent of his claim) over a prior recorded mortgage on the land as long as the chattel interest is recorded within 20 days after the chattel is affixed to the land; this allows the seller to remove the chattel without having to reimburse the mortgagee for any diminution in the property's value. However, if this exception does not apply, the general rule that the first interest to be recorded prevails will be applied by the court. Here, while the retailer has a purchase money security interest in the windows, there is no indication that he made a fixture filing within 20 days of when the windows were installed. Thus, the bank's recorded mortgage interest is superior to the retailer's security interest, so the retailer will not be permitted to remove the windows. (A) is incorrect. In determining whether a chattel is a fixture in landlord-tenant cases, courts will generally allow the tenant to remove any chattel that he installed (*i.e.*, deem it not be a fixture) if removal does not cause substantial damage to the premises or the virtual destruction of the chattel. However, that reflects the probable intent of the tenant who purchased the chattel, since he has no interest in permanently improving the freehold. Here, however, the buyer was the fee simple owner of the house. The fact that he saved the old windows does not negate his intent to permanently improve the real estate with the new ones. (B) is incorrect because, as discussed above, the ease of removing the windows was for purposes of cleaning and does not negate an intent to permanently improve the real estate. (C) is incorrect, even though it states an important factor for concluding that the windows are fixtures. As discussed above, that fact would not have precluded the retailer from prevailing, had he recorded his security interest in the windows.

Answer to Question 22

(B) The bank may foreclose or sue the buyer on the debt. In the majority of jurisdictions, when a mortgagor transfers title to another, and the transferee takes "subject to" the mortgage, that means that the transferee will not be liable to the mortgagee on the promise underlying the mortgage. So the third party cannot be sued on the debt. But the mortgage follows the property and if the transferee does not make the payments, the mortgagee may foreclose on the mortgage. In any event, the mortgagor, the buyer, remains liable on the mortgage after the transfer and she can be sued on the debt. If the facts showed that the third party had "assumed" the mortgage, rather than merely taking "subject to" it, then he could have been sued on the debt. (A) is incorrect. The buyer signed the mortgage and promised to pay the debt. She will always continue to be liable for her promise regardless of whether the third party is liable. And, since the mortgage follows the land, the mortgagee may always foreclose. (C) is incorrect. The third party did not "assume" the mortgage. He can thus not be held liable on the underlying debt, although if he does not make the payments, the mortgagee may foreclose, since the mortgage always follows the land. (D) is incorrect. Only the buyer is liable on the underlying debt since the third party only took "subject to" the mortgage. Because the mortgage follows the land, the mortgagee may always foreclose if the mortgage is not paid.

Answer to Question 23

(C) The daughter will not prevail because her title is not marketable. The daughter did satisfy all six requirements of adverse possession of the portion of the neighbor's property. She possessed it exclusively for more than the statutory period, her possession was continuous and adverse to the rights of the true owner, and her possession was visible for all to see. But, even though she did acquire title by adverse possession, that title is not marketable until a judicial action is taken to quiet title. The law does not require purchasers to have to go to court to clearly establish title. Since the daughter had not done this, the title she contracted to convey was not, in fact, marketable. Thus, (C) is correct. (A) is wrong because mere satisfaction of the elements of adverse possession is not enough to make title marketable; the adverse possessor must quiet title in a court action. (B) is incorrect. While the doctrine of marketable title merely requires a title that a reasonable person would accept, a discrepancy of one acre in a tract this small could in no way be considered "minor." (D) is incorrect. The daughter's fencing in of the neighbor's acre was hostile since she neither owned it nor had any right to fence it in. The true owner's knowledge (or lack of it) of an adverse possessor's actions is irrelevant to adverse possession.

Answer to Question 24

(D) The grandson will lose, and the daughter owns the farm. Since the half-sister was the legal owner at the time the aunt transferred to her nephew, any claimant out of the nephew's will must rely on adverse possession to defeat the half-sister's daughter's claim. The only possible persons who could have possessed it adversely are the nephew, the son, the grandson and the neighbor. The nephew did not get title by adverse possession because he possessed for only five years. The son did not succeed either because there is no evidence he ever possessed the farm and, in any event, it could not have been for more than a year because of his transfer to the neighbor. The neighbor did have possession of the house, although not the rest of the farm, but his possession was interrupted by his five-year job in a distant city. He did not continuously possess any part of the farm for seven years. The grandson may have claimed the property as his own for 10 years, but adverse possession requires actual possession and he never actually possessed any of the farm. Since all adverse possession claims fail, the daughter must own the property in fee simple. (A) and (B) are incorrect. As indicated above, the neighbor did not continuously adversely possess any part of the farm for the necessary seven years. Thus, he has no claim to any of the farm, even the farmhouse he occupied. (C) is incorrect. The grandson never took possession of the farm for that 10-year period. The mere fact that he claimed it during that time will not serve as a basis for adverse possession.

Answer to Question 25

(C) The developer will be strictly liable only for the damage to the land. A landowner is strictly liable to the adjacent landowner for support of the land, and this liability does not depend on negligence. But the strict liability rule extends only to the land and not to the improvements if it is shown that the land would not have collapsed had it not been for the weight of the improvements. So the manufacturer can recover for the value of the land itself. As to the improvements, the manufacturer can recover in strict liability if their weight did not help cause the collapse; if it did, the manufacturer has to show negligence in excavation by the developer. (A) is wrong because it does not recognize the rule of strict liability for failure to support adjacent land. (B) is incorrect. This fails to note that the strict liability rule goes to the land itself and only to the improvements if it can be shown that the land would have collapsed even if it had not had the improvements on it. (D) is incorrect. If the excavation was done negligently, ordinary tort rules apply. The adjacent landowner can recover for the buildings if a reasonable person would not have excavated the land as the developer did. All tort principles apply.

Torts

Questions and Analytical Answers

barbri®

Torts

1. Ⓐ Ⓑ Ⓒ Ⓓ
2. Ⓐ Ⓑ Ⓒ Ⓓ
3. Ⓐ Ⓑ Ⓒ Ⓓ
4. Ⓐ Ⓑ Ⓒ Ⓓ
5. Ⓐ Ⓑ Ⓒ Ⓓ

6. Ⓐ Ⓑ Ⓒ Ⓓ
7. Ⓐ Ⓑ Ⓒ Ⓓ
8. Ⓐ Ⓑ Ⓒ Ⓓ
9. Ⓐ Ⓑ Ⓒ Ⓓ
10. Ⓐ Ⓑ Ⓒ Ⓓ

11. Ⓐ Ⓑ Ⓒ Ⓓ
12. Ⓐ Ⓑ Ⓒ Ⓓ
13. Ⓐ Ⓑ Ⓒ Ⓓ
14. Ⓐ Ⓑ Ⓒ Ⓓ
15. Ⓐ Ⓑ Ⓒ Ⓓ

16. Ⓐ Ⓑ Ⓒ Ⓓ
17. Ⓐ Ⓑ Ⓒ Ⓓ
18. Ⓐ Ⓑ Ⓒ Ⓓ
19. Ⓐ Ⓑ Ⓒ Ⓓ
20. Ⓐ Ⓑ Ⓒ Ⓓ

21. Ⓐ Ⓑ Ⓒ Ⓓ
22. Ⓐ Ⓑ Ⓒ Ⓓ
23. Ⓐ Ⓑ Ⓒ Ⓓ
24. Ⓐ Ⓑ Ⓒ Ⓓ
25. Ⓐ Ⓑ Ⓒ Ⓓ

Question 1

At a little league game, a seven-year-old boy was called out on strikes. The boy's father was so infuriated with the umpire's decision that he shouted in a loud voice, "Kill the umpire." The boy, who was still holding his bat, swung the bat at the umpire. The umpire ducked and the bat flew out of the boy's hands and struck a spectator, who was seriously injured.

In a tort action by the umpire against the boy:

(A) The umpire could recover only on an assault theory.

(B) The umpire could recover either on an assault theory or a negligence theory.

(C) The umpire could recover only on a negligence theory.

(D) The umpire could not recover.

Question 2

A physician performed scheduled surgery on her patient's right ear for a condition caused by prolonged and repeated infections in that ear. During the surgery, the physician determined that her patient had been particularly susceptible to this condition due to a previously unsuspected anatomical abnormality. The physician reasonably believed that this same abnormality was likely to exist in the patient's left ear. Though the patient had not had many infections in the left ear, if a similar course of recurring infections were to transpire involving that ear, it would probably develop the same condition as the right and require surgery. The physician therefore decided to perform surgery on her patient's left ear, although she had received his consent only to operate on the right ear. The surgery was performed with due care and was successful. The applicable jurisdiction permits the extension of an operation beyond the consented procedure only in emergency situations.

In an action by the patient against the physician:

(A) The patient will not recover because the extension of the operation was successful.

(B) The patient will not recover because the extension of the operation was carried out with due care.

(C) The patient will recover at least nominal damages on a negligence theory.

(D) The patient will recover at least nominal damages on a battery theory.

Question 3

Two men stopped to have a drink together at a bar, where five other people were also gathered. The two men had a few drinks and began to argue, hurling insults at each other. After the first man threw a punch, a fight ensued, and the second man was struck in the back of the head with a heavy object from behind. He never saw who had struck the blow and he was knocked unconscious. He was hospitalized for a severe concussion and still suffers from severe headaches.

The injured man sues the first man as well as the five other persons present in the bar at the time he was struck, and presented the evidence above.

The injured man will:

(A) Prevail, because the first man was the aggressor.

(B) Prevail, because the first man acted unreasonably.

(C) Not prevail, because he cannot prove that there was concerted action against him.

(D) Prevail, because of the doctrine of res ipsa loquitur.

Question 4

A man and a woman who were fierce business competitors were both competing for a large job. The man submitted his bid and then went to the woman's office and told her, "If you leave this office, I'm going to get you!" The woman merely laughed and said, "I'm about finished with my bid and will be leaving in a few minutes." The man left the office but placed a large, heavy couch across the entrance to the woman's office, hoping to keep her from leaving. Meanwhile, the woman finished the bid and tried to leave her office, but found that she could not open the door. She pushed against the door as hard as she could and was eventually able to force it open, then ran all the way to the place where bids were being taken and got her bid in with one minute to spare. As usual, her bid was slightly lower than the man's, and she was awarded the contract.

If the woman sues the man, she has a cause of action for:

(A) Assault, but not false imprisonment.

(B) False imprisonment, but not assault.

(C) Both assault and false imprisonment.

(D) Neither assault nor false imprisonment.

Question 5

A college student was holding a loud party at her house. The next door neighbor was getting increasingly angry with the noise, and several complaints to the local police station brought no results. The neighbor called the student on the phone and told her that if she did not stop the noise, he would "come over there and cut your throat." The visibly shaken student told her guests what had just happened, and they all decided to leave immediately. The student was unable to sleep that night and thereafter purchased an alarm system for her house and a gun that she kept next to her bed.

If the student brings an action for intentional infliction of emotional distress and succeeds, it will be because:

(A) The neighbor had the apparent present ability to make good on his threat.

(B) The student suffered some physical harm as a result of her distress.

(C) The student suffered pecuniary injury as a result of his threat.

(D) The neighbor's conduct was extreme and outrageous.

Question 6

While returning from transporting a group of children to summer camp, a bus driver and his assistant were caught in the leading edge of a forest fire raging down the high mountains. Hurrying ahead of the flames and smoke, the driver reached the last half-mile of a dirt road that ran to the main highway and safety, but he discovered that the road ahead was already blocked by fallen, burning foliage. Separating the driver's bus from the main highway, which angled off to the right, was the fenced property of a rancher. The bus driver drove across the property to reach the main highway, damaging some turf and a fence, and proceeded to the city.

If the rancher asserts a claim against the bus driver, the rancher will probably:

(A) Lose, because the bus driver was acting to protect the lives of himself and his assistant.

(B) Lose, because the bus driver acted as would any reasonably prudent person under the circumstances.

(C) Win, because the bus driver damaged the rancher's property when he drove through the fence to get to the main highway.

(D) Win, because the bus driver intentionally drove across the property, knowing it would cause damage.

Question 7

Two members of a backgammon club owned identically sized, red backgammon boards. The first member's board was made of cheap material while the second member's board was quite expensive. One night, after a competitive tournament, the two members met in the finals, playing on a borrowed board. The second member won and the first member, visibly upset, mistakenly grabbed the other's board and drove home. As was her custom, she left the board in the trunk of her car. Meanwhile, the owner of the board discovered the board switch and drove to the first member's apartment to make an exchange. The first member took the second to her parking place and saw that her car had been stolen. The police recovered the car days later, with no backgammon board in the trunk. The second member demanded a replacement board, but was refused.

In an action to recover the board's value, the second member will:

(A) Recover, because when the first member took the board she committed a trespass to chattel.

(B) Recover, because when the board was stolen along with the car, the first member became liable for conversion.

(C) Not recover, because the first member believed in good faith that the board was hers when she took it from the club.

(D) Not recover, because the board was lost through no fault of the first member.

Question 8

A teenager who was totally blind in one eye and had only 10% vision in the other could not obtain a driver's license. Nevertheless, on his 18th birthday, he borrowed his father's car and took his girlfriend for a ride. With his 10% vision in one eye, he was able to stay in the correct lane and avoid oncoming traffic, but he failed to see a jogger on the edge of the highway. The teenager's car hit the jogger, causing serious bodily injury.

If the jogger prevails in a negligence suit against the teenager, it will be because:

(A) The teenager failed to exercise ordinary and reasonable care under the circumstances.

(B) The teenager failed to exercise the amount of care that an 18-year-old of like education, intelligence, and experience would have exercised.

(C) The teenager failed to exercise the ordinary and reasonable care that a person with the teenager's disability would have exercised.

(D) The teenager violated the law when he drove without a license.

Question 9

A passenger departed on an ocean liner, knowing that it would be a rough voyage due to predicted storms. The ocean liner was not equipped with the type of lifeboats required by statute. The passenger was swept overboard and drowned in a storm so heavy that even a lifeboat that conformed to the statute could not have been launched.

In an action against the operator of the ocean liner brought by the passenger's representative, will the representative prevail?

(A) Yes, because the ocean liner was not equipped with the statutorily required lifeboats.

(B) Yes, because in these circumstances common carriers are strictly liable.

(C) No, because the passenger assumed the risk by boarding the ocean liner knowing that it would be a rough voyage.

(D) No, because the storm was so severe that it would have been impossible to launch a statutorily required lifeboat.

GO ON TO THE NEXT PAGE

Question 10

A driver traveling the speed limit in the evening on a quiet country road rounded a curve and struck a bicyclist who was riding in the same lane. The driver stopped the car and inspected the bicyclist, who had a broken leg. The driver thought it best not to try to move the bicyclist, so he told him that he would go to get help. The driver drove away and left the bicyclist by the side of the road. After the driver had left the scene, he realized that he had forgotten his wife's birthday, so he stopped to buy a gift and hurried home. He did not remember the bicyclist until a few hours later, but assumed that by that time someone would have come along to render assistance. However, the bicyclist was not rescued until the following morning. By then, he had contracted pneumonia as a result of exposure.

The bicyclist sued the driver to recover damages for his broken leg and the pneumonia.

If the jury finds that the driver was not negligent in his operation of his automobile, the bicyclist will most likely:

(A) Recover for both the leg injury and the pneumonia.

(B) Recover for the leg injury but not the pneumonia.

(C) Recover for the pneumonia but not the leg injury.

(D) Not recover for either the leg injury or the pneumonia.

Question 11

A pilot was flying her small airplane when she realized that she was rapidly losing fuel and would not make it to the nearest airport. Looking down, she could find no large open space on which to attempt a landing except for a highway off to her left and a nearby lake about a mile to her right. She considered ditching the plane in the water but decided against it under the circumstances. As the pilot maneuvered over the highway and saw a long section free of any overpass or obstruction, her engine sputtered and died. In a barely controlled glide, the pilot descended onto the highway, but her left wing sideswiped the median and her plane veered to the right, crashing into a car. The plane and car catapulted into a fence, severely injuring both the pilot and driver.

The driver brought an action for personal injuries against the pilot. At trial, the above facts were established, and the parties stipulated that the sudden loss of fuel was due to a defect in the fuel system that could not have been discovered by the pilot. At the close of the evidence, both parties moved for a directed verdict.

The court should:

(A) Deny both motions, because the jury could decide that the pilot's selection of the highway rather than the lake was not a reasonable choice under the circumstances.

(B) Grant the driver's motion, because the evidence establishes that his injuries were the result of a defect in the pilot's plane.

(C) Grant the pilot's motion, because the parties stipulated that she was not negligent in failing to discover the defect in her fuel system.

(D) Grant the pilot's motion, because she made the decision to land on the highway rather than the lake under emergency conditions.

Question 12

The parents of an eight-year-old boy at a public school told the school principal that their son said he had been molested by his teacher. The next day, the principal confronted the teacher with the accusation. The teacher admitted sexually molesting the boy, but he pleaded with the principal for another chance, promising never to do it again. Although the principal believed him, he still insisted that the teacher must leave. The teacher then threatened to blackmail the principal with information he had about a former student of the principal who had an affair with him when he taught at the local high school. Fearful that he would lose his position if this accurate information ever came to light, the principal allowed the teacher to continue teaching, and told the family that the boy's charges were unfounded. Two weeks later, the teacher molested the boy again, and the teacher was arrested and charged with both incidents.

In a suit against the principal on the boy's behalf, the parents will:

(A) Win, because the principal is vicariously liable for the teacher's torts.

(B) Win, because the principal was aware that the teacher was a child molester and did nothing.

(C) Lose, because the principal did not molest the boy.

(D) Lose, because the principal believed the teacher when the teacher told the principal that he would not molest children again.

Question 13

A landowner owned several dozen acres of mountain land near a national forest. A plaintiff who was injured by a condition on the owner's land brought an action for personal injury against the landowner.

The plaintiff is most likely to win if she was:

(A) A 10-year-old trespasser who was swept onto some rocks while attempting to cross a swiftly flowing river.

(B) A five-year-old trespasser who fell into a mineshaft from which the owner had removed all warning signs, but the plaintiff was not attracted onto the owner's land because of the mineshaft.

(C) A five-year-old trespasser who inadvertently stepped into a badger hole that was obscured in the undergrowth.

(D) A 10-year-old niece visiting the landowner who stepped into a badger hole that the landowner did not know was present but that could have been discovered by inspection.

Question 14

Striking construction employees snuck onto their employer's construction site on a Saturday night, started up a backhoe, and dug a huge trench diagonally across a roadbed. The following morning, company officials discovered the trench, and determined that it would probably take all day Monday to repair it. The company placed warning barriers with flashing yellow lights at intervals along the trench and left the site. Arrangements were made to have private security guards around the heavy equipment starting that evening.

That same afternoon, two neighborhood eight-year-olds entered the construction site to play on the idle heavy equipment, which they had done on the past few Sundays. Both children noticed the warning barriers and saw the trench, which was about five feet wide. One child decided to leap over it, but she stumbled and fell into the trench, breaking her leg.

In a negligence action brought on behalf of the child against the company:

(A) Judgment for the company, because the intentionally tortious actions of the strikers are an independent intervening cause of the child's injury that supersedes any negligence by the company.

(B) Judgment for the company, because the company erected warning barriers and the child saw them and knew of the presence of the trench.

(C) Judgment for the child, if she was unable to appreciate the danger presented by the trench.

(D) Judgment for the child, because the company owed her the same duty a landowner owes to a trespassing child.

Question 15

While approaching an intersection with the red light against him, a motorist suffered a heart attack that rendered him unconscious. The motorist's car struck a child crossing the street with the green light in her favor. Under the state motor vehicle code, it is an offense to drive through a red traffic light.

The child sued the motorist to recover for her injuries. At trial it was stipulated that (i) immediately prior to suffering the heart attack, the motorist had been driving within the speed limit, had seen the red light, and had begun to slow his car; (ii) the motorist had no history of heart disease and no warning of this attack; and (iii) the motorist was unconscious when his car ran the red light.

On cross-motions for directed verdicts on the issue of liability at the close of the case, the court should:

(A) Grant the motorist's motion, because he had no history of heart disease or warning of the heart attack.

(B) Grant the child's motion, because, in the circumstances, reasonable persons would infer that the motorist was negligent.

(C) Grant the child's motion, because the motorist ran a red light in violation of the motor vehicle code.

(D) Deny both motions and submit the case to the jury, to determine whether, under the circumstances, the motorist's conduct was that of a reasonably prudent person.

Question 16

A hunter had packed his shotgun in the backseat of his car for hunting deer. On the way to the woods, the hunter gave his cousin a ride to his friend's house. Without the hunter's knowledge, the cousin took the shotgun when he left the car and used it to shoot a member of a gang that he had been in a fight with.

The gang member recovered a judgment for his injuries against the hunter as well as the cousin, on grounds that the hunter was negligent in allowing the cousin to obtain possession of the gun and was therefore jointly and severally liable with the cousin for the gang member's damages. The jurisdiction has a statute that allows contribution based on comparative fault and adheres to the traditional common law rules on indemnity.

If the hunter fully satisfies the judgment, he will have a right to recover from his cousin:

(A) Indemnity for the full amount of the judgment, because the cousin was an intentional tortfeasor.

(B) Contribution only, based on comparative fault, because the hunter himself was negligent.

(C) One-half of the amount of the judgment.

(D) Nothing, because the hunter's negligence was a substantial proximate cause of the shooting.

Question 17

A hunter constructed an outfit which made him appear, from the waist up, to be a 16-point buck. Below the waist he wore camouflage pants and hiking boots. The day hunting season opened, the hunter stationed himself in a heavily populated deer area and awaited his prey. Meanwhile, a second hunter, who had had numerous alcoholic drinks before embarking on opening day hunting, caught sight of the first hunter in his deer costume and fired his shotgun. One of the bullets grazed the first hunter's head, blasting the deer mask off and knocking the hunter unconscious.

The first hunter brings an action to recover damages for his personal injuries against the second hunter in a jurisdiction retaining traditional contributory negligence rules.

What result?

(A) The second hunter will win, because he did not have the requisite intent to justify imposing liability for an intentional tort on the first hunter.

(B) The second hunter will win, if he can prove that he did not have the last clear chance to avoid injuring the first hunter.

(C) The first hunter will win, if he can establish that the second hunter's act of hunting while intoxicated was reckless and wanton conduct.

(D) The first hunter will win, if he can show that the second hunter was negligent in hunting while intoxicated.

GO ON TO THE NEXT PAGE

Question 18

A pedestrian crossed the street at a crosswalk without looking for oncoming traffic. He was struck first by a car and then by a truck. The pedestrian sued both the driver of the car and the driver of the truck for negligence. The jury determined that the pedestrian was 60% at fault, the driver of the car 30%, and the truck driver 10%. The jury also determined that the pedestrian suffered damages of $100,000. The driver of the car is insolvent.

In a pure comparative negligence jurisdiction retaining traditional joint liability rules, how much can the pedestrian collect from the driver of the truck?

(A) Nothing.

(B) $10,000.

(C) $40,000.

(D) $100,000.

Question 19

Because of a farmer's default on his loan, the bank foreclosed on the farm and equipment that secured the loan. Among the items sold at the resulting auction was a new tractor that had been recently purchased by the farmer. The auctioneer did not inspect the tractor before it was sold. Shortly after purchasing the tractor at the auction, the buyer was negligently operating the tractor on a hill when it rolled over, in part due to a defect in the tractor's design. The buyer was injured as a result. The buyer sued the auctioneer, alleging strict liability in tort. The jurisdiction has adopted a comparative fault rule in strict liability cases.

In this suit, the result should be for the:

(A) Buyer, because the auctioneer sold a defective product that injured the plaintiff.

(B) Buyer, because the auctioneer failed to inspect the tractor for defects prior to sale.

(C) Auctioneer, because the accident was caused in part by the buyer's negligence.

(D) Auctioneer, because he should not be considered a "seller" for purposes of strict liability in tort.

Question 20

A tenant moving into a new apartment bought a spool of "10-pound test" fishing line, manufactured by a fishing tackle and accessories company, for the purpose of hanging pictures, all of which she knew weighed less than 10 pounds. The spool came with no guidelines or warnings about using it for hanging objects. She attached the fishing line to either end of the pictures and hung them on hooks on the wall. The next week, a friend visiting the tenant was hit and injured while sitting on the couch by a picture that fell when the fishing line broke. It is common knowledge in the sporting goods industry that "10-pound test" indicates that the line will stand a pull of 10 pounds, but is not intended to support a 10-pound weight over a period of time. However, it is also common knowledge in the industry that the public in general uses fishing line to support heavy hanging objects over a period of time.

If the friend asserts a claim against the tackle company for damages caused by his injury, will he prevail?

(A) Yes, because the line failed to support a weight of less than 10 pounds.

(B) Yes, because the label did not warn the consumer against relying on the term "10-pound test" for purposes other than fishing.

(C) No, because the line was not being used for its intended purpose, fishing.

(D) No, because the line conformed to the accepted standard for "10-pound test line."

Question 21

A driver on a 3,000-mile cross-country trip in his new car tried to drive the entire trip without stopping, but fell asleep at the wheel, causing the car to strike a bridge abutment and roll over. The driver was seriously injured by the rollover, and suffered additional injuries when the turn signal rod broke off and punctured his lung.

The driver had purchased the car from his local auto dealer. The car was manufactured by a local manufacturer, and the turn signal rod was manufactured by a subcontractor whom the manufacturer had used for many years. Tests after the accident established that the turn signal rod was defective and that the defect was the reason it broke off. The defect was not discoverable through reasonable inspection and the manufacturer had had no prior indication of any defects.

If the driver sues the manufacturer in strict liability, what is the likely result?

(A) The driver will be awarded damages for all injuries incurred as a result of the accident.

(B) The driver will be awarded damages for injuries incurred because the turn signal rod was defective, but he will not recover for other injuries incurred in the accident.

(C) The manufacturer will prevail, because the accident was caused by the driver's negligence.

(D) The manufacturer will prevail, because the driver cannot show that the manufacturer knew or should have known that the turn signal rod was defective.

Question 22

A trucker owned and operated a small truck which he used commercially to haul dynamite to construction sites. Unbeknownst to the trucker, there was a hidden defect in the latch that held the rear panel of the truck. The trucker was hauling a load of dynamite one morning and exceeding the speed limit when his truck struck a bump in the road, the latch malfunctioned, and the rear panel of the truck flew open. One box of dynamite fell out of the truck and struck a pedestrian, breaking her foot.

If the pedestrian sues the trucker under strict liability for his injuries, the pedestrian will:

(A) Win, because hauling dynamite is an abnormally dangerous activity.

(B) Win, because the trucker was speeding while driving with the dynamite.

(C) Lose, because the defect in the latch was not discoverable upon reasonable inspection.

(D) Lose, because the dynamite did not explode.

Question 23

After accounts of a confidential congressional hearing on a national security matter were published, the chief counsel at the hearing made a statement to a major newspaper accusing a popular network news anchorman of leaking the story and endangering national security. The network immediately fired the anchorman. When facts came to light a few weeks later showing that the allegation was not true, the anchorman was rehired and restored to his position.

The anchorman sued the newspaper for defamation, claiming compensatory and punitive damages, and made allegations legally sufficient to sustain those damages if proved. No affirmative defenses were allowed.

The best defense of the newspaper would be that:

(A) It was not negligent in printing the chief counsel's remarks.

(B) The anchorman was restored to his position within a few weeks.

(C) The publication was not made with knowledge that it was false nor with reckless disregard for the truth.

(D) The statement was protected by the Speech and Debate Clause.

Question 24

A famous comedian was asked by the host of a popular late night television talk show what brand of cigars he smoked. He responded, "I smoke only [the manufacturer's] cigars, because they're the best."

Two weeks later the manufacturer of those cigars began a national advertising campaign featuring billboards, posters for use in retail stores, and full-page ads in high circulation magazines. The advertising featured a picture of the comedian with the manufacturer's cigar in his hand, and the copy quoted his statement from the show. The manufacturer had not received the comedian's permission to use either his picture or the statement that had been made during the interview.

Will the comedian prevail in an action against the manufacturer for using his picture and statement?

(A) Yes, because the comedian has been defamed.

(B) Yes, because the comedian's likeness was appropriated for a commercial purpose without his consent.

(C) No, because the advertising accurately reflects what the comedian said publicly before millions of television viewers.

(D) No, because the comedian's appearance on television created an implied consent to reasonable use of anything he might say.

Question 25

A horse breeder owned a small but exceptionally well-tended horse farm for many years. The county in which the farm was located had no zoning or land-use regulations, but that had never been a problem until a half-acre plot of land next to the farm was recently purchased by a salvage company. The company let the weeds grow high on the land and it became littered with smelly, unsightly garbage and rusting metal. The breeder complained to the company on several occasions but was ignored. In addition, business started to taper off at the breeding farm due to the noise, smells, and general disarray of the junkyard.

If the breeder brings an action for nuisance against the company, how will the court rule?

(A) For the breeder, because the breeder was a property owner in the area long before the company bought the lot and opened his business.

(B) For the breeder, if he can show a substantial interference with the use and enjoyment of his land.

(C) For the company, because it is using the land for legal purposes.

(D) For the company, unless the breeder can objectively demonstrate that the value of the farm has declined.

STOP

Answer to Question 1

(A) The umpire could recover on an assault theory. Even though the boy did not hit the umpire, his action still constitutes an assault because it can be shown that he intended to cause harmful contact and actually created an apprehension of contact. Children are liable for their intentional torts when they are capable of forming the requisite intent. For assault, the intent required is to bring about the offensive or harmful contact; knowledge of its wrongfulness is not an element of that intent. The fact that he swung the bat at the umpire strongly indicates that he believed his bat would hit the umpire and that the boy desired this result. Therefore, it can be assumed that the boy had the capacity to form an intent to hit and that he did form that intent, which is a required element of the tort of assault. Thus, (C) and (D) are incorrect. The umpire could not recover on a negligence theory because the facts do not suggest that the umpire suffered any physical harm as a result of the boy's act. Specifically, most jurisdictions hold that recovery for negligent infliction of mental distress can only be had when the plaintiff has actually sustained physical contact as a result of defendant's actions or has suffered actual physical harm. These facts do not indicate that the harm done to the umpire is the kind of harm compensable in negligence. Therefore, (B) and (C) are incorrect.

Answer to Question 2

(D) The patient will recover at least nominal damages. The patient here need only show that the extension of the operation was an intentional, unpermitted, offensive contact in order to recover at least nominal damages in battery. The patient may recover in battery regardless of whether he was harmed. Battery is a tort where no physical harm need be shown, and no actual damage need be proven. (A) is incorrect because the patient here can show that the extension of the operation was an intentional, unpermitted, offensive contact. Therefore, the patient may recover in battery regardless of whether or not he was harmed. Battery is a tort where no physical harm need be shown, and no actual damage need be proven. Actual harm is an element of the prima facie case of negligence, but is not required for most intentional torts. (B) is incorrect because the patient may recover in battery regardless of whether he was harmed and whether or not the physician's conduct was incompetent (*i.e.*, negligent). Battery is a tort where no physical harm need be shown, and no actual damage need be proven. Also, no negligence or incompetence need be shown in battery. The patient here need only show that the extension of the operation was an intentional, unpermitted, offensive contact. (C) is incorrect because, in a negligence action, actual harm must be shown. The plaintiff must establish that he suffered damage as a result of the defendant's conduct. Damages will not be presumed and nominal damages cannot be awarded in a negligence action. Nominal damages are only appropriate in a suit based on an intentional tort where no actual harm can be shown.

Answer to Question 3

(C) The injured man will not prevail. While concerted action would create joint and several liability among all parties sued by the injured man, he has presented no evidence of this and therefore cannot prevail. (A) and (B) are incorrect. The fact that the first man was the aggressor or acted unreasonably does not, by itself, impose liability on the other persons sued. (D) is incorrect because res ipsa loquitur does not apply when more than one party may have been in control of the instrumentality causing injury. It requires that the instrumentality causing the injury be in the defendant's sole control. Furthermore, res ipsa loquitur creates a prima facie case for negligence, and the striking of the second man involves an intentional tort.

Answer to Question 4

(B) The woman has a cause of action for false imprisonment only. The woman has no cause of action for assault, because there was no act by the man that created a reasonable apprehension in the first person of immediate harmful or offensive contact. The man's words, unaccompanied by any act, constitute at most a threat of future contact. Such a threat is insufficient to create the requisite apprehension of immediate harmful or offensive contact. Because there is no assault, (A) and (C) are incorrect. The woman has a cause of action for false imprisonment because the man placed a physical barrier across the entrance to the woman's office, intending to confine the woman therein. The man's action caused the woman to be confined to the office. The fact that the woman apparently was confined for only a short time is immaterial to the false imprisonment action, as is the apparent absence of actual damages. Thus, (B) is correct and (A) and (D) are incorrect.

Answer to Question 5

(D) If the student wins, it will be because the neighbor's conduct was extreme and outrageous. Intentional infliction of emotional distress requires proof that: (i) the conduct was extreme and outrageous; (ii) it was also intentional, or at least reckless; and (iii) severe emotional distress resulted. If the threat is deemed to be extreme and outrageous, the student will prevail because the other elements are present. (A) is incorrect because an apparent present ability to make good on a threat is required for an action of assault, but it is not specifically required for an action for intentional infliction of emotional distress, the tort at issue here. (B) is incorrect because the requirement of physical harm only applies in cases of negligent infliction of emotional distress. This is a case of intentional infliction of emotional distress. (C) is incorrect because pecuniary injury is not required in an action for intentional infliction of emotional distress. While severe emotional distress must be shown, an action will lie even if no actual monetary harm was caused.

Answer to Question 6

(C) The rancher will probably win. A person who intentionally intrudes upon land in the possession of another is guilty of the tort of trespass to land. The bus driver has clearly met all the elements of this tort. However, the bus driver has the defense of private necessity, because it was necessary to drive onto the rancher's land to avoid the forest fire. Although private necessity is a defense to trespass to lands, it does not relieve the bus driver of liability for damage done to the property. Hence, (A) and (B) are incorrect. Note that the call of the question merely asks what the outcome of the rancher's claim against the driver would be, not whether the driver has committed a trespass. (D) is not as good a choice as (C) because it focuses on the driver's intent in committing a trespass rather than on whether the land was damaged.

Answer to Question 7

(B) The plaintiff will win because the defendant committed a conversion. A conversion occurs when the defendant intentionally causes serious interference with the chattel of the plaintiff. The intent involved refers to the physical act that results in the conversion, not to the defendant's desires regarding the ultimate disposition of the property. Therefore, the first member was guilty of conversion when she intentionally (*i.e.*, volitionally) took the second's board, which resulted in its loss, even though the first member did not intend to lose it or even realize that she had taken the property of another. (A) is not the best answer because complete loss of a chattel is too serious an interference to be classified a mere trespass. (C) is wrong because the first member's good faith is irrelevant in a conversion action. (D) is wrong because the fact that the first member's car was stolen does not relieve her of liability.

Answer to Question 8

(C) If the jogger prevails, it will be based on failure to exercise ordinary care of someone with the teenager's vision problem. In a lawsuit based on negligence, the usual standard of care is ordinary and reasonable care under the circumstances. The standard changes when the defendant has a major physical disability such as blindness. In that situation, the standard becomes ordinary and reasonable care for a person with that disability. Therefore, (C) is a more accurate answer than (A). (B) is wrong because it states the standard to be applied to children, which would not be applied to an 18-year-old car driver. (D) is a true statement. However, the statutory violation of failure to obtain a license was not the cause of the accident.

Answer to Question 9

(D) The representative will not prevail because of the severity of the storm. A common carrier does have a duty to aid an injured passenger. However, the storm was so severe that no aid could be rendered. In addition, because the statutorily required lifeboat could not have been used, it also prevents recovery on a negligence per se theory, because the failure to have the proper lifeboats was not a cause of the harm suffered by the passenger. (A) is incorrect. To be liable for negligence based on failure to conform to a statute, the statute must impose criminal liability and the harm suffered by the plaintiff must be the same as the statute sought to protect. Even if the statute applies here, its application only establishes negligence per se, *i.e.*, duty and breach of duty. As discussed above, the statutory violation was not a cause of the harm that occurred. (B) is incorrect because common carriers are not strictly liable to their passengers. They have only a special duty to render assistance to a passenger in need. (C) is incorrect because the assumption of the risk defense to negligence requires that the plaintiff knowingly enter or stay in a position of danger. The passenger's boarding of a standard ocean liner knowing that it would be a rough voyage was not such a risk but a reasonable travel choice.

Answer to Question 10

(C) The bicyclist will most likely recover for the pneumonia but not for the leg injury. The facts indicate that the driver was not driving negligently when the accident occurred. Therefore, he is not liable for the leg injury caused by the accident, and (A) and (B) are incorrect. However, where the defendant's actions have placed another person in peril or caused another's injury, the defendant has a duty to make reasonable efforts to rescue the imperiled person or render aid to his victim. The driver's neglect of the bicyclist after injuring him will make him liable for the resulting pneumonia. Therefore, (B) and (D) are incorrect.

Answer to Question 11

(A) The court should deny both motions and submit the case to the jury. Through process of elimination, this has to be a negligence action. Clearly the pilot did not commit an intentional tort, and the driver cannot sue the pilot, the plane's owner, in strict liability. The jury could determine that the pilot was negligent in selection of the landing site; hence, the court should deny the pilot's motion. The court should also deny the driver's motion because this is not a strict liability action; negligent conduct needs to be established. Hence, (B) is incorrect. (C) is incorrect because even though the pilot was not negligent in discovering the defect, she could have been negligent in selecting the landing site. (D) is incorrect because in an emergency, the pilot is held to the standard of care of a reasonable person in an emergency. It is up to the jury to determine whether she acted reasonably under the emergency circumstances.

Answer to Question 12

(B) The parents will win because the principal was aware of the teacher's conduct and did nothing. The principal and the teacher are in an employer/employee relationship. Normally, intentional torts of the employee are deemed not within the ambit of the employment relationship, except in jobs such as that of a bill collector or club bouncer. There is no evidence that intentional tortious conduct is part of this employment relationship. So the principal cannot be vicariously liable for the teacher's intentional torts and (A) is incorrect. However, there is a cause of action against the principal under a negligence theory. The principal knew that the teacher was a child molester. The principal initially indicated that the proper thing to do was for the teacher to leave. He backed down only under threats. Clearly action of some sort should have been taken, and the parents should have been told the truth about the teacher. The fact that the principal did nothing is clearly negligence on his part. (C) is incorrect because, as explained above, the principal can be liable for negligence even if he did not molest the boy. (D) is wrong because, even though the principal believed the teacher, he had a duty to take action to protect the schoolchildren from the teacher.

Answer to Question 13

(B) The child who fell into the mineshaft is most likely to win. Under the attractive nuisance doctrine, a child trespasser who is injured by a dangerous artificial condition need not have been attracted onto the property by the condition. (A) is wrong because generally there is no obligation for a landowner to warn trespassers, whether they are children or adults, of dangerous ***natural*** conditions. (C) is wrong for the same reason. (D) is wrong because, as a licensee, the plaintiff need only be warned of dangerous natural conditions of which the land owner is in fact aware and which are unknown to the licensee or unlikely to be discovered by her, and here the landowner did not know of the hole.

Answer to Question 14

(C) The child will win if she was unable to appreciate the danger. As a child trespasser, if the child was unable to appreciate the danger presented by the trench, the company's placement of warning barriers at intervals along the trench would be insufficient to protect the child from the dangerous artificial condition. (A) is wrong because the company's negligence consisted of its response to the dangerous condition created by the strikers. Once aware of the condition, the company had a duty to child trespassers to warn or make safe. (B) is incorrect because, if the child was too young to appreciate the danger of the trench, the warning barriers and her knowledge of the trench's presence would not preclude her from recovering for the company's negligent failure to make it safe as to her. (D) may be a true statement, because the company may be acting on behalf of the landowner, but does not address the determinative issue of the child's ability to understand the danger presented by the trench.

Answer to Question 15

(A) The court should grant the motorist's motion. For the motorist to be liable he must have been negligent. The facts stipulate that the motorist took all reasonable care while driving and that his heart attack was unforeseeable. Therefore, the court should grant the motorist's motion for a directed verdict. (C) is incorrect. While the unexcused violation of a statute or ordinance establishing negligence per se against the defendant would be a basis for a directed verdict, here the motorist was unconscious when he ran the red light and had no control over this violation of the motor vehicle code. Thus, his violation is excused. (D) is incorrect. For a directed verdict to be granted, there must be no issue for the jury to decide. Based on the uncontested facts, the motorist did not breach his duty of care, so submitting this case to a jury would be improper because there is nothing for the jury to decide. (B) is incorrect because it would be up to the jury to infer whether the motorist was negligent. Here, as noted above, there is no issue for the jury to decide because the facts establish that the motorist was ***not*** negligent.

Answer to Question 16

(A) The hunter may recover indemnity from the cousin. The general rule with respect to joint tortfeasors is that if one tortfeasor satisfies the judgment, he can only proceed against his fellow tortfeasors for contribution and cannot collect the total amount he paid by way of indemnification. The exception to that rule is where one tortfeasor (in this case, the hunter) is liable in tort because of negligence, and his fellow tortfeasor is liable in tort because he intentionally injured the plaintiff. In that case, the negligent tortfeasor can proceed against the intentional tortfeasor by way of indemnification rather than contribution. (B) is incorrect. If each of the tortfeasors were liable because each were negligent, the contribution based on the comparative fault standard would apply to the right of the hunter to collect from his cousin. Here, however, the cousin engaged in intentional conduct, whereas the hunter was only negligent. The hunter therefore can proceed by way of indemnification rather than contribution. (C) is incorrect for the same reason as (B), and also because in the jurisdiction here, the contribution rule has been modified so that it is based on comparative fault rather than equal shares. (D) is incorrect because the issue is not whether the hunter is liable to the plaintiff. That has been determined. The issue is whether the hunter can collect from his cousin. Because the cousin is a joint tortfeasor who is also liable to the plaintiff, the hunter can collect from the cousin after he satisfies the judgment. In this case, he can collect 100% of what he paid on an indemnification theory because the cousin committed an intentional tort, whereas the hunter was only negligent.

Answer to Question 17

(C) The first hunter will win if the second hunter's conduct was reckless or wanton. Because the first hunter was contributorily negligent in making himself appear to be a deer on opening day of deer hunting season, his recovery depends on the effect of his contributory negligence. Without comparative negligence principles, the first hunter's contributory negligence might bar his recovery unless he can show that the second hunter was reckless and wanton, as to which conduct contributory negligence is no defense. Thus, (C) is the correct pick. (A) is wrong because the second hunter's liability is not dependent on intentional tort theories. (B) is not the best answer because, even if the second hunter did not have the last clear chance (which overcomes contributory negligence), he may still be liable if his actions are characterized as reckless and wanton. (D) is wrong because, absent the factors discussed above, the second hunter's negligence would be counterbalanced by the first hunter's contributory negligence.

Answer to Question 18

(C) The pedestrian can collect $40,000 from the driver. In a pure comparative negligence jurisdiction, the plaintiff can recover even if he was over 50% at fault. Thus, (A) is wrong. The recovery will be limited to the percentage of damage attributed to the defendant(s), in this case 40%. The jurisdiction retains the rule on joint and several liability. Therefore, each defendant is responsible for the combined liability of all defendants. (C) is therefore correct and (B) is incorrect. (D) is wrong because, in a comparative negligence jurisdiction, the plaintiff's recovery is reduced due to his negligence.

Answer to Question 19

(D) The auctioneer should prevail. The auctioneer is not liable under a strict liability theory because he is not a manufacturer or supplier who is normally engaged in selling tractors. (A) is therefore incorrect. (B) is incorrect; because the auctioneer is not a manufacturer or supplier who is normally engaged in selling tractors, he had no obligation to inspect the tractor prior to its sale. (C) is incorrect because the jurisdiction applies comparative fault to these cases. Therefore, even if the buyer was partly at fault, this would only reduce his recovery against the auctioneer, not prevent it entirely. Proximate cause in strict liability actions is analyzed the same as it is in negligence actions. Generally, any type of ordinary negligence by an intermediary, such as the failure to discover or warn of a defect, is foreseeable and therefore not a superseding cause.

Answer to Question 20

(B) The friend will prevail on grounds of inadequate warnings. Where a product presents an unreasonable risk of injury to users and bystanders, the fact that there is no sufficient warning of the danger may be a dangerous defect that will invoke strict products liability. The facts establish that the fishing tackle company knew that purchasers of its fishing line commonly used that line to support heavy hanging objects, and that the line would not support the weight rating in that type of use. Thus, the fishing tackle company's failure to provide a warning is a defect that will permit the friend to recover in strict liability. (A) is incorrect. The fact that the line would not support a hanging weight of less than 10 pounds is not alone sufficient to constitute a dangerous defect; it is the fact that the fishing tackle company knew of the danger represented and failed to provide a warning to such users that makes the injury to the friend actionable. (C) is incorrect because the foreseeable misuse of a dangerously defective product by a purchaser or user does not relieve the manufacturer of the product of liability for injuries that are caused by the defect. Here, the known use of fishing line to support heavy hanging weights is what prompts the need for a warning, the absence of which makes the product dangerously defective. (D) is incorrect because, as indicated above, the presence or absence of a dangerous defect, and the responsibility for injuries caused by the defect, is not controlled by whether a product meets standards of performance measured solely by the use intended by the manufacturer. The fact that the fishing line performed adequately under industry standards when used for fishing does not mean that it cannot be dangerously defective when used for another purpose, when such use is known or reasonably should have been known by the manufacturer.

Answer to Question 21

(B) The driver will be awarded damages for injuries from the turn signal rod. Even though the defective turn signal rod was not the proximate cause of the accident, the driver can recover from the manufacturer for the additional injuries suffered due to the defective turn signal rod, because those are identifiable as caused by that defect. The manufacturer is strictly liable under a products liability theory for injuries caused by that defect, even though a subcontractor manufactured the rod. Thus, (B) is the correct answer. (C) and (D) can be eliminated because they deal with negligence theories, and the suit is being filed under a strict liability theory. Because liability attached only for the damages actually caused by the defective turn signal, (A) is incorrect.

Answer to Question 22

(D) The pedestrian will lose in this suit. The defendant is strictly liable for engaging in certain activities when the dangerous propensity of that activity injures the plaintiff. Although hauling dynamite is an unusually dangerous activity, it was not the dynamite's dangerous propensities that caused the accident. Instead, it was a defective latch in the truck. Thus, (A) is incorrect. (B) and (C) can be eliminated because they deal with negligence issues and the pedestrian is suing under a strict liability theory. (D) is the best answer. Note that if the dynamite had exploded, even though it fell out due to the defective latch, there would have been liability under a strict liability theory.

Answer to Question 23

(C) The newspaper's best defense is that the publication was not made with actual malice. A public figure suing for damages in a defamation action must prove actual malice. Mere hostility or dislike of the plaintiff does not constitute malice. To establish malice, a plaintiff must show "that the utterance was false and that it was made with knowledge of its falsity or with reckless disregard of whether it was false or true." [New York Times v. Sullivan (1964)] Reckless disregard is not measured by whether a reasonable person would have investigated before publishing. There must be sufficient evidence to permit the conclusion that the defendant in fact entertained serious doubts as to the truth of the communication when it was published. (A) is incorrect because negligence is not the standard which will apply in this case to determine the defendant's fault. As the anchor of a popular news show, the anchorman is a public figure, and a public figure suing for damages in a defamation action must prove actual malice. (B) is incorrect because the fact that the anchorman was restored to his position quickly is relevant to the issue of damages, but it does not help the newspaper on the issue of liability. (D) is incorrect. The Speech and Debate Clause provides immunity from defamation, but only for communications in one of the houses of Congress. The chief counsel's statement outside of Congress would not be covered.

Answer to Question 24

(B) The comedian will prevail on invasion of privacy grounds. (B) is a correct statement of the law defining the invasion of the comedian's privacy by appropriating his likeness for a commercial purpose (*i.e.*, using the comedian's picture to promote the sale of a commercial product without the comedian's consent). (A) is incorrect because the comedian lacks a prima facie case for defamation (there was no defamatory statement causing damage to the comedian's reputation) and, in any case, what the manufacturer printed was true. (C) is relevant to defamation, but is incorrect here, because accuracy is not a defense to privacy torts. (D) is incorrect because consent to commercial appropriation must be specific; it may not be implied from the comedian's statements on the television program.

Answer to Question 25

(B) The court will rule for the breeder. A private nuisance is a substantial, unreasonable interference with another's use or enjoyment of his own property; hence, (B) is correct because it states an element that the breeder must prove. (A) is incorrect because the fact that the plaintiff owned the property first does not establish the nuisance case. (C) is also incorrect. The fact that the defendant is using his property for legal purposes is not a defense to a nuisance action. (D) is incorrect, because a decline in the property's value is not an element of the prima facie case of nuisance.

100 Question Exam

Questions and Analytical Answers

Multistate Practice Exam

100 QUESTION EXAM

Time—3 hours

You will be given three hours to work on this test. Be sure that the question numbers on your answer sheet match the question numbers in your test book. You are not to begin work until the supervisor tells you to do so.

Your score will be based on the number of questions you answer correctly. It is therefore to your advantage to try to answer as many questions as you can. Give only one answer to each question; multiple answers will not be counted. If you wish to change an answer, erase your first mark completely and mark your new choice. Use your time effectively. Do not hurry, but work steadily and as quickly as you can without sacrificing your accuracy.

YOU ARE TO INDICATE YOUR ANSWERS TO ALL QUESTIONS ON THE SEPARATE ANSWER SHEET PROVIDED.

DIRECTIONS

Each of the questions or incomplete statements in this test is followed by four suggested answers or completions. You are to choose the ***best*** of the stated alternatives. Answer all questions according to the generally accepted view, except where otherwise noted.

For the purpose of this test, you are to assume that Articles 1 and 2 of the Uniform Commercial Code have been adopted.

The Federal Rules of Evidence are deemed to control.

The terms "Constitution," "constitutional," and "unconstitutional" refer to the federal Constitution unless indicated to the contrary.

You are also to assume that there is no applicable statute unless otherwise specified; however, survival actions and claims for wrongful death should be assumed to be available where applicable. You should assume that joint and several liability, with pure comparative negligence, is the relevant rule unless otherwise indicated.

DO NOT OPEN THE TEST UNTIL YOU ARE INSTRUCTED TO DO SO.

100 Question Exam

1. Ⓐ Ⓑ Ⓒ Ⓓ
2. Ⓐ Ⓑ Ⓒ Ⓓ
3. Ⓐ Ⓑ Ⓒ Ⓓ
4. Ⓐ Ⓑ Ⓒ Ⓓ
5. Ⓐ Ⓑ Ⓒ Ⓓ

6. Ⓐ Ⓑ Ⓒ Ⓓ
7. Ⓐ Ⓑ Ⓒ Ⓓ
8. Ⓐ Ⓑ Ⓒ Ⓓ
9. Ⓐ Ⓑ Ⓒ Ⓓ
10. Ⓐ Ⓑ Ⓒ Ⓓ

11. Ⓐ Ⓑ Ⓒ Ⓓ
12. Ⓐ Ⓑ Ⓒ Ⓓ
13. Ⓐ Ⓑ Ⓒ Ⓓ
14. Ⓐ Ⓑ Ⓒ Ⓓ
15. Ⓐ Ⓑ Ⓒ Ⓓ

16. Ⓐ Ⓑ Ⓒ Ⓓ
17. Ⓐ Ⓑ Ⓒ Ⓓ
18. Ⓐ Ⓑ Ⓒ Ⓓ
19. Ⓐ Ⓑ Ⓒ Ⓓ
20. Ⓐ Ⓑ Ⓒ Ⓓ

21. Ⓐ Ⓑ Ⓒ Ⓓ
22. Ⓐ Ⓑ Ⓒ Ⓓ
23. Ⓐ Ⓑ Ⓒ Ⓓ
24. Ⓐ Ⓑ Ⓒ Ⓓ
25. Ⓐ Ⓑ Ⓒ Ⓓ

26. Ⓐ Ⓑ Ⓒ Ⓓ
27. Ⓐ Ⓑ Ⓒ Ⓓ
28. Ⓐ Ⓑ Ⓒ Ⓓ
29. Ⓐ Ⓑ Ⓒ Ⓓ
30. Ⓐ Ⓑ Ⓒ Ⓓ

31. Ⓐ Ⓑ Ⓒ Ⓓ
32. Ⓐ Ⓑ Ⓒ Ⓓ
33. Ⓐ Ⓑ Ⓒ Ⓓ
34. Ⓐ Ⓑ Ⓒ Ⓓ
35. Ⓐ Ⓑ Ⓒ Ⓓ

36. Ⓐ Ⓑ Ⓒ Ⓓ
37. Ⓐ Ⓑ Ⓒ Ⓓ
38. Ⓐ Ⓑ Ⓒ Ⓓ
39. Ⓐ Ⓑ Ⓒ Ⓓ
40. Ⓐ Ⓑ Ⓒ Ⓓ

41. Ⓐ Ⓑ Ⓒ Ⓓ
42. Ⓐ Ⓑ Ⓒ Ⓓ
43. Ⓐ Ⓑ Ⓒ Ⓓ
44. Ⓐ Ⓑ Ⓒ Ⓓ
45. Ⓐ Ⓑ Ⓒ Ⓓ

46. Ⓐ Ⓑ Ⓒ Ⓓ
47. Ⓐ Ⓑ Ⓒ Ⓓ
48. Ⓐ Ⓑ Ⓒ Ⓓ
49. Ⓐ Ⓑ Ⓒ Ⓓ
50. Ⓐ Ⓑ Ⓒ Ⓓ

51. Ⓐ Ⓑ Ⓒ Ⓓ
52. Ⓐ Ⓑ Ⓒ Ⓓ
53. Ⓐ Ⓑ Ⓒ Ⓓ
54. Ⓐ Ⓑ Ⓒ Ⓓ
55. Ⓐ Ⓑ Ⓒ Ⓓ

56. Ⓐ Ⓑ Ⓒ Ⓓ
57. Ⓐ Ⓑ Ⓒ Ⓓ
58. Ⓐ Ⓑ Ⓒ Ⓓ
59. Ⓐ Ⓑ Ⓒ Ⓓ
60. Ⓐ Ⓑ Ⓒ Ⓓ

61. Ⓐ Ⓑ Ⓒ Ⓓ
62. Ⓐ Ⓑ Ⓒ Ⓓ
63. Ⓐ Ⓑ Ⓒ Ⓓ
64. Ⓐ Ⓑ Ⓒ Ⓓ
65. Ⓐ Ⓑ Ⓒ Ⓓ

66. Ⓐ Ⓑ Ⓒ Ⓓ
67. Ⓐ Ⓑ Ⓒ Ⓓ
68. Ⓐ Ⓑ Ⓒ Ⓓ
69. Ⓐ Ⓑ Ⓒ Ⓓ
70. Ⓐ Ⓑ Ⓒ Ⓓ

71. Ⓐ Ⓑ Ⓒ Ⓓ
72. Ⓐ Ⓑ Ⓒ Ⓓ
73. Ⓐ Ⓑ Ⓒ Ⓓ
74. Ⓐ Ⓑ Ⓒ Ⓓ
75. Ⓐ Ⓑ Ⓒ Ⓓ

76. Ⓐ Ⓑ Ⓒ Ⓓ
77. Ⓐ Ⓑ Ⓒ Ⓓ
78. Ⓐ Ⓑ Ⓒ Ⓓ
79. Ⓐ Ⓑ Ⓒ Ⓓ
80. Ⓐ Ⓑ Ⓒ Ⓓ

81. Ⓐ Ⓑ Ⓒ Ⓓ
82. Ⓐ Ⓑ Ⓒ Ⓓ
83. Ⓐ Ⓑ Ⓒ Ⓓ
84. Ⓐ Ⓑ Ⓒ Ⓓ
85. Ⓐ Ⓑ Ⓒ Ⓓ

86. Ⓐ Ⓑ Ⓒ Ⓓ
87. Ⓐ Ⓑ Ⓒ Ⓓ
88. Ⓐ Ⓑ Ⓒ Ⓓ
89. Ⓐ Ⓑ Ⓒ Ⓓ
90. Ⓐ Ⓑ Ⓒ Ⓓ

91. Ⓐ Ⓑ Ⓒ Ⓓ
92. Ⓐ Ⓑ Ⓒ Ⓓ
93. Ⓐ Ⓑ Ⓒ Ⓓ
94. Ⓐ Ⓑ Ⓒ Ⓓ
95. Ⓐ Ⓑ Ⓒ Ⓓ

96. Ⓐ Ⓑ Ⓒ Ⓓ
97. Ⓐ Ⓑ Ⓒ Ⓓ
98. Ⓐ Ⓑ Ⓒ Ⓓ
99. Ⓐ Ⓑ Ⓒ Ⓓ
100. Ⓐ Ⓑ Ⓒ Ⓓ

Question 1

A "wind farm" was constructed on the open land next to a gas station where a mechanic is employed. The huge windmills generated electrical power and oscillated at low speeds, resulting in very low-frequency but high-amplitude sound waves which caused extreme discomfort in a substantial minority of people. The mechanic is one of the people adversely affected by such sound waves; the vibrations from the windmills give him severe headaches and upset his immune system.

If the mechanic brings an action for nuisance against the owners of the wind farm and loses, it will be because:

(A) Sound waves are not the kind of physical phenomenon on which liability for nuisance can be based.

(B) The owners of the wind farm cannot generate power without producing the offending sound waves, despite their best efforts to find an alternative technology.

(C) At lease six out of 10 people are not affected by low-frequency sound waves.

(D) The mechanic neither owns nor rents the gas station at which he works.

Question 2

For several years, a landowner supplied water to the factory located on his land from a pump located on that same land. The pump drew water from a nearby creek, which provided plenty of water for all the factory's needs. Subsequently, a developer purchased property abutting the northern boundary of the landowner's land and constructed a large apartment building upstream from the creek, which also ran through her property. The building's water supply was pumped from the creek. Once the developer's building was fully occupied by tenants, there remained insufficient water to meet the needs of the factory.

If the jurisdiction follows the prior appropriation theory of water rights, when the landowner sues to stop the developer's use of the water, the result will be:

(A) The developer wins, because prior appropriation always protects upstream owners.

(B) The developer wins, because of the exception for domestic uses.

(C) The landowner wins, because he was the first to use water from the stream as a riparian owner.

(D) The landowner wins, because he first made beneficial use of the water.

Question 3

In a writer's copyright suit against various publishers of versions of his book, the writer's interrogatories asked for information concerning total sales of versions of the book by the defendant publishers the previous year. The defendants replied to the interrogatories by referring the writer to a current edition of a publication industry journal for the information.

If, at trial, the writer offers that publication as evidence of the defendants' sales volume, this evidence is:

(A) Inadmissible as hearsay not within any exception.

(B) Inadmissible as lacking sufficient authentication.

(C) Admissible as an adoptive admission of the defendants.

(D) Admissible as a business record.

Question 4

Two men who had long hated each other got into a violent argument in a restaurant one night. The result of the argument was that the first man pulled out a gun and shot the second. The prosecution calls a witness to testify that he was standing in the parking lot, and, as the first man was leaving the restaurant, he dropped the gun into a nearby garbage can.

The witness's testimony regarding the first man's conduct would be:

(A) Admissible hearsay falling within the state-of-mind exception.

(B) Admissible, because nonassertive conduct is not hearsay, and it is otherwise admissible.

(C) Inadmissible, because nothing was said.

(D) Inadmissible, because the first man's acts constitute assertive conduct.

Question 5

During the nighttime, a woman broke into the house of the victim with the intention of stealing his diamond ring. When she could not find the diamond ring, she became angry, lit a match to a newspaper and threw it on the victim's bed, setting the mattress on fire. The flames destroyed the bed and a portion of the floor under the bed.

In a common law jurisdiction, the woman is guilty of:

(A) Burglary only.

(B) Arson only.

(C) Burglary and attempted arson.

(D) Burglary and arson.

Question 6

A consumer purchased an air compressor, designed for powering tools and inflating tires, to use in a remodeling project. The consumer discovered that the reservoir and nozzle for a paint compressor gun he owned fit the threads on the nozzle of his air compressor. He decided to use the manufacturer's compressor rather than buying the compressor that went with the spray gun because he needed to paint a fence. After painting for a few minutes, the paint reservoir on the spray gun exploded, causing severe injuries to the consumer. The consumer subsequently brought a strict products liability action against the air compressor manufacturer to recover for his damages.

Evidence at trial revealed the following: (i) The spray gun reservoir had exploded because the air compressor developed too much air pressure for use in a spray device; it was for this reason that the manufacturer did not manufacture a spray painting attachment for its compressor. (ii) The manufacturer purposefully chose an unusual threading for its compressor nozzle to prevent its use with most spray painting systems, but the spray gun that the consumer had was a foreign-manufactured model that happened to use the same threading. (iii) When used with the tools and attachments produced by the air compressor manufacturer, the air compressor was completely safe and suffered from no design or manufacturing defects.

If the jury finds for the manufacturer, it will be because:

(A) The manufacturer exercised due care in the design and manufacture of the paint sprayer.

(B) It was not foreseeable that the compressor would be used by consumers to attach power spray devices.

(C) The compressor suffered from no design or manufacturing defects when used in the intended manner.

(D) The consumer misused the compressor when he attached it to his spray-painting gun.

Question 7

On January 30, a company that designs and builds generators to standard industrial specifications received a telephone call from a buyer who ordered two generators at a price of $25,000 each. The parties agreed that delivery of the first generator would be on March 15, and the second on April 30. Payment was to be made no more than 30 days after delivery. On March 12, the company delivered the first generator, which the buyer accepted. On April 22, the company completed the second generator but had not yet notified the buyer. On April 23, the buyer, having made no payment to the company, canceled the agreement. The company brings an action against the buyer for breach of contract.

How much should the company recover in damages?

(A) Nothing.

(B) $25,000 only.

(C) Damages for total breach of contract for the sale of two generators, because the buyer accepted part performance.

(D) Damages for total breach of contract for the sale of two generators, because the goods were made for the buyer.

Question 8

A manufacturer of washing machines telephoned a company that built motors and asked for a price quote on an order for 250 washing machine motors built according to the specifications that the manufacturer had sent to the motor-building company the previous week. The company responded that it would sell the motors to the washing machine manufacturer at a cost of $20 apiece, with delivery in 30 days. The washing machine manufacturer agreed to the terms and instructed that its order be entered. The motor-building company immediately started work on the motors, and had made a substantial beginning on their manufacture (having completed 110 motors) when the washing machine manufacturer notified the company that it would not honor the contract. The motor-building company stopped work on the motors and sued the washing machine manufacturer, who raised the Statute of Frauds as a defense. The motor-building company responded that the specially manufactured goods exception takes the contract out of the Statute of Frauds.

If the motor-building company loses, it will be because:

(A) It had not substantially completed work on the contract.

(B) It had completed work on less than half of the motors.

(C) It stopped work on the motors before the job was completed.

(D) It could have sold the motors in the ordinary course of its business.

Question 9

A developer prepared and recorded a subdivision plan, calling for 100 home sites on half-acre lots. There were five different approved plans from which a purchaser could choose the design of the home to be built on his lot. Each deed, which referred to the recorded plan, stated that "no residence shall be erected on any lot that has not been approved by the homeowners' association."

A lawyer purchased a lot and built a home based on one of the approved designs. However, many of the lots were purchased by investors who wanted to hold the lots for investment purposes. Two years after the lots went on the market, one such investor sold her lot to an architect by a deed that did not contain any reference to the recorded plan nor the obligation regarding approval by the homeowners' association. In fact, because very few residences had been built in the subdivision since the lots were first available for purchase, no homeowners' association meetings had been held in two years.

The architect, at a great expense, built a very modernistic house on her one-half acre. The lawyer, who had been unaware of the fact that this house was being built, brings an action to have the house torn down.

The probable result of this action will be in favor of:

(A) The architect, because her deed contained no restrictive covenants.

(B) The architect, because any restrictive covenant in her deed can only be enforced by the opposite party to the covenant or that person's successor in title.

(C) The lawyer, because the recorded subdivision plan, taken with the fact that all lots were similarly restricted and the architect had notice of this, gave him the right to enforce the covenant on her property.

(D) The lawyer, because his deed contained the restrictive covenant.

Question 10

The federal government has complete jurisdiction over certain parkland located within a state. To conserve the wildlife inhabiting that land, the federal government enacts a statute forbidding all hunting of animals in the federal park. That statute also forbids the hunting of animals that have left the federal park and have entered the state. A hunter has a state hunting license, authorizing him to hunt deer anywhere in the state. On land within the state located adjacent to the federal park, the hunter shoots a deer he knows has recently left the federal land.

The hunter is prosecuted for violating the federal hunting law. The strongest ground supporting the constitutionality of the federal law forbidding the hunting of wild animals that wander off federal property is that:

(A) This law is a necessary and proper means of protecting United States property.

(B) The animals are moving in the stream of interstate commerce.

(C) The police powers of the federal government encompass protection of wild animals.

(D) Shooting wild animals is a privilege, not a right.

Question 11

A husband and wife were both professors at the United States Naval Academy. The husband made a speech criticizing United States foreign policy with respect to a Middle Eastern country and was dismissed from his teaching position soon thereafter. Six months later, he accepted new employment in another state.

The man's wife has commenced suit in federal court claiming that the Naval Academy violated her husband's right to due process and his right of free speech when it fired him.

The most likely ground on which the court will dismiss the suit is:

(A) The political question doctrine, because foreign policy is in the domain of the executive branch.

(B) The case is moot, because the husband has a new job.

(C) The plaintiff has no standing.

(D) There is no federal question presented.

Question 12

After having much too much to drink at the corner bar, the defendant decided it was time to go home. However, because of her intoxication, she did not notice that she grabbed an expensive and distinctive fur coat instead of her inexpensive cloth coat from the bar's coat room. The owner of the fur coat, who noticed the defendant staggering out of the bar and down the street, ran out of the bar and shouted for the defendant to stop. A police officer on foot patrol heard the shout and immediately apprehended the defendant.

If charged with larceny of the fur coat, the defendant should be found:

(A) Guilty, because her mistake was unreasonable.

(B) Guilty, because voluntary intoxication is not a defense to a charge of larceny.

(C) Not guilty, because the defendant did not reach a place of temporary safety and thus did not complete the crime.

(D) Not guilty, because she was too intoxicated to realize the property did not belong to her.

Question 13

For many years, a farmer has grown and harvested a sizeable wheat crop on his land. On May 1, the farmer entered into an agreement with a bakery to supply the bakery with 10,000 bushels of wheat at $15 a bushel. The agreement called for the farmer to deliver the bushels to the bakery's plant on or before September 1. In mid-July, it became apparent that the year's wheat crop grown in the United States was going to be substantially smaller than originally anticipated. As a result, the price of wheat on August 1 rose to $35 a bushel. On August 10, the farmer informed the bakery that he would be unable to deliver any bushels to the bakery on September 1, because he had sold his entire harvested crop to other consumers.

If the bakery sues the farmer for breach of contract, the bakery will:

(A) Prevail, as long as it files suit on or after September 1.

(B) Prevail, regardless of whether it sues before or after September 1.

(C) Lose, because the sharp increase in the price results in a commercial frustration of the original deal, which excuses the farmer's performance.

(D) Lose, because the unforeseen rise in price is a substantial change of circumstances which excuses both parties.

Question 14

Two partners bought a commercial building from an owner. They paid cash for the building and took title as joint tenants with right of survivorship. Several years later, the first partner executed a mortgage on the building to secure a personal loan to a bank. The second partner had no knowledge of the mortgage to the bank. The state in which the commercial building is located recognizes the lien theory of mortgages. The first partner died before paying off his loan. He left all of his property by will to his daughter, his only heir.

Who has title to the commercial building?

(A) The second partner has title free and clear of the mortgage.

(B) An undivided one-half is held by the second partner free and clear of the mortgage, and the other one-half is held by the daughter, subject to the mortgage.

(C) An undivided one-half is held by the second partner and the other one-half by the daughter, with both halves subject to the mortgage.

(D) The second partner has title to the entire property, with an undivided one-half being subject to the mortgage.

Question 15

A drug dealer was convicted in federal court of possession of 10 kilos of cocaine with intent to distribute. She was sentenced to a prison term. Subsequently, a federal grand jury indicted the dealer under a separate statute for conspiracy to distribute the same 10 kilos of cocaine. She moved to dismiss the indictment.

Her motion should be:

(A) Granted, because the Double Jeopardy Clause protects her against a second prosecution for the same criminal conduct.

(B) Granted, because the Due Process Clause protects her against double punishment for the same criminal conduct.

(C) Denied, because the Double Jeopardy Clause does not apply when the second prosecution is for violation of a separate statute.

(D) Denied, because each prosecution requires proof of an element that the other does not.

Question 16

A defendant calls a secretary present at a meeting between the defendant and the plaintiff in which attempts were made to negotiate a settlement. The secretary offers to testify that the plaintiff said at the meeting, "Well, maybe it wasn't fraud—I'll settle for refund of the purchase price plus $50,000." The plaintiff objects.

The offered testimony is:

(A) Admissible hearsay (under the admission exception to the hearsay rule) to show the plaintiff's recognition of the weakness of his case.

(B) Admissible, because statements made in the course of settlement negotiations are admissible where relevant, even though offers to compromise are excluded.

(C) Inadmissible, because of public policy.

(D) Inadmissible, because the statement was made in the office of the defendant, an attorney, and hence privileged.

Question 17

A Hispanic woman was a citizen of a foreign country but had lived in the United States for 10 years. She had properly acquired resident alien status and regularly complied with all regulations pertaining to resident aliens, such as annual registration at the local post office. Several of her friends had been called for jury service and she thought it would be interesting to serve on a jury. Thus, she went to the county courthouse and asked the clerk how she could apply to be a juror. The clerk replied, "You can't. We draw names, and if we want you we'll call you." Nevertheless, she was very diligent, and after tedious research she discovered that no Hispanic female alien had ever served on a jury in the county where she lived; in fact, no person of that class had ever been in a venire panel.

May she compel the county officials to include her and other persons of her class in venire panels through a lawsuit in federal district court?

(A) Yes, because there is a consistent pattern of discrimination against persons of her class.

(B) Yes, because alienage is a suspect category.

(C) No, because certain privileges, such as jury service, may be constitutionally denied to aliens.

(D) No, because she lacks standing, in that she is not involved in a case or controversy where the lack of jurors in her class might prejudice her right to a fair trial.

Question 18

On September 1, after lengthy negotiations, an import company agreed to sell to a clothing retailer, and the retailer agreed to buy, 10,000 imported, plaid woolen earmuffs for $8 apiece, to be delivered to the retailer's principal place of business no later than October 31. The agreement was reduced to a writing signed by both parties. A month later, the importer telephoned the retailer and explained that a strike in the manufacturer's main factory had reduced the number of earmuffs available. The parties agreed in that same phone call that the importer would deliver 7,000 earmuffs instead of the 10,000 originally called for in the contract, but that the price would still be $8 per earmuff. However, no earmuffs were delivered to the agreed-upon location on or before the contract date, and repeated telephone calls to the importer went unanswered. Finally, the retailer brought an action for breach of the modified agreement against the importer.

Which of the following is the strongest justification for the trial court to dismiss the complaint?

(A) The retailer will be unable to prove the terms of the modification, due to the parol evidence rule.

(B) The Statute of Frauds renders the modification unenforceable.

(C) The modification is unenforceable because it is not supported by adequate consideration.

(D) A written contract may not be modified by a subsequent oral agreement.

Question 19

A stockbreeder kept his prize bull in a fenced enclosure on his property. The stockbreeder's neighbor, who raised sheep, was driving his tractor inattentively and drove the tractor over the stockbreeder's fence, creating a four-foot hole in the fence. The neighbor was unaware of the damage he caused and drove the tractor to another part of his farm. Later, the bull wandered through the hole in the fence onto the neighbor's property. The bull was peacefully munching on hay left out for the sheep when the neighbor's sheepdog began barking loudly and harrying the bull, nipping at the bull's heels. The bull became enraged and stampeded over the neighbor's property. Several sheep had the misfortune of finding themselves in the bull's path and were either gored or trampled to death. The neighbor sued the stockbreeder for the death of his sheep.

Which of the following is most helpful to the neighbor?

(A) A bull is livestock and its owner is strictly liable for damages caused by its trespass.

(B) The neighbor was unaware that he knocked the fence down.

(C) The fence was down for several hours before the bull wandered through it.

(D) A bull is a dangerous animal and its owner is strictly liable for damages caused by its actions.

Question 20

A man and woman who shared an apartment were arrested and charged with murder. The woman's attorney moved to have the defendants tried separately. The motion was granted. The woman was tried first and was acquitted of the crime. The man's trial began one month later. The man's attorney called a witness, who was now living with the man, to testify that, shortly after she was acquitted of murder, the woman had told the witness that she (the woman) had killed the victim because the victim owed her money, and that the man was not involved at all in the victim's death.

The witness's testimony should be:

(A) Admissible as an admission by a co-conspirator.

(B) Admissible as a declaration against penal interest.

(C) Inadmissible, because it is hearsay not within any exception.

(D) Inadmissible, because the woman is estopped from contradicting the jury verdict of acquittal.

Question 21

A farmer crossing a cattle breeder's land with permission noticed that the breeder had forgotten to put the prize bull in his barn as usual, and the bull noticed the farmer at the same time and charged. The farmer bolted for the nearest safety—the fence between the pen and a melon grower's melon patch. Leaping over, the farmer landed on and shattered several melons. Hearing the melee, the melon grower ran from a hiding place where he had been waiting to try to catch some children who had been stealing melons. He pointed his shotgun, which was loaded with rock salt, and exclaimed, "Stop or I'll shoot." Just then two juvenile melon thieves decided to make their escape and ran from where they had been crouching. The melon grower aimed his shotgun at them and prepared to fire but slipped on the shattered and slimy melons, and the load of rock salt struck the farmer, whom the melon grower had recognized and had not intended to hit.

Has the melon grower committed an assault against the farmer?

(A) Yes, because he actually pointed the shotgun at the farmer.

(B) Yes, if the farmer reasonably believed that the melon grower might shoot him.

(C) No, because the shotgun was only loaded with rock salt.

(D) Yes, because assault is included within the tort of battery, and the melon grower committed a battery when he shot the farmer in the shoulder.

Question 22

A small group of terrorists hijacked a foreign airliner. Ten prominent bankers from the United States were among the airline passengers. The terrorists demanded that three individuals imprisoned in a state prison be released. Although these individuals were properly convicted of violation of state laws, the terrorists contended that they were political prisoners and that their convictions were merely a subterfuge to prevent them from inciting the local populace. The President of the United States agreed to release the three prisoners in return for the freedom of the 10 bankers. He issued official pardons and ordered the state governor to release the prisoners. The governor refused to do so, contending that the President had overreached his constitutional powers and had violated the concept of federalism.

The best argument for the governor's position is that:

(A) The President had no power to make an agreement with the terrorists because his treaty power extended only to dealings with the legitimate governments of other nations.

(B) The Constitution immunizes a governor acting pursuant to a state constitution from inconsistent orders by a federal official.

(C) The President's duty to see that the laws are faithfully executed prevents him from ordering state officials to release prisoners.

(D) The President's constitutional powers to grant pardons extends only to prisoners who have violated federal laws.

Question 23

A state is operating a nuclear power plant on a river. The plant uses river water for cooling and discharges water back into the river 10 degrees warmer than when it was taken in. While the discharged water quickly cools, it has adversely affected the business of a downstream ice cutting operator, located in a neighboring state. The ice cutter successfully urged his state to bring suit in the United States Supreme Court against the state operating the power plant, alleging damage to its environment and seeking an injunction against the thermal discharge.

The United States Supreme Court should:

(A) Dismiss the action, because the suit is really one by the ice cutter against the state operating the power plant and is barred by the Eleventh Amendment.

(B) Hear the matter on the merits, because the ice cutter's state is suing in its own right and jurisdiction is proper.

(C) Dismiss the action, because it does not have original jurisdiction.

(D) Remand the case to the district court for trial, because it does not have the time to function as a trial court.

Question 24

A homeowner agreed to sell his home to an accountant. He gave the accountant a general warranty deed and the accountant gave him $86,000, his asking price. The deed was recorded. A few years later, the accountant sold the property to a doctor, who paid her $125,000 for the property. To save on attorney's fees, the accountant went to her local office supply store to purchase a general warranty deed form. The store was out of those forms, but the clerk suggested that she use the form labeled "Quitclaim Deed," asserting that it would transfer the title just as well as the other form. The accountant purchased the form and filled in the blanks with the appropriate information she copied from her old deed. The doctor did not hire a lawyer to represent him in the purchase of the house.

The doctor accepted the deed from the accountant and gave her $125,000. Soon after the doctor moved into the house, it was discovered that the homeowner's title was not good. The true owner now demands that the doctor vacate. Title is judicially determined to be with the true owner, and the doctor is forced out.

Does the doctor have any action against the homeowner or the accountant based on any covenant for title?

(A) Yes, the doctor can sue both and can recover $125,000.

(B) Yes, the doctor can sue the homeowner, but not the accountant, and can recover his full $125,000.

(C) Yes, the doctor can sue the homeowner, but not the accountant, and can recover only $86,000.

(D) No, the doctor can sue neither the homeowner nor the accountant.

Question 25

A defendant is on trial for robbing a liquor store. The store clerk testified that the defendant came into the store at about 11 p.m., pointed a .45 automatic pistol at him, and demanded that he give him all the money in the cash register. The clerk testified that the store was well lit and that the defendant was not wearing a mask. The defendant's attorney called the clerk's employer to testify that when the clerk gave her a report of the robbery, he told her that the defendant pointed a .38 revolver at him.

The trial judge should find this testimony:

(A) Admissible, because it tends to show that the clerk is an unreliable witness.

(B) Admissible, because it has bearing on the clerk's truthfulness and veracity.

(C) Inadmissible, because it is extrinsic evidence of a collateral matter.

(D) Inadmissible, because it is hearsay not subject to any exceptions.

Question 26

A mountain lodge catered to cross-country skiing enthusiasts. Every winter, the owner of the lodge, along with his assistants, marked and groomed trails on his extensive lands. He charged a fee for a day's use of the trails. He also supplied equipment for those who needed it and provided lodging and meals for skiers staying more than one day. A woman on her first cross-country skiing outing was striding along a groomed trail when, with a loud crack, the rotten limb of a huge oak under which the trail passed separated from the tree because of the load of ice and snow it bore. It came crashing down on top of the woman, killing her instantly. The woman's heirs brought a wrongful death action against the lodge owner.

If the lodge owner prevails, it will be because:

(A) The oak limb was a natural condition of the land.

(B) The lodge owner did not know that the oak limb was rotten and was likely to fall.

(C) The lodge owner could not reasonably have discovered the rotten limb by inspecting his property.

(D) The ice and snow was an intervening force that caused the limb to fall.

Question 27

A textile company and the local textile union were involved in a bitter labor dispute that had required the governor to use the National Guard. The Guard took up positions surrounding the company's main plant and issued orders that no more than 20 picketers could picket at any one time and that all employees who were on strike were forbidden to cross the perimeter established by the Guard. In spite of this order, union marchers approached the plant and refused to obey the commander's order to disperse. As they crossed the perimeter, the Guard was ordered to fire on the marchers. As a result, seven strikers were injured.

The seven strikers brought a claim for damages against the state, which has abolished governmental immunity. Evidence indicates that the use of weapons was not necessary to protect anyone, but that the Guard used the weapons because it had previously experienced trouble in controlling civil disorders.

The best basis for recovery by the strikers is a claim based on:

(A) Battery.

(B) Unusually dangerous activity.

(C) Negligence.

(D) Strict liability in tort.

Question 28

A hotelier who operated a string of inns across the country decided to open a new inn in the Pacific Northwest. On June 1, he sent letters to all known hotel and motel suppliers, alerting them to his need for such items as ashtrays, televisions, linen, and mattresses. The hotelier received a letter dated June 8 from an ashtray company, stating that the company had 250 ashtrays left in stock and will sell them to the hotelier for $1 each. The company added that it must receive the hotelier's answer by November 1 and will hold the ashtrays for the hotelier until then. On July 1, the company sold 200 of the ashtrays to a competing hotel chain, who had recently opened a hotel on the East Coast. On July 2, the company sent the hotelier a fax stating it had only 50 ashtrays left for sale. The hotelier received the fax that day, but put it aside and never read it. On July 10, the hotelier notified the company that he was accepting the company's offer to sell 250 ashtrays. The company, upon receiving the hotelier's acceptance, shipped the remaining ashtrays. The hotelier sues the company for failing to deliver all 250 ashtrays.

Will the hotelier prevail?

(A) No, because the hotelier is not an ashtray merchant.

(B) No, because the company's offer was to remain open for more than three months.

(C) Yes, because the company promised in a signed writing to hold the offer open.

(D) Yes, because the hotelier never read the company's July 2 fax.

Question 29

A bathroom fixture company, in a signed writing, contracted with the developer of an apartment building for the sale to the building of 50 identical sets of specified bathroom fixtures, 25 sets to be delivered on March 1, and the remaining 25 sets on April 1. The agreement did not specify the place of delivery, or the time or place of payment. On March 1, the fixture company tendered 24 sets to the developer and explained that one of the 25 sets was damaged in transit from the manufacturer to the company. The fixture company also promised to deliver a replacement within five days.

Which of the following statements is correct?

(A) The developer is entitled to accept any number of the 24 sets, reject the rest, and cancel the contract both as to any rejected sets and the lot due on April 1.

(B) The developer is entitled to accept any number of the 24 sets and to reject the rest, but is not entitled to cancel the contract as to any rejected sets or the lot due on April 1.

(C) The developer must accept the 24 sets but is entitled to cancel the rest of the contract.

(D) The developer must accept the 24 sets and is not entitled to cancel the rest of the contract.

Question 30

The victim's home was not well maintained, which caused much conflict with his neighbors. The neighbors to the north and south of the house, a mechanic and a doctor, had finally had enough and planned to place a smoke bomb on the victim's front porch. The doctor and mechanic consulted with another neighbor, an army veteran who was known to be an explosives expert, to help them. The army veteran agreed, but unbeknownst to the two neighbors, the army veteran manufactured a bomb containing a lethal quantity of explosives. He gave the bomb to the mechanic and doctor, along with a timed fuse. In the middle of the night, the two men set the bomb on the victim's porch. A few minutes later, a huge explosion rocked the neighborhood. Although nobody was injured, the blast blew away the front of the victim's house.

Who, of the following, is likely to be found guilty of attempted murder?

(A) The doctor, mechanic, and the army veteran.

(B) The army veteran and the mechanic, but not the doctor.

(C) The army veteran, but not the doctor and the mechanic.

(D) Neither the mechanic nor the doctor nor the army veteran.

Question 31

A defendant is on trial for robbing a state bank. She testified that she was in another state at the time of the robbery. The defendant calls her friend as a witness to testify that two days before the robbery the defendant told him that she was going to spend the next three days in the other state.

The witness's testimony is:

(A) Admissible, because the statement falls within the present sense impression exception to the hearsay rule.

(B) Admissible, because a statement of plans falls within the hearsay exception for then-existing state of mind.

(C) Inadmissible, because it is offered to establish an alibi by the defendant's own statement.

(D) Inadmissible, because it is hearsay not within any exception.

Question 32

A rancher deeded his ranch "to my son so long as he lives, and on his death to my son's widow for the remainder of her life, and on her death to each of her lineal descendants who are living on her death, to share and share alike." The deed was validly executed, delivered, and recorded. At the time of the conveyance, the son was married but had no children. Three years later, the rancher died. His will left all of his estate to his sister. Two years after the rancher's death, the son was killed in an automobile accident, leaving his widow with twin girls. Upon the widow's death many years later, she was survived by both girls, her only lineal descendants.

Who now owns the ranch?

(A) The girls are tenants in common, with each owning an undivided one-half; their interest vested on the son's widow's death, well within the period of lives in being plus 21 years.

(B) The girls are tenants in common, with each owning an undivided one-half; they received a vested remainder, which is not subject to the Rule Against Perpetuities.

(C) The sister owns the ranch in fee simple, because the Rule Against Perpetuities voided the gift over to the son's widow and the following gift to her lineal descendants.

(D) The sister owns the ranch in fee simple, which she received upon the death of the son's widow.

Question 33

A landowner conveyed his parcel of land "to my sister and her heirs so long as it is used for residential purposes, but if it is ever used for other than residential purposes, then to the local community center."

Five years later, the landowner died, devising all of his real estate to his friend and leaving his daughter as his only heir.

The following year, the landowner's sister and the landowner's daughter entered into a contract with a third party to sell the parcel to him in fee simple for $100,000. After examining title, the third party refused to perform under the contract because he believed the sister and the daughter could not deliver good title.

The jurisdiction follows the common law Rule Against Perpetuities and has a statute providing that all future estates and interests are alienable, descendible, and devisable in the same manner as possessory estates and interests.

If the sister and the daughter sue the third party for specific performance, their request will be:

(A) Granted, because the sister owns the parcel in fee simple.

(B) Granted, because the sister and the daughter together own the parcel in fee simple.

(C) Denied, because the local community center has a valid interest in the parcel.

(D) Denied, because the friend has a valid interest in the parcel.

Question 34

The police had long suspected that an appliance store owner was selling stolen merchandise, but were unable to prove it. One night, under the direction of the police, an informant approached the store owner and offered to sell him a microwave that was represented as stolen. In fact, the oven belonged to one of the officers. The store owner indicated that he was interested and suggested meeting at a local park to complete the sale. The informant showed up at the scheduled time, but the store owner did not. When the informant saw the owner again, he asked why he had not shown up. The owner replied, "I wanted to make sure you were not working for the police." The two men then set up another meeting in the park, at which time the owner purchased the microwave for $25. Shortly thereafter, the owner was arrested by the police with the microwave in his possession.

On the issue of entrapment, the court should find:

(A) The conduct of the police amounted to entrapment, because it directly implanted a criminal intent in the mind of the owner.

(B) The conduct of the police amounted to entrapment, because the informant was not a member of the police department.

(C) The conduct of the police amounted to entrapment, because he performed a necessary act for the crime of knowingly receiving stolen property by making the property available to the owner for purchase.

(D) The conduct of the police did not amount to entrapment, because the owner already had a preexisting criminal intent to buy stolen property, and the action of the informant merely afforded him an opportunity to carry out his criminal intent.

Question 35

The police suspected that an 18-year-old living with his mother was selling marijuana to his high school classmates. The police went to the house without a search warrant and secured the mother's permission to search the teen's bedroom. In the bedroom, they found a locked suitcase under the teen's bed. The mother said that it was her son's suitcase but that they could search it. The police then broke the lock, opened it and found a substantial amount of marijuana. The police charged the teen with possession of marijuana with intent to distribute it.

If the teen should bring a pretrial motion to suppress the marijuana, that motion should be:

(A) Granted, because the mother was not informed of her right to refuse consent to the search.

(B) Granted, because the mother's consent to search the suitcase was invalid.

(C) Denied, because the mother had authority to consent to a search of anything within her home.

(D) Denied, under the doctrine of in loco parentis.

Question 36

After being fired from his job, an accountant drank heavily and decided to ride the bus home. While on the bus, he saw a briefcase that he mistakenly thought was his own. So, he picked up the briefcase. The owner of the briefcase tried to take the briefcase back from the accountant, and a struggle for the briefcase ensued. During the struggle, the accountant knocked the passenger to the floor, took the briefcase, and fled. The accountant was arrested and charged with robbery.

He should be:

(A) Acquitted, because he used no threats and was intoxicated.

(B) Acquitted, because his mistake negated the required specific intent.

(C) Convicted, because his intoxication was voluntary.

(D) Convicted, because mistake is no defense to robbery.

Question 37

A gardener entered into a contract with a landowner under which, for a monthly fee of $200, the gardener would provide the landowner with monthly gardening services for the calendar year. On June 1, the gardener told the landowner that she could no longer afford to work for $200 a month and demanded that she be paid $400 a month. The landowner refused, stating that he already had a valid contract with her and that he did not have to pay any more. The gardener again insisted that she would not work for less than $400. As a result, the gardener and the landowner agreed in writing on July 1 that the gardener would thereafter be paid $400 a month for the gardening services and that the term of the agreement would be extended through the end of next year.

Is the gardener legally entitled to receive a monthly fee of $400 from the landowner after July 1 of this year?

(A) Yes, but only for the period from January 1 to December 31 of next year.

(B) Yes, because the gardener and the landowner mutually agreed to modify their original contract.

(C) No, because the gardener used economic duress in order to obtain the landowner's agreement to the modification.

(D) No, because the gardener was under a preexisting duty to perform the gardening services for $200 a month.

Question 38

Due to anti-American sentiment that was sweeping through a foreign country, the President of the United States announced that unless incidents of insult and injury to American diplomatic personnel are stopped, he would sever diplomatic relations with that country. The Supreme Council of that foreign country countered with an announcement that all property of United States citizens or the United States government would be confiscated and forfeited if diplomatic relations were severed.

A naturalized American citizen who immigrated to the United States from that foreign country in 1965 now owns several businesses and a considerable amount of land in that country. He wants to bring a suit to prevent the President from severing diplomatic relations with the country, asserting that such an act would deprive him of property without due process of law.

As his attorney, you should advise him that a federal court would probably:

(A) Refuse to hear the suit, because the naturalized citizen lacks standing to sue.

(B) Refuse to hear the suit, because there is no diversity of citizenship between the naturalized citizen, who lives in Washington, D.C., and the President.

(C) Refuse to hear the suit, because it involves a political question.

(D) Hear the suit on the merits.

Question 39

A tire company is the manufacturer of, and owns the patent for, a new and unique type of truck tire. The company is the largest employer in the state in which it is located. That state enacted a law requiring all trucks using its highways to be equipped with the company's unique truck tires. An out-of-state trucking company filed suit against the state, and eventually the United States Supreme Court held that the state's statute violated the Commerce Clause.

Subsequently, Congress enacted a law that required all trucks engaged in interstate commerce to use the company's unique tires. This federal law should be held:

(A) Constitutional, because Congress's control over interstate commerce is plenary.

(B) Constitutional, only if Congress can demonstrate that the use of tires of another design somehow unduly burdens interstate commerce.

(C) Unconstitutional, if most states permit tires of another design.

(D) Unconstitutional, because the federal law reverses a decision of the Supreme Court, and the Supreme Court is the sole arbiter of constitutional issues.

Question 40

A pregnant woman visited her family doctor to seek relief from arthritis in her hips. The doctor prescribed a steroid-type drug. The pregnant woman took the drug as prescribed and obtained relief from her pain. The pharmaceutical company which manufactured the drug enclosed information concerning the drug in the packages it shipped to drugstores and with samples provided to physicians. This literature warned that the drug should not be prescribed for pregnant women because it caused enlargement of the ears of male children. The enlargement occurred when the children reach puberty. Studies confirming this result were published in various medical journals. The pregnant woman gave birth to a son soon thereafter. Although the son had a normal early childhood, his ears grew disproportionately large when he reached age 16, and he has suffered severe emotional distress because of his appearance. Now 17, the son has brought suit against the doctor for malpractice.

In that lawsuit:

(A) The son will prevail if he can prove that most doctors would not have prescribed the drug for his mother.

(B) The son will prevail unless the doctor establishes that he had not read the journals reporting on the side effects of the drug.

(C) The doctor will prevail because the statute of limitations has run on the son's claim.

(D) The doctor will prevail because no duty is owed to an unborn child.

Question 41

Several years ago a number of employees of the state transportation department formed a workers' organization, a voluntary association incorporated under the laws of the state. The organization has grown in size over the years and has become very powerful politically. Nearly 85% of all state highway maintenance workers are members of the organization, which is supported entirely by the dues of its members. Membership is not required as a condition of employment or advancement in the state transportation department. After a vote of its entire membership on the question, a member was expelled from the organization solely because she is an active, knowing member of an organization that seeks to propagate the concept of white racial supremacy. The expelled member brings suit in an appropriate court seeking reinstatement of her membership. The suit alleges that her expulsion violates rights guaranteed her by the First and Fourteenth Amendments.

Which of the following is the strongest constitutional defense that the organization may assert to this suit?

(A) The First and Fourteenth Amendments do not apply to the actions of the organization.

(B) Active, knowing membership in organizations with overtly racist objectives is not protected by the First and Fourteenth Amendments.

(C) The organization could reasonably believe that it has a compelling interest in eliminating from its membership active, knowing members of organizations with overtly racist objectives.

(D) The expulsion of the member took place only after a vote of the organization's entire membership.

Question 42

A large oil producer wanted to expand into the oil refinery business. It contacted a small oil refinery company and offered to purchase the company's refining facilities as well as its output of petroleum products from its remaining production facilities.

Lawyers for the oil producer prepared a written agreement specifying the sale price for the smaller company's refining business. The agreement also included provisions permitting the oil producer, at its option, to purchase 100% of all petroleum products removed from the earth by the smaller company for the following 15 years, at current market prices. The agreement was signed by both parties. One month after the sale of the refining facilities, the oil producer sent a fax to the smaller company stating that it would be exercising its option to purchase the smaller company's oil output for the next 15 years.

The written agreement between the oil producer and the smaller company is:

(A) Unenforceable, because the provision permitting the oil producer to purchase all of the smaller company's output was not supported by any consideration.

(B) Unenforceable, because the provision permitting the oil producer to purchase all of the smaller company's output for 15 years was indefinite and uncertain.

(C) Enforceable as to the sale of the smaller company's refining facilities, but unenforceable as to the output provision.

(D) Enforceable in its entirety.

Question 43

A successful stockbroker and his best friend, a land developer, were pleased that their only children were about to marry each other. The stockbroker and the developer wanted to get the marriage off to a good start. Thus, on July 1, the two agreed in writing that, on July 15, the stockbroker would deliver to the land developer a check for one-half of the market value of a two-bedroom condominium owned by the developer, and the developer would simultaneously deed the condominium to the bride and groom.

On July 10, the newlyweds learned of the agreement but neither assented to it nor changed their position in reliance on it. On July 12, the stockbroker and the developer mutually agreed to cancel their agreement.

If the newlyweds were to sue the developer and the stockbroker for breach of contract:

(A) The newlyweds would prevail because their rights as intended beneficiaries vested when the contract was made on July 1 and a later revision was ineffective in affecting their rights.

(B) The newlyweds would prevail because they received notice of the contract on July 10, and the rescission thereafter was ineffective.

(C) The stockbroker and developer would prevail because they had the right to mutually rescind their agreement.

(D) The stockbroker and developer would prevail because the newlyweds were incidental beneficiaries and had no right to enforce the contract.

Question 44

A tool producer was in the business of manufacturing and selling various hardware. The owner of a retail hardware store ordered 1,000 hammers from the tool producer, using the standard form that the tool producer's sales personnel used. Shortly after the hardware store placed their order, the tool producer's headquarters caught fire. All the purchase and sale records were destroyed in the fire. Afterwards, the hardware store owner asserted that the salesperson had agreed that the price for the hammers would be $5,000. The tool producer maintained that the price was $5,500. The tool producer then sued the hardware store. At the trial, the tool producer's director of the order department took the stand. After establishing that the original order had been destroyed by fire, the director sought to testify that the price of the order was $5,500.

Such testimony is:

(A) Inadmissible, because it is self-serving and untrustworthy.

(B) Inadmissible, because of the best evidence rule.

(C) Inadmissible, because it is not the best degree of secondary evidence.

(D) Admissible.

Question 45

A candidate was running for state senator. His campaign manager made the following statement to a potential contributor: "If you want to maintain high moral standards in this community, you should donate to my client's campaign. His opponent is a child molester and a thief, but all of that has been hushed up." A journalist overheard these statements and took detailed notes while the campaign manager was speaking, recording verbatim what the campaign manager said. The potential contributor also told several friends what the campaign manager had said, and the candidate's opponent sued the campaign manager for defamation.

At the trial, the candidate's opponent called the journalist to testify. The journalist is prepared to testify as to what he heard, but he is not willing to produce his notes containing the campaign manager's statement. The defense objects to the journalist's testimony.

The testimony is:

(A) Inadmissible under the best evidence rule.

(B) Inadmissible as hearsay not covered by an exception.

(C) Admissible as relevant evidence based on firsthand knowledge.

(D) Admissible, because the journalist's notes are protected by the journalist's privilege.

Question 46

While walking down the street, a pedestrian accidentally bumped into a street performer. The performer told the pedestrian to pay attention to where she was going. The pedestrian got mad and slapped the performer across the face. The performer, afraid that the pedestrian would continue the assault and escalate it to the point of murdering him, pulled out a gun and shot the pedestrian, killing her instantly.

The performer is most likely to be convicted of manslaughter in a state that:

(A) Recognizes the heat of passion resulting from adequate provocation as a mitigating circumstance.

(B) Applies the doctrine of diminished responsibility.

(C) Recognizes the misdemeanor-manslaughter rule.

(D) Recognizes the imperfect self-defense doctrine.

Question 47

An owner of 40 acres of mountain land sold the western 20 acres to a buyer. Because no access to any public road existed on the western side of the property, the deed conveying title to the buyer included an easement for ingress and egress that ran along the southern border of the owner's land. This deed was duly recorded. About the same time that this sale took place, the county extended the public road so that it abutted on the buyer's 20 acres. The buyer then built a cabin on the property.

Later, the owner and the buyer both sold their 20 acres to the owner's cousin. The cousin then sold the 20 acres acquired from the buyer to his lawyer and sold the other 20 acres to a doctor. All deeds involved in the various conveyances of the 20-acre parcels were validly recorded. Neither the cousin-lawyer deed nor the cousin-doctor deed made any mention of easements or rights-of-way. In fact, no use was ever made of the easement.

A few years later, the lawyer sold his 20 acres to a development company that wished to build a hunting lodge on the property. The development company now wants to construct a road across the doctor's property in the manner contemplated in the deed from the original owner to the buyer.

What is the strongest argument as to why the development company should not be permitted to construct the road?

(A) Any easement that might have existed was extinguished by abandonment because of nonuse.

(B) Any easement that once existed was terminated by merger.

(C) The county's subsequent expansion of the public road removed the necessity of using the easement across the eastern parcel.

(D) Neither the cousin-doctor deed nor the cousin-lawyer deed made any mention of the easement.

Question 48

Twenty-five years ago, a property owner placed a large sewer line (to service a single-family house he built on the property) across a neighbor's property without the neighbor's permission. Three years ago, the owner tore down the house in preparation for the construction of an apartment building on the land, and made an agreement with municipal authorities to take an easement across the neighbor's property and install a new sewer line to service the apartment building. The municipal authorities failed to perform their agreement, and the owner constructed the apartment building last year using the existing sewer line. The state has a 20-year statute for acquiring property interests by adverse use.

If the neighbor attempts to enjoin the use of the sewer line to service the apartment building, she will:

(A) Prevail, because the agreement with the municipal authorities estopped the owner from using the existing line to service the apartment building.

(B) Prevail, because the increased flow of sewage from the apartment building was beyond the prescriptive rights acquired.

(C) Not prevail, because the original sewer line was a license which ripened into an implied easement.

(D) Not prevail, because the use was within the scope of the prescriptive easement acquired.

Question 49

On January 1, state legislation was enacted that prohibited private employers, under penalty of civil fines, from hiring any person who had not been a resident of that state for 10 years. The legislation also required private employers to immediately discharge any employee who had not resided in the state for a minimum of 10 years. The new statutes additionally provided that the applicable civil fines would be assessed by the state department of employment inspectors, at their sole discretion, any time they believed that an employer had hired or failed to discharge a person not meeting the residency requirements, and that the civil fines would be imposed on any employer who had hired or failed to discharge such persons on or after January 1.

An employee within the state, who is a nonresident, brought suit challenging the state statute. Which of the following arguments would most likely result in a favorable result for the challenger?

(A) The statute is an unconstitutional Bill of Attainder.

(B) The statute violates the Privileges and Immunities Clause of Article IV.

(C) The statute violates the Equal Protection Clause of the Fourteenth Amendment.

(D) The statute violates the Ex Post Facto clause.

Question 50

The police set up an undercover "sting" operation in which they posed as fences of stolen property and bought and sold such property to anyone who came into their downtown warehouse. A defendant is being prosecuted for receiving stolen property in connection with his arrest by the undercover operatives, and the prosecution attempts to introduce a videotape showing the defendant offering to sell a television set to one of the police officers.

If this evidence is held to be inadmissible, the most likely reason is that:

(A) It is hearsay not within any exception.

(B) It violates the defendant's privilege against self-incrimination.

(C) A proper foundation was not established for its introduction into evidence.

(D) Criminality may not be proven by specific instances of misconduct.

Question 51

A driver left her car parked on the side of a hill. Two minutes later, the car rolled down the hill and struck and injured a pedestrian.

In the pedestrian's negligence action against the driver, the pedestrian introduced into evidence the facts stated above, which are undisputed. The driver testified that, when she parked her car, she turned the front wheels into the curb and put on her emergency brakes, which were in good working order. She also introduced evidence that, in the weeks before this incident, juveniles had been seen tampering with cars in the neighborhood. The jury returned a verdict in favor of the driver, and the pedestrian moved for a judgment notwithstanding the verdict.

The pedestrian's motion should be:

(A) Granted, because it is more likely than not that the driver's negligent conduct was the legal cause of the pedestrian's injuries.

(B) Granted, because the evidence does not support the verdict.

(C) Denied, because, given the driver's evidence, the jury was not required to draw an inference of negligence from the instances of the accident.

(D) Denied, if the driver was in no better position than the pedestrian to explain the accident.

barbri

Question 52

A husband purchased a cabin with his separate property. The husband provided in his will that the cabin be devised "to my sister-in-law for so long as my wife is alive, remainder to my son." Shortly thereafter, the husband died. When the sister-in-law learned of her interest in the cabin, she decided to lease the property. She entered into a valid written lease for a term of three years with a tenant, who agreed to pay $3,000 per year rent, with $1,500 due in advance every six months. The tenant paid the first $1,500 and took possession of the property. Two years later, one week after the tenant had paid the $1,500 due for the ensuing six-month period, the wife died. The son demanded that the tenant surrender possession of the cabin, but the tenant refused.

In an appropriate action for possession of the disputed property, the son will probably:

(A) Prevail, because his rights are superior to the tenant's.

(B) Prevail, if he reimburses the tenant for the portion of the six months' rent already paid to the sister-in-law that is attributable to the period after the tenant surrenders possession.

(C) Lose, because he did not wait to bring the action until the period for which the tenant had already paid rent had elapsed.

(D) Lose, because the tenant has the right to remain in possession for the last year of his lease as long as he pays the final $1,500.

Question 53

A motorcyclist had just bought a new motorcycle. One week later, while still learning how to ride the motorcycle, he saw a classmate from school that he did not like walking along the sidewalk. He tried to scare him by swerving onto the sidewalk at a driveway, planning to swerve back onto the street at the next driveway just in front of the classmate. As the motorcyclist attempted to swerve back onto the street, the motorcycle's front tire blew because of a latent defect, causing him to lose control of the steering. He attempted to apply the brakes, but due to his inexperience, hit the accelerator by mistake. The motorcycle struck and seriously injured the classmate. The classmate sues the motorcyclist for battery.

Who is likely to prevail?

(A) The classmate, because the motorcyclist intended to frighten the classmate.

(B) The classmate, unless the motorcyclist's negligence in hitting the accelerator was the proximate cause of the accident.

(C) The motorcyclist, because he did not intend to inflict bodily harm on the classmate.

(D) The motorcyclist, because the injury was proximately caused by the defective front tire.

Question 54

A speaker was addressing an audience in a city park on a subject that was highly offensive to many in the crowd that gathered to hear him speak. After awhile, the crowd became unruly and there was muttering and pushing, so the dozen police officers that were present formed a cordon around the speaker. A few members of the crowd indicated that if the police did not get "that S.O.B." to stop, they would do it themselves. At this point, two spectators picked up pieces of lumber from a construction site next door. The police officer in charge stepped in and demanded that the speaker stop speaking, to keep a fight from breaking out. When he refused, the police officer arrested him and he was convicted of disorderly conduct.

If the speaker appeals his conviction on constitutional grounds, it will be:

(A) Reversed, because the speaker's arrest constituted an interference with his First Amendment right to freedom of speech.

(B) Reversed, because the speaker's arrest constituted undue interference with the audience's right to assemble peaceably under the First Amendment.

(C) Sustained, because this speech caused an immediate and substantial threat to public order.

(D) Sustained, because it was the speaker's duty to obey a police officer where there were other times and places to convey his message.

Question 55

A mechanic noticed that his neighbor had a "for sale" sign on his old car. The mechanic thought it would be fun to have an old car to fix up and customize, and he asked his neighbor how much he wanted for the car. The neighbor told him that he would sell the car for $400, and the mechanic responded that he would buy the car for $400. They agreed that the mechanic would come to the neighbor's house by 6 p.m. the next day with the money. At 9:15 the next morning, the neighbor called the mechanic and told him that when he agreed to the sale the preceding day, he forgot that he had just put two new tires on the car and, therefore, would need to be paid an extra $50. The mechanic agreed to bring $450 in cash to his neighbor's house at six o'clock that night.

Is the mechanic legally bound to pay his neighbor the additional $50?

(A) Yes, because the original contract was not in writing.

(B) Yes, because the contract, as modified, does not exceed the minimum dollar amount required to invoke the Statute of Frauds.

(C) No, because no additional consideration was given for the oral modification.

(D) No, because contracts for the sale of goods can only be modified by merchants.

Question 56

An owner of land who was also a home contractor agreed in writing with a buyer to build a house on his (the contractor's) land and then sell the house and lot to the buyer. The contract provided that the sale must be completed by March 1. On March 5, after discovering that the house had not yet been completed, the buyer notified the contractor in writing of the buyer's election to cancel the contract because of the contractor's failure to deliver title by March 1. The contractor responded that, due to an unanticipated strike in the construction industry, performance had been unforeseeably delayed and that the house would be ready by March 20. The buyer responded that he would no longer accept delivery of the home and land. The contractor then brought an action to recover damages for breach of contract.

Who will prevail?

(A) The buyer, because the express date listed in the contract indicates that time was of the essence.

(B) The contractor, because the strike was truly an unforeseeable intervening event.

(C) The buyer, because there is a showing of good faith in the buyer's efforts to terminate the contract.

(D) The contractor, because he acted with due diligence in completing the house.

Question 57

A hunter drove to one of his old spots for target shooting. When he arrived at the spot, he noticed that an adjacent area that had formerly been an open field now contained a new housing tract with a playground where children were playing. The hunter tacked a paper target to a tree that was located between the playground and the point from which he planned to shoot. He fired a number of shots at the target, and all but one hit the target. The one shot that missed that went wide of the target, ricocheted off a tree, and flew into the playground, striking a child in the head, killing the child.

If the hunter is tried for the death of the child, the most serious crime that he can be convicted of is:

(A) Murder, because the hunter's intent to shoot the child can be inferred from his conduct.

(B) Murder, because the hunter acted with wanton recklessness when he chose to shoot the gun in an area near the playground.

(C) Manslaughter, because the hunter did not intend to kill the child.

(D) Neither murder nor manslaughter, because the hunter's shooting was negligent, and mere negligence is insufficient to support conviction for a homicide crime.

Question 58

After a bitter breakup with his ex-girlfriend, a man sank into a dark depression. It was deepened when he bumped into her at a store and she shouted at him, "Get away from me and stay away from me! You have the characteristics of a garden slug." He decided to commit suicide, which was a crime in the jurisdiction, by sitting in his running car in a closed garage. However, a neighbor discovered him and dragged him unconscious from the vehicle. The man was hospitalized for carbon monoxide poisoning but survived.

If the man sues the ex-girlfriend for his injuries, he is likely to:

(A) Prevail, because the ex-girlfriend's comments caused the man to suffer emotional distress.

(B) Prevail, if the ex-girlfriend intended to cause the man emotional distress.

(C) Lose, because the man's injuries resulted from his own voluntary choice.

(D) Lose, because the man's injuries resulted from his attempt to commit an illegal act.

GO ON TO THE NEXT PAGE

Question 59

A somewhat portly executive who was very prominent in business and social circles was aghast when he saw an article in the local paper describing the growing popularity of nude beaches. It was accompanied by a photograph of people enjoying themselves at a nearby nude beach. The picture was cropped so that nothing inappropriate was revealed, but the bather in the foreground of the picture was clearly the executive. The executive did enjoy visiting the nude beach on occasion, but he had never mentioned this to people in his social circle. Needless to say, he was quite embarrassed by the publication of the photograph, and he filed suit against the newspaper demanding damages from the newspaper for violation of his privacy rights.

Which of the following is the newspaper's best defense?

(A) There was no intrusion by the newspaper into the executive's private affairs.

(B) The newspaper did not place the executive in a false light.

(C) The picture was taken in a public place and appropriately accompanied by a newsworthy story.

(D) The newspaper did not use the photograph in any way to promote its circulation or advertising revenue.

Question 60

A defendant was on trial before a jury for murder. The state's prosecuting attorney had six witnesses prepared to testify against the defendant. After three of these witnesses completed their testimony, but before the prosecutor called her other witnesses to testify, the presiding judge called the prosecutor and the defense attorney to the bench. The judge told the prosecutor, "Frankly, your case stinks! You don't have enough evidence to convict this man of first degree murder. You are wasting our time. Reduce the charge to manslaughter and maybe you can strike a bargain with the defendant." The prosecutor replied, "No, your honor, I want to finish my case." The defendant heard the conversation, rose to his feet, and said, "Your honor, I'll plead guilty to manslaughter!" The judge, over the prosecutor's protestations, agreed to accept the plea and found the defendant guilty of manslaughter. The state appealed and the case was remanded for retrial.

Can the state retry the defendant for murder?

(A) Yes, because double jeopardy does not attach until the jury retires for deliberations.

(B) Yes, because the judge unconstitutionally forced a plea bargain, violating the Separation of Powers Clause.

(C) No, because double jeopardy attaches when the first witness is sworn.

(D) No, because the defendant was actually convicted of a lesser-included offense.

GO ON TO THE NEXT PAGE

Question 61

A homeowner leased his home to a tenant for three years. The following year, the homeowner conveyed the house to a buyer, who never recorded her deed nor did anything with regard to the house. The tenant continued paying rent to the homeowner.

Three months after the conveyance to the buyer, the homeowner conveyed the property to his proctologist, who knew nothing of the prior conveyance to the buyer. The homeowner took the proctologist's money and skipped town. The proctologist told the tenant he now owned the house and that all rents should be paid to him. The tenant complied.

Six months later, the proctologist went to his local bank for a loan. He offered to put up the property as security. One of the bank's title searchers discovered that the proctologist had never recorded his deed and that, just two weeks prior to his loan application, the buyer had recorded a deed to the house that bore an earlier date than the deed the proctologist had shown the bank. Because of this cloud on the title, the bank refused the loan request. When the tenant discovered this, she quit paying rent to the proctologist. The state has a notice recording statute.

If the proctologist sues the tenant to compel the payment of rent, the proctologist will likely:

(A) Win, because the tenant is estopped from denying a landlord-tenant relationship with the proctologist, since she had paid rent for many months.

(B) Win, because the proctologist was a bona fide purchaser when he bought the property from the homeowner.

(C) Lose, because the proctologist failed to record his deed to the property.

(D) Lose, because the proctologist did not have good title to the property and cannot demand rent from tenants in possession.

Question 62

A biker sued a driver for injuries allegedly sustained in an automobile accident. The driver's defense was that the biker was the cause of the accident, since the biker ran a red light and crashed into the driver's car. The driver's principal witness testified that he was standing on the corner when the accident occurred, and he observed the biker run the red light and crash into the driver's car. On cross-examination of the witness, the biker's lawyer asked, "Isn't it true that on the day of the accident you were 300 miles away from the scene attempting to extract protection money from the owner of a seaside restaurant?" The driver's attorney objected to the question, but the objection was overruled by the court. The witness then refused to answer the question, invoking the privilege against self-incrimination.

The biker's attorney moved to have the witness's direct testimony stricken from the record.

The court should:

(A) Grant the motion, because the privilege against self-incrimination is not applicable to civil cases.

(B) Grant the motion, because the biker has not had an adequate opportunity for meaningful cross-examination.

(C) Deny the motion, because the witness has a right to refuse to answer.

(D) Deny the motion, because the jury can assess the weight to be given to the witness's testimony.

Question 63

At 3 a.m. on the state turnpike, a driver was stopped for driving 30 m.p.h. over the posted speed limit. Because of the speed at which she was traveling and because the driver possessed an out-of-state driver's license, the officer decided to place the driver under arrest and take her to the station house. Under state law, such an arrest is valid. At the time of the arrest, the officer searched the passenger area of the automobile, and under the front seat he found a small package containing what he immediately determined to be marijuana.

If the driver is charged with possession of marijuana, her motion to suppress the marijuana will most likely be:

(A) Granted, unless the officer had probable cause to believe the car contained items that were legitimate to seize.

(B) Granted, because the search was of an area outside the control of the arrestee.

(C) Denied, because the search was incident to a valid arrest.

(D) Denied, if the court determines the officer had a reasonable fear of the driver.

Question 64

Two police officers stopped an automobile for improperly proceeding through a red light. When one of the officers approached the car, he observed some hand-rolled cigarettes on the dashboard. He ordered the driver out of the car, examined the cigarettes, and determined that they were joints of marijuana. The officer then arrested the driver and guarded him in the back seat of the police cruiser while the second officer searched the entire car, including the trunk. In the trunk, he found two rare paintings that had recently been stolen from the city's art museum.

The driver was charged with possession of stolen goods and brought a motion to suppress the introduction of the paintings into evidence.

This motion is most likely to be denied because the second officer properly conducted:

(A) A search incident to an arrest.

(B) An automobile search.

(C) A custody search.

(D) An inventory search.

Question 65

Under a program created by Congress, the federal government allocated $5 million to one of the nation's leading energy producing states "to be used solely for the development of synthetic materials to replace petroleum." The state accepted the funds and distributed $3 million from those funds to a state university, an agency of the state government. The university applied the $3 million to its ongoing energy research program, which included projects investigating the creation of synthetic replacements for petroleum products, solar power, geothermal power, biomass, and fusion power generation. The Justice Department brings suit in federal district court seeking to enjoin the expenditure of the funds in the University research programs.

The court should rule that:

(A) The University expenditure is unconstitutional because Congress has improperly delegated its power to spend for the general welfare to a state government.

(B) The expenditure is unconstitutional as a violation of the Supremacy Clause.

(C) The expenditure is constitutional because it conforms substantially with the purpose and goals of the federal program.

(D) The expenditure is constitutional because the federal government's attempt to control the actions of a state agency violates the concepts of federalism.

GO ON TO THE NEXT PAGE

Question 66

A famous chef entered into a written agreement with his friend, a very famous interior decorator respected for his unique designs. The decorator agreed, for a fixed fee, to design the interior of the chef's new restaurant, and, upon the chef's approval of the design plan, to decorate and furnish the restaurant accordingly. The agreement was silent as to assignment or delegation by either party. Before beginning the work, the decorator sold his decorating business to a rival third party. Under their agreement, the decorator assigned to the third party, and the third party agreed to complete, the chef-decorator contract. The rival third party, also an experienced decorator of excellent repute, advised the chef of the assignment, and supplied him with information confirming both the third party's financial responsibility and past commercial success.

Is the chef obligated to permit the third party to perform the chef-decorator agreement?

(A) Yes, because the agreement contained no prohibition against assignment or delegation.

(B) Yes, because the chef received adequate assurances of the third party's ability to complete the job.

(C) No, because the decorator's duties were of a personal nature, involving his reputation, taste, and skill.

(D) No, because the decorator's purported delegation to the third party of his obligations to the chef affected a novation.

Question 67

A landowner in fee simple signed a promissory note for $10,000 to a bank, and secured the note by a mortgage of her land to the bank. The mortgage was duly recorded. The landowner then sold the property to an attorney, who assumed and agreed to pay the mortgage to the bank on the land. The attorney did not make payments on the mortgage note to the bank. The bank, following appropriate statutory procedures, foreclosed the mortgage and gave notice to both the landowner and the attorney that it intended to sue for any deficiency. At the foreclosure sale, the property sold for $6,000. The bank now sues both the landowner and the attorney for $5,000, which is the remaining amount of the unpaid principal and interest on the note plus costs of foreclosure.

The bank will be successful in obtaining a judgment against:

(A) Only the landowner.

(B) Only the attorney.

(C) Either the landowner or the attorney.

(D) Both the landowner and the attorney.

Question 68

A developer owned an office building subject to a first mortgage with a creditor in the amount of $1 million. Subsequently, the developer borrowed $100,000 from a bank secured by a second mortgage on the building to help pay the first mortgage and other expenses of the building. The developer's financial condition worsened, and he was unable to make the required payments on the first mortgage to the creditor. The developer approached the creditor and offered to give her a deed to the building in satisfaction of all of his obligations to the creditor. The developer delivered to the creditor a quitclaim deed to the building, which recited as consideration the release of the developer from all liability on the mortgage to the creditor. The deed was duly recorded.

Shortly thereafter, the office market greatly improved, and the building was worth $1.5 million. The developer then brought an action against the creditor, claiming that the deed was an equitable mortgage, and the bank served notice on the creditor that it was preparing to foreclose its mortgage on the building.

In appropriate actions, the creditor will prevail against:

(A) The developer only.

(B) The bank only.

(C) Both the developer and the bank.

(D) Neither the developer nor the bank.

Question 69

A driver negligently drove his car into a pedestrian, breaking her leg. The pedestrian's leg was put in a cast, and she used crutches to get about. While shopping at the market, the pedestrian did not notice when she put one of her crutches on a piece of banana peel, even though she was using her crutches with care. The peel had been negligently left on the floor by the manager of the produce department. The pedestrian's crutch slipped on the peel and she fell to the floor, breaking her arm. Had the pedestrian stepped on the peel when she did not have to use crutches, she would have regained her balance.

If the pedestrian sues the driver and the market for her injuries, she will be able to recover from:

(A) The driver, for her broken leg only.

(B) The driver, for both of her injuries.

(C) The market, for both of her injuries.

(D) The driver, for her broken leg only, and the market, for her broken arm only.

Question 70

A bank executive was on trial for embezzling $10,000 from the bank where he worked. A key witness for the prosecution was called to testify, but on the stand he had difficulty remembering the specifics of a conversation he had with the executive regarding the executive's accounting procedures. To refresh the recollection of the witness, the prosecutor showed the witness a memorandum that the witness had written for his file, detailing the conversation. The witness reviewed the memorandum, and then testified that he recalled the conversation. He proceeded to testify about the specifics of the conversation.

The defense counsel then asks that the memorandum be introduced into evidence. The court should:

(A) Exclude the evidence if it determines that the witness's memory was refreshed.

(B) Exclude the evidence if it determines that a reasonable jury would conclude that the witness's memory was refreshed.

(C) Admit the evidence if it determines that the witness's memory was not refreshed.

(D) Admit the evidence if it was used to refresh the witness's recollection.

Question 71

A boater and a water skier were involved in a boating accident. Shortly after the accident, the water skier prepared a written summary of the events surrounding the accident. At trial two years later, the water skier is on the stand and is unable to accurately recall the details of the accident so she is asked to read to the jury the aforementioned account of the accident. The trial judge should rule her proposed testimony:

(A) Inadmissible, because the best evidence is the writing itself.

(B) Admissible, because her memory of the actual event is imperfect.

(C) Admissible, because it refreshes her recollection.

(D) Admissible, even though hearsay, because the out-of-court declarant is on the stand and is capable of being cross-examined.

Question 72

Of the following, which power is not specifically given to the Senate in the Constitution?

(A) To raise revenue.

(B) To declare war.

(C) To impeach.

(D) To regulate commerce.

Question 73

A local farm switched from vehicular application of pesticide to aerial spraying. When the aerial spraying began, the farm foreman discovered that, for the first time, the farm was experiencing appreciable drift of the insecticide, a portion of which drifted onto a nearby private school. The school filed an action seeking to have the aerial spraying enjoined as a nuisance.

If the farm prevails, it will be because:

(A) The farm's aerial spraying is in conformity with the general practices in the industry and was conducted with reasonable care.

(B) One landowner may not maintain an action for nuisance.

(C) The maintenance of vehicular application systems will greatly increase the farm's costs of operation.

(D) The drift of the insecticide does not substantially interfere with the use and enjoyment of the school's property.

Question 74

A landlord entered into a written four-year lease with a tenant for an apartment in the landlord's apartment house. The tenant's lease, and all leases in the apartment house, prohibited the playing of musical instruments between 10 p.m. and 8 a.m. The lease required the tenant to pay the rent on a monthly basis. Two years into the lease, the tenant assigned the lease to a nurse with the landlord's permission. The nurse then assigned the lease to his brother with the landlord's permission. The brother went into possession. A neighboring tenant in the same apartment house insisted upon playing a trumpet in a loud manner between 2 a.m. and 4 a.m. The brother complained to the landlord without success. Unable to sleep each night, the brother abandoned his apartment after occupying it for two months.

If the landlord sues the nurse for the rent due during the period after the nurse's brother left, the nurse's best defense would be:

(A) A breach of the landlord's covenant of quiet enjoyment.

(B) Estoppel, because the landlord consented to a further assignment.

(C) Lack of privity of estate.

(D) Constructive eviction.

Question 75

A defendant shot and wounded a victim in the victim's home late one night. The defendant was subsequently prosecuted for burglary under a statute that defined burglary as "the trespassory entering of the dwelling house of another with intent to commit a felony therein." At trial, the prosecution attempted to prove that the defendant had picked the lock on the victim's front door while the victim slept, crept into the house, awakened the victim at gunpoint, and demanded money, shooting the victim when he attempted to wrest the gun from the defendant's hand. The defendant testified on his own behalf, and told the jury that he had been invited into the house by the victim, who then pulled a knife and attempted to force him to pay an asserted debt. The defendant explained that he had shot the victim when the victim attempted to stab him after he denied owing any money. The judge then instructed the jury, among other things, that they should find the defendant not guilty if they believed, by a preponderance of the evidence, either that the victim had invited the defendant into the house or that the defendant had shot the victim when the latter attempted to stab him with a knife. The defendant was convicted of burglary and appealed.

The appellate court should:

(A) Reverse, because the jury instruction as to the trespassory entering was unconstitutional.

(B) Reverse, because the jury instruction as to self-defense was unconstitutional.

(C) Reverse, because both jury instructions were unconstitutional.

(D) Affirm, because both jury instructions were constitutional.

Question 76

During a defendant's trial for murder, the state introduced circumstantial evidence tending to establish her guilt, but could not provide direct evidence that she had committed the murder. No one had seen the killer going into or coming out of the victim's office around 2:30 p.m., the time of the victim's death by strangulation. During her defense case, the defendant took the stand and testified that she could not have committed the charged murder, because on the day of the victim's death she had been on a business trip 3,000 miles away. The prosecution then called a rebuttal witness. The witness will testify that, at 1 p.m. on the day of the charged murder, he had put his hand on the defendant's knee while both sat at a bar across town. The defendant had then coquettishly removed his necktie and attempted to strangle him with it until bystanders pulled her away and she left the bar. The defendant objects to admission of the witness's testimony.

How should the trial judge rule?

(A) For the defendant, because she did not place her character at issue in the trial.

(B) For the defendant, because the testimony is character evidence not directed at her character for truth and veracity.

(C) For the state, because the testimony established that the defendant had the opportunity to commit the charged crime.

(D) For the state, because the testimony established that the defendant has a character for violence.

Question 77

On April 4, a homeowner hired an electrician to evaluate his home's wiring. The electrician found the wiring to be faulty, called it a fire hazard, and urged the homeowner to fix it soon. That day, the homeowner entered into a written contract with the electrician, whereby the electrician agreed to repair the wiring for $1,600. The contract provided that the repair would take place prior to April 30, on a day when the homeowner would be home. On April 26, the work had yet to be done so the homeowner called the electrician to pin down a date. The electrician suggested April 29, and the homeowner agreed. On the morning of April 29, the electrician arrived ready to do the repair work. However, he discovered that no one was home, and he could not get inside. Earlier that morning, the homeowner had been rushed to the hospital for an emergency appendectomy, and the homeowner did not return home from the hospital until May 1. On that day, the faulty wiring caused a fire that severely damaged the house.

Will the electrician succeed in a breach of contract action?

(A) Yes, because the homeowner made and breached an implied-in-fact promise to make the house available to the electrician before April 30.

(B) Yes, because any recovery by the electrician will be subject to a setoff by the homeowner on account of his damage from the fire.

(C) No, because the electrician did nothing about the agreement between April 4 and April 26.

(D) No, because the homeowner's obligations under the contract were subject to an express condition precedent that failed because of supervening impossibility.

Question 78

A developer purchased a downtown lot on which she intended to have an office building constructed. She entered into a written agreement with a construction company to build a 50-story office tower for $250 million. The agreement specified that monthly progress payments of $20 million were to commence one month after the foundation was in place, with all remaining amounts due upon approval of the completed structure by the developer's architect. Construction commenced on March 10, and by April 1 the foundation was completed. On the night of April 30, a terrorist group detonated 500 pounds of explosives in the partially completed structure, totally destroying the building plus all of the construction equipment involved in the project. The construction company was forced into bankruptcy when its casualty insurer classified the loss as having occurred in an "undeclared war," and refused to replace the lost equipment. The developer engaged another construction company to construct the 50-story tower as originally planned at a price of $260 million. The trustee in bankruptcy has now brought an action against the developer to recover all payments due the company for the work completed prior to the terrorist act.

The trustee will probably recover:

(A) $20 million.

(B) The difference between $20 million and the cost to the construction company of the work completed at the time of the terrorist attack.

(C) The reasonable value of the labor and materials expended by the construction company at the time of the terrorist attack.

(D) Nothing.

Question 83

A doctor and nurse were coworkers. The doctor admired the nurse's wristwatch and frequently said how much he wished he had one like it. The nurse decided to give the doctor the watch for his birthday the following week. On the weekend before the doctor's birthday, the two attended a hospital picnic. The nurse took his watch off and left it on a blanket when he went off to join in a touch football game. The doctor strolled by, saw the watch on the blanket, and decided to steal it. He bent over and picked up the watch. Before he could pocket it, however, the nurse returned. When he saw the doctor holding the watch, he said, "Doc, I know how much you like that watch. I was planning to give it to you for your birthday. Go ahead and take it now." The doctor kept the watch.

The doctor has committed:

(A) Larcency.

(B) Attempted larcency.

(C) Embezzlement.

(D) No crime.

Question 84

A nursing home, as a matter of policy, admitted patients known for violent behavior. Each night before the patients went to bed, all doors were locked so that intruders could not enter the premises without forcing an entry. One morning an elderly and docile patient was found beaten in her bed. The doors had been locked and there were no signs of forced entry into the building during the previous night.

If the patient should sue the nursing home for her injuries and establishes the above facts, she is likely to:

(A) Recover, because an occurrence such as this would not ordinarily happen unless the nursing home was negligent.

(B) Recover, because the nursing home is strictly liable for the patients in its care.

(C) Not recover, unless the patient can prove that the beating was caused by an employee of the nursing home.

(D) Not recover, because the beating was caused by the criminal act of a third party.

Question 85

A seller entered into a written land sale contract with a buyer on May 20, whereby the seller agreed to sell a home to the buyer for $60,000. The closing date was set at August 1. The buyer put up $6,000 as earnest money, as provided by the contract. The contract stated that if the buyer failed to perform by tendering the balance due on the house on August 1, the $6,000 could be treated as liquidated damages "at the option of the seller."

On July 21, the week before the closing, the house burned to the ground because of a freak lightning strike during a thunderstorm. When August 1 arrived, the buyer refused to tender $54,000 to the seller. The buyer asked the seller for the refund of his earnest money because the house had been destroyed. The seller refused and filed suit, asking for specific performance. The buyer countersued, demanding refund of the $6,000 earnest money.

How should the court rule on the suits?

(A) The court will order specific performance by the buyer.

(B) The court will order the seller to return the $6,000 to the buyer because of frustration of purpose of the contract.

(C) The court will award the seller $6,000 as liquidated damages.

(D) The court will award neither party the relief sought because of mutual mistake.

Question 86

A state statute requires all corporations doing business in the state and making over $1 million per year in purchases to make at least 50% of their purchases from vendors located in the state.

Which of the following arguments is most likely to succeed if the plaintiff is alleging that the statute deprives him of due process of law?

(A) It applies to businesses not affected with the public interest.

(B) Materials needed for some businesses cannot be purchased locally.

(C) The object of the statute is not within the scope of the police power.

(D) The means used by the statute are unrelated to the law's objective.

Question 87

A pedestrian suffered serious injuries and amnesia after being struck by a car. The pedestrian sued the driver of the car. During case preparation, the pedestrian's attorney was frustrated by his client's inability to remember any of the facts surrounding the accident. He therefore hired a qualified hypnotist to question the pedestrian. While hypnotized, the pedestrian described details of the accident, stating that the car that struck him ran a red light, and the car's license plate number was XYZ356. It so happens that XYZ356 is the license number of the driver's vehicle. At trial, the driver stipulated that his car struck the pedestrian, but asserts a defense that he was not negligent and that the light was green when he entered the intersection. Because the pedestrian's amnesia persists at the time of trial, the pedestrian's attorney wishes to call the hypnotist to the stand to testify as to the statements made by the pedestrian under hypnosis. The driver's attorney objects.

How should the court rule on the objection?

(A) Sustained, because the hypnotist's testimony would be hearsay not within any recognized exception to the hearsay rule.

(B) Sustained, because the jury was not given a limiting instruction on the weight that should be given to testimony under hypnosis.

(C) Overruled, because the accuracy of the license plate number establishes that the testimony is reliable.

(D) Overruled, because the testimony falls within the catch-all exception to the hearsay rule.

Question 88

A witness who was unable to speak was an eyewitness to a robbery in the park. He went to the police station shortly after the crime was committed, and when asked who committed the robbery, pointed to the defendant in a police lineup in which there were several men who were dressed like the defendant and were the defendant's size. The defendant was then indicted for robbery. The witness died before trial, and the sergeant in charge of the lineup desires to testify at the defendant's trial that the witness pointed to the defendant at the lineup.

His testimony is:

(A) Admissible as evidence of prior identification.

(B) Admissible to prove the defendant committed the crime.

(C) Inadmissible, because the sergeant's testimony is hearsay.

(D) Inadmissible, because the defendant's counsel was not present at the lineup.

Question 89

A socialite purchased a hotel and hired an experienced hotelier to manage the property. The hotelier signed a three-year management contract for an annual salary of $150,000 per year, payable in monthly checks. After a year of hotel ownership proved too demanding on her social schedule, the socialite told the hotelier she was selling the hotel to a buyer. Along with the sale, the socialite assigned to the buyer the hotelier's management contract. The written contract between the socialite and the hotelier had no clause dealing with assignment of the contract. After the sale, the hotelier worked for the buyer for one year, for which the buyer paid the hotelier his $150,000 salary. The buyer then dismissed the hotelier for no apparent cause. The hotelier asserted that he is owed $150,000 for the year remaining on his contract, but the buyer refused to pay him. The hotelier has been unable to obtain further employment.

Can the hotelier recover in a suit for breach against the buyer?

(A) Yes, because the buyer accepted the hotelier's services and paid him for a year; that constituted an implied acceptance of the terms of the contract between the socialite and the hotelier.

(B) Yes, because a novation occurred, binding the buyer.

(C) No, because the assignment of the original contract was improper and no contract existed between the buyer and the hotelier; hence, there could be no breach.

(D) No, because the original contract between the socialite and the hotelier was not assignable, even with the hotelier's consent.

Question 90

The President of the United States issued an executive order banning conversation by all executive employees with members of the press unless prior permission had been obtained from a supervisor. Executive Department employees were subject to dismissal for violation of the order. An employee of the United States Department of Agriculture spoke to a reporter and told the reporter that the USDA sanctioned the approval of a dangerous pesticide because of payoffs made by lobbyists to a high-ranking USDA official. The newspaper printed the story and quoted the employee by name. After a hearing in line with civil service regulations, the employee was found to have violated the executive order barring unauthorized conversations with news media reporters, and the employee was fired. The employee brought suit in federal court for reinstatement, back pay, and other benefits and also prayed that the court should strike down the executive order as unconstitutional.

If the employee's case reaches the United States Supreme Court, the justices should rule that the executive order is:

(A) Constitutional, because the President has plenary power to control Executive Department employees.

(B) Constitutional, because government employment is a privilege and not a right.

(C) Unconstitutional, because Congress, rather than the President, has authority to set the terms of federal employment.

(D) Unconstitutional, because the President cannot broadly limit all executive employees' freedom of speech and association.

Question 91

A mother had her lawyer prepare and execute two deeds: one conveying a 640-acre farm to her daughter and the other conveying a 590-acre farm to her son. The mother produced the deed to the daughter, who told her mother to keep the deed just in case the daughter misplaced it. The mother held on to the deed. The next day, the mother went to her lawyer's office to have the deeds recorded, but she forgot the daughter's deed at home. The mother gave the lawyer the son's deed and promised to bring the daughter's deed in the next day. Later that afternoon, the lawyer recorded the son's deed. That night, the mother suffered a stroke and died in her sleep. The daughter's deed was never recorded but was found in the mother's home after her death. In her will, the mother left all of her property to her daughter, her son, and the local animal shelter, in three equal shares. Aside from her modest home and some small bank accounts, the mother had no appreciable estate.

If the animal shelter challenges the deeds to the farms on grounds of lack of proper delivery, it will:

(A) Win on both farms.

(B) Lose on both farms.

(C) Win on the 640-acre farm but lose on the 590-acre farm.

(D) Win on the 590-acre farm but lose on the 640-acre farm.

Question 92

Thirty years ago, a telephone company purchased an easement from an owner to install, inspect, repair, replace, and maintain underground transmission cables within a specified portion of the owner's property. The deed granting the easement was validly recorded, and the telephone company shortly thereafter laid underground long distance lines traversing the owner's land beneath the area described in the easement deed.

Fifteen years later, the owner sold a 50-acre portion of his land to a buyer. This portion included part of the easement granted to the telephone company. The buyer erected a residence on the purchased land and planted 49 acres of walnut trees. He granted an easement to the telephone company to string aerial telephone wires. The underground easement was never disclosed.

Last year, the telephone company informed the buyer that it would have to excavate underground cables and replace them with new ones. This was the first the buyer knew of the cables lying under his land. The cables, lying within the easement, are directly beneath a row of black walnut trees running the length of the buyer's property. Black walnuts have become extremely valuable, and the buyer estimates that their value is approximately $400,000.

The buyer seeks an injunction prohibiting the telephone company from undertaking the planned excavation. The trial court should rule for:

(A) The telephone company, because the benefits of installing the new cables outweigh the harm done to the buyer.

(B) The telephone company, because ownership of the easement permits it to make the excavation.

(C) The buyer, because the telephone company concealed the existence of the underground easement from the buyer when it acquired the overhead easement from him.

(D) The buyer, because the deed by which he purchased his property made no mention of the easement, and he had no actual knowledge of it.

Question 93

A tourist was hit at a street crossing by an automobile. The accident was witnessed by a bystander and by the tourist's wife. The tourist was hospitalized for several weeks and when it was apparent that he was about to die, the tourist cried out in anguish, "Why didn't the driver stop for the red light?" The tourist died immediately thereafter. The wife later brought an action against the driver for wrongful death, alleging excessive speed, failure to observe traffic signals, and defective brakes.

A witness for the driver was called to testify that the driver enjoyed a reputation for being a safe and prudent driver based on his personal knowledge of the driver's driving habits. The trial judge should rule the witness's testimony:

(A) Admissible, because, where there are no unbiased eyewitnesses to an accident, reputation as a safe driver may be used to prove the driver acted in conformity with that reputation at the time in question.

(B) Admissible, because the witness first testified that he has personal knowledge of the driver's driving habits.

(C) Inadmissible, because evidence of a reputation as a safe and prudent driver cannot be used to prove that the driver acted in conformity with that reputation at the time in question.

(D) Inadmissible, because, in a civil case, character evidence may be used only after the plaintiff has attacked the character of the defendant.

Question 94

A homeowner raked up numerous dead, dry leaves that had fallen on his yard and set fire to the pile, even though the wind was blowing at 15-20 miles per hour that day, and a county ordinance made it unlawful to burn leaves on any day when the wind speed exceeded 10 miles per hour. After the homeowner went into his house, the wind whipped the burning leaves into the air and deposited some of them, still burning, on the wood-shingled roof of a neighboring house, setting the house on fire. A driver was passing by and saw the burning roof of the neighbor's house. He pulled over, got out of his car and ran across the street towards the neighbor's yard so that he could warn the occupants of the house. The driver was struck by a paramedic's vehicle just arriving in response to a telephone report of the fire. In a jurisdiction that follows the traditional common law rules applicable to contributory negligence, the driver brought an action against the homeowner to recover for the injuries he suffered from being struck by the emergency vehicle.

How should the court rule in this action?

(A) For the driver, because the homeowner's negligence was a proximate cause of the driver's injuries.

(B) For the driver, because the homeowner's conduct constituted negligence per se.

(C) For the homeowner, because the emergency vehicle was the actual cause of the driver's injuries.

(D) For the homeowner, because the driver would not have been injured if he had not stopped and run across the street.

GO ON TO THE NEXT PAGE

Question 95

A business traveler met a woman at a bar in the town the traveler was visiting. After an evening of drinking, when the traveler was very drunk, the woman went with the traveler to his hotel room. The woman did not intend to have sexual intercourse with the traveler; rather, she intended to drug him and steal his money. When they arrived at his room, the traveler attempted to have sexual intercourse with the woman. She told him that before they had sex they had to have one more drink. The traveler did not want another drink and used force in attempting to have intercourse with the woman. She violently resisted, and when it became clear to the traveler that she was strong enough to physically resist, he agreed to have another drink first. The woman drugged his drink, he passed out, and she completed the theft.

If the traveler is charged with attempted rape, his best defense would be:

(A) The woman consented to sexual intercourse.

(B) The traveler was too drunk to form the mens rea necessary for the crime.

(C) It was impossible to complete the crime of rape, as the woman never intended to have sex with the traveler.

(D) The woman is a thief.

Question 96

A bus company was a private corporation that operated over fixed city routes under a franchise granted to it by the city council. To enhance revenues, the bus company rented advertising space on its vehicles. Although the city received a certain fixed percentage of the fare revenues from the company, it received nothing from the advertising fees. The management of the bus company had learned through bitter experience that any advertising that could be characterized as "controversial" led to complaints from riders and sometimes to losses in revenue. To that end, management employs a firm "no controversial advertising" policy. Thus, they refused to take ads for X-rated movies, abortion clinics, political candidates, and anything else that might be deemed "controversial." A candidate for city council was waging a populist campaign for the job and among his targets were the local utilities and the bus company. The candidate demanded that he be allowed to buy advertising on the buses, but the company's advertising manager refused, citing the company ban on all political ads. The candidate filed suit in federal district court, asking that the court require the company to accept his ads.

Which of the following is the company's best argument against the candidate's constitutional claim?

(A) The company is a privately owned company, and thus there is insufficient "state action" to invoke the United States Constitution.

(B) Commercial speech receives less protection under the First Amendment than most other forms of speech.

(C) Bus riders have First and Fourteenth Amendment rights to see the type of advertising they desire, and past experience has shown that there is substantial opposition by riders to controversial ads.

(D) The candidate has many other sources of advertising available and he does not need ads on the company's vehicles to get his message to the public.

Question 97

A software designer and software programmer ran into each other at a crowded software convention. The designer suggested to the programmer that they become partners. The programmer quickly retorted, "Look buddy, I like you, you're a nice guy and all that, but I'd never become your business partner, because when it comes to software design, you are totally incompetent." This remark was overheard by the private secretary to the CEO of a major software company that often subcontracted portions of jobs to smaller software design businesses, although it had never used this designer before.

If the designer sues the programmer for defamation, who is likely to prevail?

(A) The programmer, if her statement about the designer's competence is true.

(B) The programmer, because there was no publication.

(C) The designer, unless the programmer did not know her statement could have been overheard.

(D) The designer, if he suffered pecuniary loss as a result of the programmer's statement.

Question 98

A large wholesaler of European clothing sent out a circular to all of its customers advertising fine quality coats for sale at a price of $300 each when purchased in lots of 100 coats. The circular also stated that payment for each lot was to be made in three $10,000 installments, the first payment due within 10 days of delivery and the subsequent installments within 40 and 70 days of delivery, respectively. The day after receiving the circular, a retailer sent the wholesaler a standard order form with price, quantity, and delivery date terms filled in by the retailer, clearly indicating that the retailer was ordering one lot of 100 coats. The wholesaler shipped the coats to the retailer, and they arrived on September 10. The retailer accepted delivery of the coats and, on September 11, mailed to the wholesaler a check for $29,400. The check had the words "payment in full" written on it conspicuously. In addition, the retailer enclosed a letter with the check stating, in relevant part, "By cashing the enclosed check in the amount of $29,400, we assume that you accept our standard policy of taking a 2% discount for early payment." The wholesaler received the check on September 13 and cashed it on September 14.

Assuming that the relevant common law rules have not been modified by the check cashing rules of Article 3 of the Uniform Commercial Code in the jurisdiction, what is the legal effect of the wholesaler's cashing of the retailer's check?

(A) The entire debt is discharged, because there has been an accord and satisfaction.

(B) The entire debt is discharged on the basis of account stated.

(C) The retailer remains liable for the unpaid portion of the debt, because the discount provision was never accepted as part of the contract.

(D) Cashing the check merely satisfied a portion of the debt, and the retailer remains liable for the unpaid portion.

Question 99

A suspect was captured in a high-speed police chase five minutes after a bank robbery. The robbers had handed the teller a handwritten note demanding the money. The suspect was taken to the police station where, over his protests, he was required to write out the words of the note. After introducing the robbers' note to the teller, the prosecution also offered in evidence the writing which the suspect had been required to make by the police.

On appropriate objection, the court should rule the writing to be:

(A) Admissible.

(B) Inadmissible, because he was not advised that his handwriting sample could be admitted into evidence against him.

(C) Inadmissible, because he was not advised of his right to refuse to give a handwriting sample.

(D) Inadmissible, because he had not been informed he had a right to have counsel present.

Question 100

A large apple farm sells its product to various producers in the area who market apple products for commercial use. Prior to the harvesting season—the period when apple producers normally negotiate with processors and wholesalers for sale of the apples to be harvested—the farm was contacted by a health foods corporation that agreed in writing to purchase all of the farm's harvested apples. After the contract was signed, but before the harvest had begun, a rival apple farm offered to sell its apples to the corporation for 20% less than the price agreed to by the first farm. The corporation signed a contract with the rival farm for the purchase of raw apple products early enough before the beginning of the harvest so that the first farm had plenty of time to obtain another buyer for its apples. The corporation informed the first farm that its requirements for apples for the next year would be about 5% of the farm's total production.

If the first farm seeks specific performance of its contract with the corporation, the court should find for:

(A) The farm, because performance of the corporation-rival farm contract will automatically breach the first farm's contract.

(B) The farm, because its contract was prior in time to the rival farm's contract.

(C) The corporation, because the first farm can resell its apples elsewhere and then seek damages, if any, from the corporation.

(D) The corporation, because a seller of goods cannot obtain specific performance.

ANSWER KEY AND SUBJECT KEY

	Answer	Subject
1.	D	Torts
2.	D	Real Property
3.	C	Evidence
4.	B	Evidence
5.	D	Criminal Law
6.	B	Torts
7.	B	Contracts
8.	D	Contracts
9.	C	Real Property
10.	A	Constitutional Law
11.	C	Constitutional Law
12.	D	Criminal Law
13.	B	Contracts
14.	A	Real Property
15.	D	Criminal Law
16.	C	Evidence
17.	C	Constitutional Law
18.	B	Contracts
19.	C	Torts
20.	C	Evidence
21.	B	Torts
22.	D	Constitutional Law
23.	B	Constitutional Law
24.	C	Real Property
25.	C	Evidence
26.	C	Torts
27.	A	Torts
28.	C	Contracts
29.	D	Contracts
30.	D	Criminal Law
31.	B	Evidence
32.	D	Real Property
33.	D	Real Property
34.	D	Criminal Law
35.	B	Criminal Law
36.	B	Criminal Law
37.	B	Contracts
38.	C	Constitutional Law
39.	A	Constitutional Law
40.	A	Torts
41.	A	Constitutional Law
42.	D	Contracts
43.	C	Contracts
44.	D	Evidence
45.	C	Evidence
46.	D	Criminal Law
47.	B	Real Property
48.	D	Real Property
49.	B	Constitutional Law
50.	C	Evidence

	Answer	Subject
51.	C	Torts
52.	A	Real Property
53.	A	Torts
54.	A	Constitutional Law
55.	B	Contracts
56.	A	Contracts
57.	B	Criminal Law
58.	C	Torts
59.	C	Torts
60.	D	Criminal Law
61.	B	Real Property
62.	B	Evidence
63.	C	Criminal Law
64.	B	Criminal Law
65.	B	Constitutional Law
66.	C	Contracts
67.	D	Real Property
68.	A	Real Property
69.	B	Torts
70.	D	Evidence
71.	B	Evidence
72.	C	Constitutional Law
73.	D	Torts
74.	C	Real Property
75.	A	Criminal Law
76.	C	Evidence
77.	D	Contracts
78.	D	Contracts
79.	B	Constitutional Law
80.	D	Real Property
81.	D	Criminal Law
82.	D	Torts
83.	A	Criminal Law
84.	A	Torts
85.	A	Real Property
86.	B	Constitutional Law
87.	A	Evidence
88.	C	Evidence
89.	A	Contracts
90.	D	Constitutional Law
91.	B	Real Property
92.	B	Real Property
93.	C	Evidence
94.	A	Torts
95.	B	Criminal Law
96.	A	Constitutional Law
97.	A	Torts
98.	A	Contracts
99.	A	Criminal Law
100.	C	Contracts

Answer to Question 1

(D) A private nuisance is a substantial and unreasonable interference with the use and enjoyment of real property. Because the mechanic does not own or rent the property where he works, he may not pursue a claim based on interference with that real property's use and enjoyment. (A public nuisance is an interference with the rights of the community at large—a situation not presented by the fact pattern.) (A) is wrong because sound waves may be a basis for a nuisance action. (C) is wrong because, if 40% of the people are bothered by the sound waves, they probably are a nuisance. It is not necessary for a majority of the population to be affected for there to be a nuisance, but more than one must be affected. The choice between (B) and (D) is a difficult one. Nuisance requires an ***unreasonable*** interference with the property, and if the facts in (B) were true, the defendants could arguably be acting reasonably. However, (D) is more clearly an incorrect answer than (B).

Answer to Question 2

(D) Under the prior appropriation doctrine, the first party to make beneficial use of water from the water source is protected, regardless of whether the party is a riparian owner or not. Others may use whatever water is left in the stream or lake, but they may not diminish the water being used by the prior appropriation. (A) is an incorrect statement of the law. (B) would be the correct answer if the jurisdiction followed the riparian doctrine. Under the riparian doctrine, natural uses (*e.g.*, household consumption) prevail over artificial uses (*e.g.*, manufacturing). (C) is incorrect because the prior use must be beneficial (not just any use), and the individual need not be a riparian owner.

Answer to Question 3

(C) By referring the plaintiff to the publication industry journal for the information concerning sales figures, the defendants have adopted it to the same extent as if they had said or written the words contained in the journal. Therefore, it is an adoptive admission and nonhearsay under Federal Rule 801(d)(2)(b). (A) is incorrect. The publication is not hearsay. (B) is incorrect. The defendants identified the publication industry journal in answers to interrogatories as the document to which the plaintiff should refer for sales information. Since the interrogatories are admissions, the answer is the equivalent of an admission by the defendants that the book is what it is claimed to be and is therefore sufficiently authenticated under Federal Rule 901(b)(1). (D) is incorrect. Although it correctly states that the document is admissible, it specifies the wrong reason. Since the statement is an admission, it is not hearsay and need not come under any exception to the hearsay rule to be admissible.

Answer to Question 4

(B) The first man's acts constitute nonassertive conduct. Alternatively, this could be considered an admission by conduct. Therefore, the testimony is direct, relevant, nonhearsay evidence. Since it is not hearsay, (A) is incorrect. (C) is incorrect because evidence is not limited to testimony regarding spoken words; a witness may testify as to what he saw. (D) is incorrect because the first man did not intend his conduct to be a substitute for words.

Answer to Question 5

(D) The woman is guilty of arson and burglary. She is guilty of arson because she deliberately set a fire that, in addition to burning the mattress, also burned part of the dwelling house of another, namely the floor. She is also guilty of burglary because she broke and entered into the dwelling house of another during the nighttime to commit a felony. The fact that she was not successful in committing the crime she intended or that she in fact committed another felony is irrelevant to her guilt for burglary; it is the intent to commit a felony at the time of the breaking and entering which is critical. (A) is incorrect. This choice correctly states that the woman is guilty of burglary, but she is also guilty of arson; she deliberately set a fire that, in addition to burning the mattress, also burned part of the dwelling house of another, namely the floor. Therefore, (B) and (C) are incorrect.

Answer to Question 6

(B) If the jury finds for the manufacturer, it will be because the misuse by the consumer was not foreseeable. A manufacturer is liable for a defective product, even if the plaintiff misuses it, as long as that misuse is foreseeable. Foreseeability in this case is an issue for the trier of fact. If the jury finds that the misuse was not foreseeable, the manufacturer will prevail. (A) is incorrect because the consumer's action is based on strict liability. (C) and (D) appear to be true based on the facts, but they ignore the key issue that the jury must decide, which is whether the consumer's misuse was foreseeable.

Answer to Question 7

(B) Contracts for goods for $500 or more must be evidenced by a writing to be enforceable. There are three exceptions to this rule: specially manufactured goods unsuitable for resale in the seller's regular course of business, contracts admitted in court, and contracts partially accepted (enforceable to the extent of the acceptance). Here, the contract was for $50,000 and was oral. Thus, it will be enforceable only if one of the exceptions applies. The buyer's acceptance of the first generator constitutes part acceptance that will make the buyer liable to the extent of the acceptance: $25,000. Therefore, (B) is correct and (A) is incorrect. (C) is incorrect because partial acceptance renders the buyer liable only for the part accepted, not the entire contract. (D) is incorrect because, while the goods were made for the buyer, they were suitable for resale in the company's business, because they were built to standard industry specifications.

Answer to Question 8

(D) This question concerns the specially manufactured goods exception to the U.C.C.'s Statute of Frauds. In order for the specially manufactured goods exception to apply, there must be all three of the following elements: (i) the goods must be specially manufactured for the buyer, (ii) the seller must have started work on the goods or else entered into a commitment to purchase them from someone else, and (iii) the goods must not be sellable in the seller's ordinary course of business. Therefore, (A), (B), and (C) are incorrect.

Answer to Question 9

(C) When a subdivision is created with similar covenants in all deeds, there is a mutual right of endorsement (each lot owner can enforce against every other lot owner) if two things are satisfied: (i) a common scheme for development existed at the time that sales of parcels in the subdivision began; and (ii) there was notice of the existence of the covenant to the party sued. Here, there was a common scheme evidenced by the recorded plan, and the fact that the covenant was in the architect's chain of title gave her constructive notice of the restriction. Therefore, not only does the covenant apply to the architect's land, but the lawyer (or any other lot owner) can enforce it as a reciprocal negative servitude. (A) is incorrect. While it is true that the architect's deed had no restrictions, those restrictions are binding if they are in her chain of title so as to give her notice of them. The restriction was in the deed from the developer to the investor, so the fact that it was omitted in the deed from the investor to the architect is of no significance. (B) is incorrect. While a covenant is normally only enforceable by the party receiving the promise (here, the developer), this is a situation of mutual rights of enforcement within a geographically defined area, a special situation that gives every lot owner in the area the right of enforcement, even though they did not directly receive the benefit of the promise. (D) is incorrect. The fact that gives the lawyer the right of enforcement is not just the fact that his deed contains the covenant, but that the same covenant was in all of the deeds from the developer, including the one to the architect's predecessor in title.

Answer to Question 10

(A) Congress has the authority to legislate to protect federal parklands. The federal law safeguards wild animals that wander off federal parklands. The Necessary and Proper Clause allows Congress to choose any means to carry out its constitutional powers. Thus, it may regulate hunting to protect the federal interest in safeguarding the wild animals. (B) is wrong because it rests on an unjustified factual statement, that the "animals are moving in the stream of interstate commerce." There are no facts describing the movement patterns of the animals. (C) is wrong because there is no federal police power to protect wild animals. Generally, the federal government lacks the police power; the police power belongs to state and local governments. Although Congress possesses the police power in legislating for federal lands, this choice is not limited to those circumstances. It speaks broadly of a federal police power to protect wild animals, and none exists. (D) is wrong because the Supreme Court has discarded the distinction between rights and privileges as a constitutional principle. Moreover, it is a distinction used to determine when the government must provide procedural due process before deprivations of property or liberty. This question does not involve the Due Process Clause.

Answer to Question 11

(C) Except for very limited exceptions, the traditional rule is that a person has standing only to raise constitutional issues which affect her personally. She cannot claim that a third person's constitutional rights were violated. The husband is the injured party and must assert his own rights. (A) is incorrect. The issue in this question is not the substance of America's foreign policy, which would be a political question, but the husband's First Amendment right to speak out about it, which is not a political question. Therefore, the court is not barred from litigating this issue under the political question doctrine. (B) is incorrect. There are damages to be assessed if the husband was improperly dismissed. Under *Mt. Healthy Board of Education v. Doyle* (1977), a public employee cannot be fired without a hearing for exercising the right to free speech, even if there is no property right in the job. The case is not moot because the husband has lost his job permanently. The case would be moot only if the husband had been reinstated to his former job at his former pay. (D) is incorrect. The subject matter of the suit—the dismissal of an employee for exercise of his First Amendment rights—presents a federal question.

Answer to Question 12

(D) Larceny is a specific intent crime that requires that the defendant intend to permanently deprive the owner of her property. If the defendant can show that she really believed the property was her own, there is no intent to deprive the owner of his property, and therefore, the defendant would not be guilty of larceny. This is true whether or not the mistake was reasonable or whether the mistake was attributable to intoxication. In the instant case, the defendant did not realize that she had taken another's coat, and thus did not have the specific intent to commit larceny. (A) is incorrect. A mistake of fact that negates the state of mind requirement for ***specific*** intent crimes need not be reasonable. ***Any*** mistake of fact, reasonable or unreasonable, that negates specific intent would be a defense. For much the same reason, (B) is incorrect. For specific intent crimes, intoxication may be a defense when it prevents the defendant from formulating the requisite state of mind. (C) is incorrect because it implies that the asportation requirement for larceny must be substantial. It need not be; any movement of the property is sufficient to satisfy the requirement. Here, the defendant walked out of the bar with the fur coat, which is a sufficient asportation.

Exam Note: Reaching a place of temporary safety may be important in a question involving killings committed during the course of a felony because it may cut off liability; it has nothing to do with the asportation requirement for larceny.

Answer to Question 13

(B) The farmer's statement of August 10 that he would be unable to deliver because he had sold all of his crop to others constitutes a repudiation of the contract, which entitles the bakery to sue at once rather than wait for the September 1 performance date. [*See* U.C.C. §2-610] The bakery will prevail unless there have been some unanticipated circumstances that would excuse performance, but a rise in price due to poor crop performance is not sufficient to excuse performance under the doctrine of commercial impracticality. The farmer appears to have repudiated merely to make a greater profit. (A) is incorrect—because the farmer repudiated, the law does not require the bakery to wait until the due date for performance to arrive. It may sue at once. [*See* U.C.C. §2-610] (C) is incorrect because the facts do not indicate that the farmer has been harmed at all by the price increase, or that he cannot perform the contract with the bakery. As a matter of fact, he is simply attempting to gain a windfall by repudiating the contract with the bakery to sell at a higher price. (D) is incorrect because the facts do not indicate that the circumstances that led to the poor crop were unforeseen. Crop performance is risky and variable, and a poor crop can certainly result in a price increase by virtue of the operation of the law of supply and demand. The farmer must be assumed to have anticipated such possibilities and taken such risks.

Answer to Question 14

(A) When the partners bought the property, they took title as joint tenants with right of survivorship. If the joint tenancy continued until the first partner's death, then the property would pass immediately on death to the second partner. Because the second partner did not sign the mortgage, she would not be subject to it, regardless of whether she knew about it. The key to answering this question is to know whether execution of the mortgage by the first partner caused a severance of the joint tenancy. If it did cause a severance, then the first partner's one-half would not pass to the second under right of survivorship but instead would pass to the first's estate, and thus by will would go to the daughter. Whether a mortgage creates a severance or not depends on whether the state follows the lien theory or the title theory of mortgages. Lien theory means no severance; title theory means severance. Because this is a lien theory state ***(majority rule on the MBE)***, there was no severance; thus, the joint tenancy remained intact. On the first partner's death, the joint tenancy ended and the first partner's interest instantly passed to the second partner. The first partner's estate got nothing; hence, the daughter could get nothing. (B) would be the correct answer if the execution of the mortgage had created a severance of the joint tenancy. The severance would have changed the joint tenancy to a tenancy in common. The second partner would keep her one-half, free of the mortgage she did not sign, and the daughter would inherit the first partner's one-half, subject to the mortgage the first partner signed. Because we are told this is a lien theory state, there was no severance when the mortgage was executed so the joint tenancy remained intact until the first partner's death. (C) is incorrect. Not only is the joint tenancy unsevered so that it remains intact to give title to the entire property to the second partner, but also under no circumstances could the second partner be held liable for a mortgage she did not enter into. (D) is incorrect. When the first partner died, the property passed free and clear to the surviving joint tenant. The mortgage signed by the first partner did not sever the joint tenancy because this is a lien theory state. The mortgage can be held only against the property the first partner has; when the first partner died, the right of survivorship operated to end the first partner's interest and automatically vested it in the survivor.

Answer to Question 15

(D) The drug dealer's motion should be denied. The defense of double jeopardy does not apply if the second crime requires an element which is not an element of the first crime and vice versa. In this case, the crime of conspiracy has an element which is not in the possession crime, namely the agreement to commit the crime with another person, and it is lacking an element, namely the actual commission of the crime. (A) is incorrect because it is possible to commit two separate crimes by the same criminal conduct, such as conspiracy and the substantive offense. (B) is incorrect because it is the Double Jeopardy Clause of the Bill of Rights that affords protection against a subsequent prosecution, not the Due Process Clause. (C) is incorrect because even if a lesser included offense to the first crime were contained in a separate statute, the defense of double jeopardy would still apply.

Answer to Question 16

(C) This question involves the admissibility of settlement offers ("I'll settle for a refund of the purchase price plus $50,000") and statements made in the context of settlement negotiations ("Well, maybe it wasn't fraud"). Both settlement offers and statements made during settlement negotiations are ***inadmissible***. [Fed. R. Evid. 408] This is because public policy favors the voluntary settlement of disputes. If a settlement offer has been made in a case that ultimately goes to trial, admission of the offer into evidence would probably prejudice the party who made the offer. Thus, if such evidence were admissible, there would be a disincentive to parties making settlement offers. Similarly, if statements made during settlement negotiations could be admitted into evidence in cases that ultimately go to trial, then that would be a disincentive to enter into settlement negotiations or to discuss settlement in a freewheeling way. In either event, the public policy favoring settlements bars use of such statements. (A), which asserts the offered testimony is admissible to show plaintiff's recognition of the weakness of his case, is plainly incorrect. Because of the public policy valuing settlements, this type of testimony would not be admissible. (A) is also incorrect because an admission is ***not hearsay*** evidence. The definition of hearsay evidence specifically excludes admissions. [Fed. R. Evid. 802(d)(2)] Thus, it is inaccurate to characterize an admission as hearsay evidence admissible under the admission exception to the hearsay rule. (B) is incorrect because it is only half true. Offers to compromise are excluded, as (B) says, but (B) is incorrect in asserting that statements made in the course of settlement negotiations are admissible where relevant. (D) is incorrect. The offered testimony involves a statement made by the plaintiff to the defendant, not a statement made by a party to the party's attorney. Thus, the attorney-client privilege is not involved. Similarly, the attorney work product privilege is inapplicable. A settlement offer made by a party or an opposing party is not attorney work product. (D)'s assertion—that any statement made in the office of an attorney is privileged—is obviously incorrect.

Answer to Question 17

(C) The Supreme Court consistently has held that the government may restrict aspects of citizenship such as voting and, here, jury service to citizens. In fact, the Court has held that laws discriminating against aliens that are related to attributes of citizenship need only meet a rational basis test. (A) is incorrect because the discrimination is constitutional as long as it is rationally related to a legitimate government purpose. Restricting jury service to citizens would be regarded as such a purpose. (B) is wrong because, although alienage is generally a suspect classification, only a rational basis test is used for discrimination related to aspects of citizenship. (D) is incorrect because she could claim an injury based on the fact that she was discriminated against. Those who claim a violation of equal protection of the law in that they have been discriminated against have standing to sue.

Answer to Question 18

(B) Because the modification involves the sale of goods for a price of at least $500, the Statute of Frauds of the U.C.C. is applicable, and thus the modification is unenforceable. (A) is wrong because the parol evidence rule is inapplicable to a ***subsequent*** agreement. The parol evidence rule only prohibits the introduction of prior oral or written evidence or contemporaneous written evidence. (C) is wrong because the U.C.C. does not require that a contract modification be supported by consideration. (D) is wrong because it is too broad a statement; a written contract can be orally modified if the Statute of Frauds does not apply or if the contract provides that an oral modification is permissible.

Answer to Question 19

(C) (A) is not helpful to the neighbor because the neighbor's negligence allowed the bull to escape, so the stockbreeder will not be strictly liable for the damages from his trespassing livestock. (B) is neutral, or possibly helpful to the stockbreeder. The neighbor's failure to realize that the fence was down suggests that the neighbor was negligent, which would help the stockbreeder. (C) clearly helps the neighbor, because it supports an argument that the stockbreeder was negligent in failing to repair the fence or restrain the bull. (D) is an incorrect statement of the law, so it does not help the neighbor. If the neighbor raised this argument, the stockbreeder could easily rebut it, since a bull is considered a domestic animal. Thus, (C) is the argument that is most helpful to the neighbor.

Answer to Question 20

(C) The witness's testimony would clearly qualify as hearsay. Since there is no applicable exception to the hearsay rule, his testimony is inadmissible. (A) is incorrect because statements by one conspirator are not admissible on behalf of another conspirator. (B) is incorrect because the woman has already been acquitted of the crime in question. (D) is an incorrect statement of law.

Answer to Question 21

(B) An assault is committed when the victim is put in reasonable apprehension of an offensive touching. If the farmer believed that the melon grower might shoot him, and the belief was objectively reasonable, then the melon grower's action amounts to assault. The conditional threat, "stop or I'll shoot," is sufficient for an assault. Since the melon grower was pointing a rifle at the farmer at the time the threat was made, the requirement of immediacy was fulfilled. The melon executory interest in the community center, it struck all the language following the comma: "but if . . ."; that left "to my sister and her heirs so long as it is used for residential purposes." The fee simple determinable is not a fee simple absolute; it is accompanied by the possibility of reverter in the grantor, and that person (or his successor) must join in the conveyance for the grantee to get a fee simple absolute. (B) is incorrect. The daughter owns nothing; the landowner devised his real property interests to the friend, so his heir takes none of it. The sister has a fee simple determinable, not a fee simple absolute. (C) is incorrect. The Rule Against Perpetuities voided the attempted executory interest in the local community center; it has nothing.

Answer to Question 34

(D) To prevail with the defense of entrapment, the defendant must establish that: (i) the idea for the crime originated with the police, and (ii) the defendant was not predisposed to commit the crime prior to solicitation by the government. On the facts, the store owner will be unable to establish the second element. (A) is wrong. The store owner was predisposed to committing the crime. (B) makes no sense. The fact that the informant was not a member of the department would not be relevant as to the issue of entrapment. (C) is wrong. Even if the police did perform an act necessary for the completion of the crime, there will be no "entrapment" if the defendant was predisposed.

Answer to Question 35

(B) A search is valid if the police reasonably believe that they obtained valid consent for the search. Generally, a homeowner has authority to consent to a search of her own home, as long as she has apparent access to the place searched. Here, nothing indicates that the teen's bedroom door was locked. Thus, the mother had apparent authority to search the teen's room. However, it appears unreasonable for the police to believe that the mother had authority to consent to a search of the suitcase because it was locked, and the police had to break the lock to open it (indicating that the mother did not have a key for the lock and so likely did not have access to the contents of the suitcase). The parent-child relationship does nothing to change this analysis. A parent of an adult teenager does not have automatic authority to search the adult teen's locked things (the rule probably is different for young children). (A) is incorrect. To be effective, a consent to search must be voluntary and given under no threat or compulsion. However, the police are under no obligation to inform the defendant or other person of the right to refuse entry. Therefore, this search is not invalid because the mother was not informed of her right to refuse entry. The issue is whether her consent was sufficient to allow the police to search the son's suitcase. (C) is incorrect because, as explained above, a homeowner does not necessarily have authority to consent to a search of everything in her home. Where it is apparent that she does not have access (*e.g.*, when something is locked and she does not have a key), the police may not reasonably believe she may consent to the search of the locked area. (D) is incorrect. The doctrine of in loco parentis is a tort doctrine under which the state is charged with a parent's responsibilities over a child in its care. The doctrine does not apply here.

Answer to Question 36

(B) Robbery is larceny from a person by violence or intimidation. Larceny requires a specific intent to steal or personally deprive the personal property of value from another's superior possessory interest. Because the accountant thought that the property belonged to him, his mistake of fact is a valid defense to the crimes of larceny and robbery. This is because the mistake negates the existence of a mental state (specific intent to steal) essential to the charged crime. (A) is incorrect. Robbery is larceny by either violence or intimidation. Knocking the passenger to the floor constitutes the necessary violence, whether or not the accountant used intimidation. Even though voluntary intoxication may be a defense to a specific intent crime (in those circumstances where the intoxication negates the specific intent), the better answer is (B), because the accountant's mistake of fact is a defense to the specific intent crime charged since he did not have the specific intent to steal. The question does not establish that the mistake of fact was a product of the intoxication. (C) is incorrect. As discussed above, although voluntary intoxication can be a defense to a specific intent crime, (B) is the better answer. (D) is incorrect. The accountant's mistake of fact negates the specific intent to steal required to convict him of robbery.

Answer to Question 37

(B) The common law rule is that a promise to modify a contract must be supported by consideration. Here, the gardener agreed to work an extra year in return for the landowner's promise to pay extra money. In the absence of facts indicating duress or unconscionability (facts not present here), courts will not inquire into the adequacy of the consideration. There is no indication that the landowner had no "meaningful choice" but to accept the price increase, and because the landowner received a year's extension in exchange, there was adequate consideration to support a modification. (A) is incorrect because, as discussed above, the modification is valid and the price increase can take effect as agreed. (C) is incorrect for two reasons: First, economic duress generally is not a good defense to contract unless caused by the party seeking to enforce the contract. Second, as mentioned above, there are no facts indicating that the landowner had no "meaningful choice" but to accept the proposed modification; nothing indicates that the landowner could not have found another gardener or could not have sued the gardener for breach if she had not performed the original contract in the absence of modification. (D) is incorrect because the gardener did not merely promise to perform a preexisting duty in exchange for the promise to pay $200 a month more. She promised a year's extension of services, and this is additional and valuable consideration.

Answer to Question 38

(C) The courts have regarded as a nonjusticiable political question the issue of proper exercise of the President's power over the foreign policy of the United States. Thus, (D) is incorrect. (A) is incorrect because the naturalized citizen, threatened by an immediate and direct injury, has standing to challenge the President's action. (B) is wrong because no diversity of citizenship is necessary in cases involving a federal question.

Answer to Question 39

(A) Congress has plenary power over interstate commerce, and it may enact laws that regulate commerce. (B) is a misstatement of the law, because Congress is not required to find that there exists some burden on interstate commerce before it enacts laws regulating commerce. (C) is wrong because it is Congress that is empowered to regulate commerce between the states. Current state laws have no effect on whether Congress can, or cannot, regulate. (D) is incorrect because the federal statute did not ***reverse*** the decision of the Supreme Court. It merely enacted a requirement as a matter of ***federal*** law, while the Supreme Court had ruled that a ***state*** law on the subject was invalid.

Answer to Question 40

(A) A fetus who is born alive has a cause of action against those who negligently cause prenatal injuries. The mother's doctor owes a duty to both mother and child not to act in a negligent manner. If a family practitioner practicing according to the standard of care required in this jurisdiction would not have treated an obviously pregnant woman with the drug, then the doctor's treatment of the pregnant woman was negligent. If the son can prove that "most doctors" would not have used this drug to treat a pregnant woman, then he has probably shown that the doctor has failed to comply with the required standard of care. Also, the statute of limitations has not run. The general rule with respect to injuries to a minor is that the statute commences running when the child reaches majority. Even where the rule with respect to minors is not in effect, the discovery rule would hold that the cause of action only accrues at the time that the patient discovers the wrong. Therefore, (C) and (D) are incorrect. (B) is incorrect. The doctor can only prevail if he can prove that treating the pregnant woman with the drug was in accord with prevailing medical procedure as practiced by a physician of ordinary care and skill. The fact that the doctor was not personally aware that the treatment he prescribed would cause injury will not allow him to avoid liability if his conduct was not in accord with the standard of care required of doctors in this jurisdiction. If he needed to read certain journals to acquire the knowledge and skill of a competent physician, then failure to do so is failure to exercise reasonable care.

Answer to Question 41

(A) First Amendment rights are made enforceable against a state through the Fourteenth Amendment. However, the amendments do not prevent private individuals or organizations from encroaching upon individual civil liberties. Since there is nothing in the facts to indicate significant state involvement (state action) with the organization, the amendments do not apply to their actions in expelling one of their members. (B) is incorrect because such membership may be protected by the First and Fourteenth Amendments. (C) and (D) would have no bearing on the alleged violation of the member's rights.

Answer to Question 42

(D) The written agreement is enforceable in its entirety. The initial contract had two components: the sale of the smaller company's refining facilities to the oil producer, and the oil producer's option to purchase the smaller company's output. Normally, the option provision would be illusory, because the oil producer's promise to purchase, ***at its option***, 100% of the smaller company's output is not a promise to do anything and therefore is not consideration. However, there is other consideration here—the oil producer's purchase of the smaller company's refining facilities. The contract must be considered as a whole, and here the oil producer promised to purchase the smaller company's refining facilities. Moreover, the specification of the quantity of 100% of output is sufficiently certain and can be enforced because the quantity of output can be estimated from prior output. The specification of the price of "current market prices" is also sufficient. Thus, the written agreement is enforceable in its entirety, and (A), (B), and (C) are incorrect.

Answer to Question 43

(C) The rights of the newlyweds, as intended beneficiaries, would have vested if they had learned of the contract made for their benefit and either accepted it at the request of the contracting parties or changed their position in reliance on it. In this case, they did neither before the donors rescinded the contract, and therefore they have no right to enforce it. (A) is incorrect. This choice correctly states that the newlyweds are intended third-party beneficiaries of the contract made by their fathers. However, their rights do not vest as of the formation of the contract. Rather, they must at least assent to the contract at the request of the contracting parties or must change their position in reliance on the contract. Thus, rescission of the contract by the stockbroker and the developer was sufficient to terminate the rights of the newlyweds. (B) is incorrect. However, their rights do not vest merely because they have received notice of the contract. They must either accept the contract at the request of the contracting parties or must substantially rely on the contract to their detriment before they would be able to prevent the original contracting parties from rescinding the contract. (D) is incorrect. Since the parties to the contract contemplated that the newlyweds would receive a benefit under the terms of the agreement, the newlyweds were intended, and not incidental, beneficiaries.

Answer to Question 44

(D) This question involves the best evidence rule, which requires the production of the original document ***when attempting to prove the contents of the document.*** [Fed. R. Evid. 1002] The director of the tool producer's order department seeks to testify that the price of the hardware store's order was $5,500. It appears that this testimony is based solely on the director having seen the standard tool producer's form on which the hardware store placed their order. Thus, the testimony is about the contents of a document—the tool producer form that the store owner completed to order hammers. At first glance, therefore, it would appear that (B) is the correct answer, that the director's testimony would be inadmissible because of the best evidence rule. However, that rule does not require production of the original ***if the original has been lost or destroyed in good faith.*** [Fed. R. Evid. 104(1)] It appears that the order form was destroyed in good faith in a fire at the tool producer's headquarters. Thus, (B) is incorrect. (C) is also incorrect. If the original of a document cannot be produced to prove its contents, ***any form of secondary evidence*** can be substituted for the original. There is no requirement, for example, that a copy of the original be produced. Testimony as to the contents of the document is equally permissible. From the standpoint of the best evidence rule, then, (D) is the correct answer. The proposed testimony of the director of the tool producer's order department is admissible. (A) is incorrect because it confuses the question of ***admissibility*** of evidence with that of the ***weight*** that a fact finder should give to the evidence. That the proposed testimony is self-serving may render it ***unpersuasive,*** but not ***inadmissible.*** Also, if the self-serving nature of testimony rendered it inadmissible, then virtually any time a party testified in support of his proposition, the testimony would have to be excluded. The law of evidence has for centuries rejected such a broad rule requiring disqualification of witnesses. In addition, (A) states that the proposed testimony of the director of the tool producer's order department is untrustworthy. There is no factual basis in the question for reaching that conclusion.

Answer to Question 45

(C) This question also involves, in part, the best evidence rule. Can the journalist testify as to the defamatory statement he overheard or is he prohibited from testifying because he also possesses notes recording the defamatory statement? Are the notes the "best evidence" that must be offered to prove the defamatory statement? The best evidence rule does ***not*** require a party to use the ***most persuasive*** evidence to prove a point. It merely requires the production of the original document ***when attempting to prove the contents of the document.*** [Fed. R. Evid.1002] If a party is attempting to prove a fact (here, the defamatory statement), as opposed to the contents of a document, any competent evidence can be used. For example, if a party is attempting to prove the fact that a valid marriage has taken place, that could be done either by presenting testimony of an eyewitness to the wedding ceremony or by presenting the marriage certificate itself; production of the marriage certificate would be only one of several permissible ways to prove the point. Since the candidate's opponent is attempting to prove that a defamatory statement was made, it is perfectly permissible to offer the testimony of a witness who heard the statement. Thus, (C) is correct; the journalist's testimony is admissible as relevant evidence based on firsthand knowledge.

(A) is wrong because, as explained above, the testimony is not made inadmissible by the best evidence rule. (B) is wrong because it states that the testimony is inadmissible as hearsay not covered by an exception. It is true that the journalist would be testifying about a declarant's out-of-court statement, but the ***purpose*** of the testimony is not to prove the truth of the matter asserted in the statement (that the candidate's opponent is a child molester and a thief). The purpose of the testimony is simply to prove that the statement was made, to prove that defamation occurred. Since the purpose of testifying about the campaign manager's statement is not to establish the truth, the testimony would not be classified as hearsay evidence. (D) is wrong for many reasons: First, the "journalist's privilege" is not recognized in the Federal Rules or in many evidentiary systems governing state courts. Second, even if a journalist's privilege were recognized, it clearly does not apply to the facts of this case. The journalist's privilege covers confidential communications between reporter and news source; it generally does not cover the reporting of a statement made to someone else (here, campaign manager's statement to the potential contributor). Finally, (D) is a logically incomplete answer. If the journalist's ***notes*** were protected by the journalist's privilege, that would not explain why the journalist's ***testimony*** would be admissible; it would only explain why the notes need not be produced. The correct answer, (C), explains why the journalist's testimony is admissible.

Answer to Question 46

(D) The imperfect self-defense doctrine applies to these facts. In states that apply the doctrine, murder is reduced to voluntary manslaughter when the defendant unreasonably, but honestly, believed in the necessity of responding with deadly force. In the instant case, the performer unreasonably, but apparently honestly, believed that the pedestrian would kill him. Thus, the performer would be guilty of voluntary manslaughter in such a jurisdiction. (A) is wrong. In order to have murder reduced to voluntary manslaughter based on a "heat of passion" theory, it must be shown that: (i) the provocation must have been one that would arouse sudden and intense passion in the mind of an ordinary person such as to cause him to lose self-control; (ii) the defendant was in fact provoked; (iii) there must not have been sufficient time to cool off; and (iv) the defendant did not in fact cool off. Adequate provocation generally consists of being subjected to a serious battery or threat of deadly force; or of discovering one's spouse in bed with another person. In the instant case, not only is it unlikely that a slap on the face would be considered a serious battery such that would provoke one to murder, the facts do not indicate that the performer acted in a fit of rage. (B) is wrong because there is no evidence of any diminution of the defendant's ability to reason. (C) is wrong. Although some states would call a killing committed during a misdemeanor "manslaughter," in the instant case there are no facts to indicate that the performer was in the process of committing a misdemeanor when he killed the pedestrian.

Answer to Question 47

(B) When the cousin bought both parcels from the owner and the buyer, the dominant (buyer) and servient (owner) estates came together in the same owner and the easement was terminated by merger. Once terminated by merger, the easement does not revive when the ownership is later split. (A) is incorrect. An easement may be terminated by abandonment, but mere nonuse is not enough. The holder of the dominant estate must perform some physical act on the property that would show the intent to abandon. The facts do not show that any holder of the western parcel did anything to indicate this intent. (C) is incorrect. The easement granted in the deed from the owner to the buyer was a valid express easement. No implied easement arose because there was no necessity for one. The later construction of the public road can have no effect if there had been no valid implied easement in the first place. (D) is incorrect. The fact that the easement was not included in the subsequent deeds is irrelevant because the easement was in the owner-buyer deed, which was recorded properly in the chain of title. That puts all subsequent purchasers on notice of the easement, and it need not be put in subsequent deeds to be given effect.

Exam Tip: Multiple transfers can be confusing on the exam. A technique to aid analysis is to make a quick chart in the margin of the exam booklet. This would have clearly shown the merger and unity of ownership:

West	***East***
Owner	**Owner**
Buyer	**Owner**
Cousin	**Cousin**
Lawyer	**Doctor**
Dev. Co.	**Doctor**

Answer to Question 48

(D) The owner has made an adverse use of the neighbor's land since the sewer line was first constructed across it. The fact that the owner tore down the house on his property does not stop the prescriptive period from running, because the mere existence of the sewer line was an adverse use and there was no intent to abandon it. Therefore, the owner's use ripened into a prescriptive easement 20 years after that use first began. Moreover, the use of the line to service the apartment building is within the scope of the easement by prescription because the same pipe in the same location will be used for the apartment building, and the amount of sewage through the pipe will not affect the neighbor's property. (A) is incorrect. By the time the owner constructed the apartment building, he had maintained the sewer line across the neighbor's property for the statutory period and therefore had acquired an easement by prescription to continue to use that line. Once the owner obtained an easement by prescription over the neighbor's property, that property right persists despite any actions by the municipal authorities with regard to the neighbor's property, or any actions by the owner with regard to the authorities. (B) is incorrect. This is not a case where the owner is using the easement to benefit a different parcel of land, only a new building on the land benefited by the easement. (C) is incorrect. The owner never had a license. A license is a permissive use of property. The owner placed the sewer line across the neighbor's property without her permission. Moreover, the use never ripened into an implied easement. Such an easement can only occur when there is a division of a large parcel of property into smaller parcels and there is a reasonable necessity for the owner of one of the parcels to continue to use rights over another part of the larger parcel. There is no such division of property here. Instead, the adverse use by the owner ripened into an easement by prescription.

Answer to Question 49

(B) State laws that discriminate against out-of-state residents in terms of the right to earn a living trigger the Privileges and Immunities Clause of Article IV and are almost always unconstitutional. (A) is incorrect. A Bill of Attainder requires, inter alia, a legislative act which is intended to "punish" an identifiable group. Punishment is an unlikely motive of the statute. (C) is incorrect. Out-of-state residents are not considered a protected class under the Fourteenth Amendment Equal Protection Clause. This would more than likely be a Fourteenth Amendment Due Process Clause violation because the government may not take a recognized "liberty" or "property" interest of a person without some procedural due process. (D) is incorrect. Only retroactive criminal laws can violate the ex post facto clause.

Answer to Question 50

(C) No single facet of the law of evidence provides a ready answer to this question. Thus, it is useful to analyze each choice and arrive at the correct answer by a process of elimination. (A) is incorrect because the videotape showing the defendant offering a television set to one of the police officers is not hearsay evidence. Even if the defendant's conduct on the videotape is considered assertive conduct and thus a "statement" within the meaning of the hearsay rule (much like nodding one's head to indicate "yes" is a statement), it still would not be a ***hearsay*** statement. Under the Federal Rules an admission of a party is not a hearsay statement. [Fed. R. Evid. 801(d)(2)] Since the defendant is a party to this criminal prosecution, his conduct, if considered a statement, would constitute an admission. It is not clear, however, that the defendant's conduct on the videotape is assertive conduct. If it is considered nonassertive conduct—conduct that is not intended to communicate a thought—it would not be a statement within the meaning of the hearsay rule. [Fed. R. Evid. 801(a)] Thus, this is an alternative reason, albeit a less clear one, why (A) is incorrect. (B) is incorrect because the privilege against self-incrimination applies to compulsory self-incrimination. The defendant was not forced to incriminate himself. He voluntarily took an action (offering to sell a television set to one of the police officers) that helps establish that he is guilty of receiving stolen property. Such an act is not covered by the self-incrimination privilege. (D) is also incorrect because specific instances of misconduct pertaining to an event (here, the receipt of stolen property) are frequently used to prove criminality. If (D) said that specific instances of past misconduct pertaining to a defendant's character (*i.e.*, propensity evidence) were inadmissible, that would be true as an abstract statement of law, but (D) does not say that, nor do the facts in the question remotely relate to propensity evidence. Thus, (A), (B), and (D) are clearly incorrect. (C), on the other hand, is a plausible answer. If the videotape is held to be inadmissible, one reason could be that a proper foundation had not been established for its introduction into evidence. A videotape, like other forms of tangible evidence, must be ***authenticated*** before it can be admitted. The failure to properly authenticate the videotape is one reason why it could have been held inadmissible.

Answer to Question 51

(C) Since cars do not ordinarily roll downhill in the absence of negligence, and since there was evidence that the driver was in control of her car at the time it was parked, the pedestrian has made out a prima facie case of negligence under the doctrine of res ipsa loquitur and has avoided a directed verdict. In this case the driver has introduced direct evidence that she was not negligent in the way that she parked her car and introduced evidence that the movement of the car could have been caused by the deliberate act of third parties. Therefore the jury was not required to find negligence on the defendant's part. (A) is incorrect. It is not the judge's right when deciding a motion for a judgment notwithstanding the verdict to determine if the plaintiff proved that the defendant was more likely than not to have been negligent. The issue of negligence is a question of fact for the jury, and it can be disturbed by the trial judge by the granting of a judgment notwithstanding the verdict only when no reasonable jury could find that there was no negligence. The pedestrian has not met this standard. (B) is incorrect. The evidence of the driver that she turned her wheels to the curb and that she applied her emergency brake, which was in good working order, supports the verdict that she was not negligent. (D) is incorrect. The relative positions of the parties to explain the accident does not protect the driver from a directed verdict, if on the evidence presented no reasonable juror could find that the driver was not negligent.

Answer to Question 52

(A) Under the husband's will, the sister-in-law's interest will terminate upon the wife's death. Regardless of whether the court determines it to be a life estate per autre vie (*i.e.*, a life estate with another's life as the measuring life) or a fee simple determinable (the wife's death being the terminating event), the sister-in-law's interest will end when the wife dies and the property will go automatically to the son. Because the sister-in-law's estate will end on the wife's death, she cannot affect any rights of any holder of a future interest that will become possessory on that event. Any lease purporting to continue after the wife's death is simply invalid as of that event. When the wife dies, the son has a fee simple and the tenant has nothing. Thus (A) is correct. (B) is incorrect. The son received a fee simple on the wife's death, and he is not bound by any actions of the holder of the life estate purporting to lease the property for any period that would extend beyond the terminating event. (C) is incorrect because the son's right to possession begins on the instant of the wife's death. The life tenant can do nothing to extend that date. (D) is incorrect. The tenant's right to possession ends on the wife's death, regardless of what the tenant's lease from the sister-in-law may say. She could give no more than she had, and her interest ended on the wife's death.

Answer to Question 53

(A) The motorcyclist intended to assault the classmate, since he drove at the classmate with the intent to scare him. Under the doctrine of transferred intent, the intent to assault is sufficient to establish a battery if a touching results. A battery requires: (i) a harmful or offensive touching to the plaintiff's person; (ii) intent; and (iii) causation. The causation element is satisfied here because the motorcyclist set in motion the force which brought about the assault and subsequent battery. (C) is incorrect because the motorcyclist's intent to commit an assault is sufficient. (B) is incorrect because the motorcyclist's potential negligence in hitting the accelerator would not be sufficient to cut off liability for his battery. (D) is incorrect because the fact that the tire may have been defective would not qualify as an intervening force sufficient to cut off the motorcyclist's liability. The classmate may have a separate claim against the motorcycle manufacturer on a products liability theory, but the motorcyclist remains liable for the battery.

Answer to Question 54

(A) The speaker's conviction will be reversed. A park is a public forum. The government can limit rights of speech in such a forum only when there is a serious and imminent threat to the public order. It can restrict the speech of a speaker because of an unruly audience only in the rare case when the police are absolutely unable to control the crowd. [*See* Feiner v. New York (1951)] In this question, it does not appear that the conditions under which the police can prevent a speaker from continuing because of an unruly crowd have been met. There were a dozen police officers, who should have been able to restrain or subdue the two spectators who appeared to be intent on committing violence. Hence, (C) is incorrect. (B) is incorrect. No one in the audience has raised any constitutional argument. The speaker probably cannot raise the audience members' First Amendment rights in this situation. Even if this argument were raised, the state has a right to limit the rights of the audience to assemble when there is imminent danger of violence. (D) is incorrect. The state may not limit access to a public forum on the sole basis that there are other times and places where the right of free speech can be exercised. The state must show a more substantial reason.

Answer to Question 55

(B) A contract for the sale of goods may be modified without consideration to support the modification if the modification was sought in good faith. No writing is required under the Statute of Frauds unless the contract, as modified, is within the Statute. Here, the parties formed a contract for the sale of goods (a car) when the mechanic agreed to buy the car for $400. (B) is correct because the contract as modified is under $500, so it is enforceable, even though it is not evidenced by a writing. (A) is incorrect because the fact that the original contract was not in writing is irrelevant. The original contract was for the sale of goods under $500 in value, and the Statute of Frauds does not apply. Thus, the mechanic could have enforced the original oral contract if he had not agreed to the modification. (C) is incorrect because under U.C.C. section 2-209, no consideration is needed for the modification of a contract for the sale of goods. (D) is incorrect because all Article 2 contracts can be modified, if done in good faith.

Answer to Question 56

(A) The contract has a set time limit in which construction "must" be completed, and thus the buyer would have a good case for a right to cancel when the contractor did not make that time limit. (B) is incorrect because, even if the strike was totally unforeseeable, the buyer could still cancel if time was of the essence (the strike would release the parties from their contract). (C) and (D) are wrong, because time was of the essence, making the buyer's good faith and the contractor's due diligence irrelevant.

Answer to Question 57

(B) Conviction for common law murder requires malice. At common law, malice is: (i) the intent to kill (express malice); (ii) intent to inflict great bodily injury; (iii) reckless indifference to an unjustifiably high risk to human life ("depraved heart"); or (iv) intent to commit a felony ("felony murder"). The hunter did not intend to kill a child when he fired at the target, so he did not meet the specific intent test. Thus, (A) is incorrect. Malice is also shown when a person acts with a wanton and reckless disregard for human life. Based on these facts, the hunter clearly acted with malice by firing a high-powered gun in front of an occupied playground; thus, (B) is the correct answer. (C) is incorrect, given that specific intent is not the only way to show malice. (D) is incorrect because the hunter's actions go far beyond simple negligence.

Answer to Question 58

(C) The man probably will not prevail because his injuries were self-inflicted, and the ex-girlfriend is not liable for intentional infliction of emotional distress. The elements of a prima facie case for intentional infliction of emotional distress are: (i) an act by the defendant amounting to extreme or outrageous conduct; (ii) intent to cause severe emotional distress; (iii) causation; and (iv) damages. (The victim must suffer severe emotional distress.) Generally, offensive, insulting language does not meet the test of outrageous conduct. There are exceptions where there is a special relationship between the parties (common carriers and innkeepers to their customers) or where the defendant knows that the victim is more sensitive than the average person. Although the man is extremely depressed, the facts do not indicate that his ex-girlfriend was aware of this. Also, there is no additional evidence that the man was extremely sensitive or that the ex-girlfriend knew about this sensitivity. Hence, the ex-girlfriend's comments do not meet the test for extreme and outrageous conduct and (A) is therefore incorrect. (B) is incorrect because even if she had the intent to cause distress, the act must be extreme and outrageous, and harsh words to an ex-boyfriend do not rise to that level. (D) is wrong because the illegality of the man's conduct would not preclude him from recovering from the ex-girlfriend if the elements of the tort were satisfied.

Answer to Question 59

(C) The best defense is that the picture was taken in a public place as part of a newsworthy story.

There are four different torts which qualify as invasions of privacy: (i) commercial appropriation of plaintiff's picture or name; (ii) intrusion on plaintiff's seclusion or private affairs; (iii) publication by defendant of facts placing plaintiff in a false light; and (iv) public disclosure of private facts about the plaintiff. (A) would be a defense to intrusion on plaintiff's private affairs. (B) is a defense to the false light tort. (D) is a defense to the commercial appropriation tort. But (C) is the best answer because it is a defense to most of the privacy torts. Because the picture was taken in a public place, the newspaper has a defense to the tort of intrusion into plaintiff's private affairs. Because the picture "accompanied a newsworthy story," the newspaper has a defense to the false light tort. Where the published matter is in the public interest (such as a newsworthy story about the growing popularity of nude beaches), plaintiff cannot recover without proof of malice. Because there is no evidence of malice, the newspaper has a defense to the false light tort. A defense to the tort of public disclosure of private facts is that, if the matter is one of legitimate public interest, the publication is privileged. Thus the newspaper's best defense, (C), is a defense to three of the four privacy torts. Although it is not a defense to commercial appropriation, there is no evidence to support a claim for commercial appropriation.

Answer to Question 60

(D) The state cannot retry the defendant for murder because he has been convicted of the lesser included offense of manslaughter. The constitutional ban on double jeopardy prohibits a second trial after the defendant has been convicted of the "same offense." For double jeopardy purposes, "same offense" covers lesser included offenses. Thus, a person cannot be convicted of the lesser included offense and later tried for the greater offense. As ***manslaughter*** is a lesser included offense of ***murder,*** the conviction of the defendant for manslaughter would bar a subsequent trial for murder. (A) is wrong because, in a jury trial, double jeopardy attaches when the jury is sworn. (C) is also wrong; it states the correct rule for a bench trial, but in this question a jury trial took place. (B) is wrong because there is no "separation of powers clause" of the Constitution. In addition, the concept of separation of powers has never applied to judicial pressure on a prosecutor to plea bargain.

Answer to Question 61

(B) When the proctologist bought the property from the homeowner, he was a bona fide purchaser who gave value and who had no notice of the earlier sale to the buyer. Not only did the proctologist not have actual notice of the earlier sale, he did not have constructive notice either because the buyer did not record before the proctologist bought. In a jurisdiction with a notice recording statute, a subsequent purchaser who gives value and takes without notice wins over the earlier grantee. If the facts had shown a jurisdiction with a race-notice recording act, the proctologist would have been in trouble. With race-notice, the proctologist would not only have to take without notice, he would have to be the first to record. Because the facts do not show that the proctologist recorded at all, he would lose. But because this is a notice act jurisdiction, the fact that the buyer finally recorded before the proctologist is irrelevant. (A) is incorrect. Simply because a tenant pays rent to someone who the tenant thinks owns the property does not create an estoppel requiring the tenant to continue paying rent to that person. The proctologist will win, but not for this reason. (C) is incorrect because it is not necessary for a grantee to record a deed to give the grantee legal title to the property. Recordation is necessary only to protect against subsequent purchasers from the same grantor. Unrecorded deeds are perfectly valid as long as the recording act does not dictate otherwise. (D) is incorrect The proctologist did in fact have good title to the property because, as a bona fide purchaser, he was protected by the notice recording act.

Answer to Question 62

(B) This question involves the interrelationship between the exercise of testimonial privilege (the privilege against self-incrimination) and the right to cross-examine a witness claiming such a privilege. Should the witness's direct testimony be stricken because he refused to answer a question on cross-examination? The answer is yes, at least in the context of this case. Here, the question on cross-examination ("Isn't it true that on the day of the accident you were 300 miles away from the scene attempting to extract protection money from the owner of a seaside restaurant?") is centrally relevant to the witness's direct testimony (pertaining to his supposed observation of the accident). Every party has a right to adequate cross-examination of a witness who has testified for an opposing party. If adequate cross-examination cannot be obtained, the remedy is to strike the direct testimony of the witness. For this reason, (B) is correct, and (D) is an incorrect answer. (C) is incorrect, although it correctly states that the witness has a right to refuse to answer. The allegation of criminal activity contained in the question he declined to answer is very clear. There is thus no doubt that it is proper for the witness to "take the Fifth Amendment" in response to the question. However, (C) is incorrect in its conclusion, that the request to strike the witness's direct testimony should be denied. It does not logically follow that, because a witness has a right to refrain from answering a question, he has a corresponding right to have his direct testimony admitted into evidence. No such "right" exists, particularly where the invocation of a testimonial privilege has the effect of depriving a party of the right to adequately cross-examine the witness claiming the privilege. (A) is incorrect because the privilege against self-incrimination is applicable ***in any setting*** (civil case, legislative hearing, custodial interrogation of a suspect, etc.). As long as the information requested of a person could then be used against him in a subsequent criminal proceeding, that person has a right to invoke the privilege against self-incrimination.

Answer to Question 63

(C) A valid arrest justifies a search incident to the arrest. Under this theory, the entire passenger area of a car can be searched. It does not matter what the arrest is for. It does not matter whether the police have reason to believe the arrestee is dangerous or that the evidence will be destroyed. A valid arrest justifies a search of the area within the control of the arrestee as a search incident to the arrest. (A) is wrong because the search of the passenger area was incident to an arrest and so probable cause is not required. (A) would be correct if a search was made of an area of the car, such as the trunk, that was beyond the immediate control of the driver. (B) is wrong because the entire passenger area is within the control of the arrestee. (D) is wrong because it is too broad a statement; a reasonable fear is not required for a search incident to a valid arrest.

Answer to Question 64

(B) Because of a lessened expectation of privacy in a car (as compared to a home) and because of the inherent mobility of a car which can prevent the police from easily obtaining a search warrant and searching it, the police are permitted to make a complete search of an automobile, if there is probable cause to believe that the car contains the fruits, evidence, or instrumentalities of a crime. [Carroll v. United States (1925)] When the police have probable cause to search an entire vehicle, they may conduct a warrantless search of every part of the vehicle and its contents. [United States v. Ross (1982)] While it is doubtful that the marijuana joints provided sufficient probable cause to search the entire vehicle, this is the best reason to deny the motion, because all of the other choices are clearly incorrect. (A) is incorrect because a lawful search of a vehicle incident to an arrest includes a search of the defendant and only the area of the vehicle within the defendant's control. [New York v. Belton (1981)] In this case, as the trunk is outside the defendant's area of control, the search went beyond the scope of a proper search incident to an arrest. Therefore, this was an invalid search incident to arrest and the driver's motion would be granted on this basis. (C) is incorrect. Technically, there is no such thing as a custody search. The correct term is an inventory search. An inventory search occurs when the officers properly impound a car and search it while it is in their control to make sure that the assets of the owner of the car are fully accounted for. [South Dakota v. Opperman (1976)] This choice is incorrect because it does not articulate a legal basis to conduct the search as the car was not impounded. (D) is incorrect. In this case, the police did not take custody of the car, so this is not the best reason to deny the motion.

Answer to Question 65

(B) The federal power to tax and spend includes the power to attach conditions to the expenditures, and to the extent the university research program conflicts with the federal legislation, the state action is superseded by the federal statute. Here, since the federal program expressly limited use of the distributed funds to development of synthetic materials to replace petroleum, the University projects involving solar, geothermal, biomass and fusion energy would be in conflict with the statutory prescription. "Substantial" conformity is not enough, so (C) is incorrect. (D) is an incorrect statement of the law. The supremacy doctrine permits Congress to effectively control the actions of a state in spending money provided by the federal government. (A) is incorrect. There is nothing unconstitutional about the means by which the funds are disbursed.

Answer to Question 66

(C) The chef is not obligated because the performance owed by the decorator was of a personal nature, involving his reputation, taste, and skill. While the third party may well be an excellent decorator, courts recognize that contractual promises of such performance are nondelegable, unless there is an affirmative agreement to allow for the delegation. (A) is incorrect but the next best answer. Except where a contract involves an inherently nondelegable duty (such as decorating an upscale restaurant), contractual obligations are freely delegable unless there is an expressed prohibition. (B) is incorrect. Where a contract calls for performance of a personal nature, the obligee is under no obligation to allow even the most talented delegatee to assume the contractual duties. Where examination choices involve adequate assurances, generally those answers are only correct when dealing with the basis for not holding a party to a contract that has anticipatorily repudiated the contract. (D) is incorrect. A novation is an agreement amongst three parties whereby an obligee agrees to release an original obligor from liability for a contract, and allows a delegatee to assume the original obligor's duty. Here, there is no release of the decorator by the chef, nor any agreement to allow the third party to assume the decorator's contractual duties.

Answer to Question 67

(D) The bank will be successful in obtaining a judgment against both the landowner and the attorney, although it may only collect once. When a grantee assumes the mortgage, the grantee expressly promises the grantor-mortgagor that he will pay the mortgage obligation as it becomes due. The mortgagee then becomes a third-party beneficiary of the grantee's promise to pay and can sue the grantee directly if the grantee fails to pay. After the assumption, the grantor-mortgagor becomes a surety who is secondarily liable to the mortgagee on the note if the grantee fails to pay. The landowner and the attorney are jointly liable, even though the attorney is primarily liable and the landowner is secondarily liable as a surety. Therefore, (A) and (B) are incorrect. (C) is incorrect.

The bank is not required to choose between the landowner and the attorney and can obtain a judgment against both, although it may only collect once. Because the attorney assumed the mortgage obligation, the bank can sue the attorney, but it can also sue the landowner in the same action as a surety. The landowner and the attorney are jointly liable, even though the attorney is primarily liable and the landowner is secondarily liable as a surety.

Answer to Question 68

(A) The creditor will be successful against the developer only. The developer initiated an agreement with the creditor to convey the property to the creditor in satisfaction of the developer's obligation to the creditor. The deed was meant to convey absolute title to the creditor, and was not intended to be another form of the mortgage that already existed. Therefore, the developer has no further interest in the property. (B) is incorrect. The creditor will not prevail over the bank. The conveyance from the developer to the creditor discharged the first mortgage on the property because the conveyance was in satisfaction of the mortgage obligation. The first mortgage, however, was never foreclosed and therefore did not wipe out the second mortgage. When the first mortgage was discharged by the conveyance, the second mortgage became a first mortgage and is still a valid encumbrance on the property. (C) and (D) are incorrect because the creditor will prevail against the developer but not against the bank.

Answer to Question 69

(B) The driver can be held liable for both of the pedestrian's injuries. The negligent intervening act of the grocer leaving the banana peel on the floor of the market did not break the causal connection to the driver. The market's ordinary, intervening act of negligence was a foreseeable result of the pedestrian's use of crutches. (A) is incorrect. The driver is liable for all foreseeable injuries to the pedestrian even when there is an intervening act of negligence. (C) is incorrect. The market's negligence did not cause (actually or proximately) the pedestrian's broken leg. (D) is incorrect. As stated above, the driver can be liable for both injuries. But for the driver's negligence, the pedestrian would not have been injured by the market's negligence.

Answer to Question 70

(D) Since the witness read the notes, and then had an independent recollection of events, this qualifies as a present recollection refreshed. Normally a writing used to refresh is ***not*** placed into evidence. However, under Federal Rule of Evidence 612, if a writing is used to refresh the recollection of a witness, ***the opposing party*** has a right to introduce the document into evidence. Thus, (A) and (B) are incorrect. (C) is incorrect because, if the witness's memory was not refreshed, the memorandum would have to be introduced as a past recollection recorded. The proper foundation has not been laid for admission of a past recollection recorded.

Answer to Question 71

(B) If the witness on the stand has insufficient recollection to testify to a relevant event fully and accurately, Federal Rule 803(5) permits the introduction of an out-of-court written record of the event made by the witness at a time when the witness's memory of the event was fresh. The fact that the witness's memory of the actual event is imperfect would be sufficient to satisfy that standard. If the past recollection recorded is admissible, the record itself may not be admitted; unless it is offered into evidence by the adverse party, the offering party may only read the record to the jury, as here. (A) is incorrect. There is no question that the document which is read must satisfy the best evidence rule and be either the original or a duplicate, or there must be a satisfactory excuse for nonproduction of an original. There is no indication in this case that the summary in the witness's possession would fail to satisfy the best evidence rule. It appears to be her original notes. The real question here is whether the document in question is admissible despite the hearsay rule. (C) is incorrect. If a written record is used to refresh the memory of a witness who then proceeds to testify from her own memory as to the matter, then the memorandum is not evidence which comes within the past recollection recorded exception under Federal Rule 803(5). A document which is used to refresh a witness's memory may not be read to the jury. Instead, the witness will testify from her refreshed memory. (D) is incorrect. The hearsay rule applies in general to any out-of-court statement, whether or not the declarant is available for cross-examination. However, this statement comes within the hearsay exception for a past recollection recorded under Federal Rule 803(5). Under that Rule, the contents of the memorandum may be read to the jury.

Exam Tip: The difference between present recollection refreshed and past recollection recorded is a recurring exam favorite.

Answer to Question 72

(C) While the Senate has the exclusive power to try impeachments, only the House of Representatives has the power to impeach. (A) is incorrect because, although all revenue bills must originate in the House, the Senate may propose amendments to such bills. (B) and (D) are specific grants of power to both the House and Senate by section 8.

Answer to Question 73

(D) The farm's spraying operations are a nuisance based on strict liability for engaging in an abnormally dangerous activity (crop dusting) only if they substantially and unreasonably interfere with the use and enjoyment of the neighboring landowner's property. If there is no substantial interference, the farm will prevail. (A) does not establish a defense to an assertion of nuisance based on strict liability; the farm could be liable even if it exercised due care. (B) is incorrect because a private nuisance action is often brought by one landowner. (C) might affect the remedy (*i.e.*, whether money damages might be substituted for an injunction), but does not state the test to be applied for determination of nuisance.

Answer to Question 74

(C) The nurse is only an assignee of the tenant. The nurse is not directly contractually obligated to the landlord. Once an assignee of the nurse goes into possession of the premises (especially with the consent of the landlord), the privity of estate between the landlord and the nurse, the prior assignee, is terminated. An assignee has no contractual obligation under the original lease and is only liable for rent during the period of his estate, *i.e.*, his possession. Thus, in this case, there is no longer any privity of estate between the nurse and the landlord, and the landlord cannot sue the nurse on the rent covenant. (A) is incorrect. The covenant of quiet enjoyment was not breached here because no one with superior title interfered with possession of the apartment. Moreover, the duty to provide quiet enjoyment is owed by the landlord only to the tenant and his successors in interest (*i.e.*, those in privity of estate). Here, there is no privity of estate between the landlord and the nurse because the nurse is an assignee who is no longer in possession at the time of his brother's abandonment, and that is the nurse's best defense. (B) is incorrect. The defense of estoppel may be invoked where a party, acting in good faith, has been induced by the conduct of the adverse party to do something that it otherwise would not have done, that resulted in his harm, and that the adverse party had cause to know would so result in harm. These facts do not support the use of the theory of estoppel to avoid the application of landlord-tenant law, because the landlord has made no representations which were relied upon by the nurse to his detriment. (D) is incorrect, if only because there is a better defense available to the nurse. The defense of constructive eviction might be available to the nurse's brother, who was in privity of estate with the landlord during the month in question. However, it is less clear that it would be derivatively available to the nurse. Moreover, it is a difficult factual defense. The landlord must be shown to have the ability to control the noise and to have failed to exercise that control. The noise must be of sufficient magnitude to deprive the nurse's brother of the reasonable beneficial use of the apartment. The defense of lack of privity of estate is clear-cut and much more beneficial to the nurse.

Answer to Question 75

(A) The prosecution must prove every fact necessary to constitute the crime beyond a reasonable doubt, but the state may require the defendant to bear the burden of proof as to defenses or other exculpating or mitigating facts. Thus, the burden of proof as to trespassory entering of the dwelling, an element of the crime, cannot be placed on the defendant, and so the jury instruction as to the entering was unconstitutional. Thus, (A) is correct, and (D) is wrong. The state may constitutionally place the burden of proving self-defense on the defendant, and so the instruction as to self-defense was valid. Therefore, (B) and (C) are wrong.

Answer to Question 76

(C) This question is ***not*** about propensity evidence. Rather, it is about evidence of prior bad acts to help prove something ***other than*** a person's propensity to act in a manner consistent with a character trait. Under Federal Rule 404(b), it is permissible to use evidence of a criminal defendant's prior bad acts to establish a motive for committing the crime, to help to identify him as the perpetrator of a crime, or, as here, to show opportunity to commit the crime. The defendant claims that she could not have committed the murder because she was on a business trip the day it occurred. The witness's testimony, however, pertaining to his encounter with the defendant in a crosstown bar on the day of the murder, is clearly relevant to show that the defendant had the opportunity to commit the murder. For this reason, (C) is correct. All the other answers are wrong because they mistakenly assume that the witness's testimony involves propensity evidence rather than prior bad acts evidence. (A) correctly states that the defendant did not place her character at issue by testifying that she was across the country when the murder occurred. That would be a reason for excluding the witness's testimony ***if*** his testimony amounted to an attack on the defendant's character (*i.e.,* propensity evidence). However, his testimony is to show opportunity; thus, it may be admitted. (B) correctly implies that propensity evidence can be used to impeach the testimony of a witness only if it addresses the ***witness's character for truth and veracity***. The defendant was a witness in the trial. ***If*** the purpose of the witness's testimony had been to impeach her testimony by attacking her character for something other than truth or veracity, the testimony would be inadmissible. Since this evidence was admitted not to impeach but to show opportunity, (B) is incorrect. (D) correctly implies that the prosecution cannot introduce propensity evidence establishing a defendant's bad character until the defendant has placed her character in issue. The defendant's testimony did not place her character in issue. Thus, ***if*** the witness's testimony amounted to an attack on the defendant's character, the testimony would be inadmissible. Because the testimony was not an attack on the defendant's character, however, (D) is incorrect.

Answer to Question 77

(D) The electrician will not succeed because there was an express condition precedent that the repairs had to be performed on a day when the homeowner would be home, and the homeowner was unable to honor that commitment due to an unforeseeable supervening event. (C) is not the best answer. Although the electrician did nothing between April 4 and April 26, he did confirm the repair date of April 29 with the homeowner. The electrician would have honored the contract but for the supervening impossibility of the homeowner being unable to stay home. (A) is a false statement. The promise to make the house available was an express condition, not an implied-in-fact contract. (B) is wrong because impossibility discharges duties on both sides.

Answer to Question 78

(D) Destruction of a building being built under a construction contract does not render the contract impossible or impracticable to perform and therefore does not discharge the contractor from his duties. The original construction company could not continue to perform because the loss of its equipment rendered it bankrupt. Therefore, it was in breach and not entitled to any contractual remedy. Neither could it recover in restitution or quasi-contract. Unlike a contract to repair or remodel, no restitutionary or quasi-contract remedy is available when the subject matter of a construction contract is destroyed.

Answer to Question 79

(B) A state has the right, under its police power, to enact legislation for the health, safety, and welfare of its citizens, provided that such legislation is not in areas reserved to the federal government or preempted by federal legislation, and provided that a state does not unduly restrain interstate commerce. The legislation in question affects only that state's banks and does not discriminate against other banks. The political process is considered the adequate method for bringing such statutes as the anti-usury statute into line with contemporary conditions. (A) is incorrect because even if a state statute does not conflict with a federal statute, the state statute may still fail under the Supremacy Clause if Congress has indicated an intent to preempt an entire field. Thus, (B) is a better answer than (A). (C) is incorrect because income level is not a "suspect" category, and the fact that the super-rich can purchase homes while everyone else cannot is an incidental result of economic conditions. Regardless of the interest rate, there will always be some citizens who cannot obtain mortgages. (D) is incorrect because the legislation affects only that state's banks. There may be a slight incidental effect on interstate commerce, but the legislation in no way discriminates in favor of that state's banks.

Answer to Question 80

(D) The judicial sale of the first son's 1/4 undivided interest caused a severance of the joint tenancy and turned it into a tenancy in common in the buyer, the farmer. That meant that, no matter what happened in the future, the farmer would always have a 1/4 interest. When the third brother died six years ago, his interest immediately went by right of survivorship to the remaining joint tenants, the second and fourth brothers. Each of them then owned an undivided 3/8, together with the farmer's 1/4. Then last year, when the fourth brother died, the right of survivorship again operated to give his 3/8 interest to the second brother. That left the second brother with 3/4 and the farmer with 1/4. Note that because the farmer got his 1/4 as a tenant in common, he had no right of survivorship and could get nothing additional when the other co-tenants died. Note also that neither the third brother's son nor the fourth brother's daughter got anything upon their fathers' deaths. The right of survivorship operates instantly on death, and the deceased's estate gets nothing. (A) is incorrect. The farmer bought the first brother's undivided interest at the judicial sale, and that interest was an undivided 1/4 of 360 acres. The fact that the first brother had farmed only 60 acres is irrelevant. (B) is incorrect. The only way the second brother and the third brother's son might own 100 acres each would be if adverse possession applied. It is very difficult for one co-tenant to get adverse possession against another co-tenant. Unless one co-tenant ousts another, or claims a right of exclusive possession, there can be no adverse possession. Neither happened here. (C) would be correct if the property had been conveyed as tenancies in common, rather than as joint tenancies. Because they were joint tenants, the right of survivorship operated on the deaths of the third and fourth brothers, so the third brother's son and the fourth brother's daughter get nothing.

Answer to Question 81

(D) ***This is a very commonly tested MBE issue.*** (A) is incorrect. It is clear from the facts that the shopkeeper manifestly intended to kill or seriously injure the gangster, and this intent is transferred to the delivery person, who was killed by mistake. (B) is incorrect because any imminent threat of death or serious injury to the shopkeeper had passed at the time he shot at the gangster. (C) is incorrect because there is nothing in the facts that indicates duress. Therefore, (D) presents the strongest argument—that the gangster's intentional near miss with the knife was sufficient provocation to mitigate the intended homicide from murder to voluntary manslaughter.

Answer to Question 82

(D) Because the pilot's wrongful death claim derives from her son's death, either the son's or the pilot's contributory negligence will defeat the claim. Thus, although (A) and (B) are correct statements, they are not as good as (D), which is more complete. (D) states that the negligence of ***either*** the pilot or the son will prevent recovery, and this is the correct rule. (C) is wrong because only one person need be negligent to bar recovery.

Answer to Question 83

(A) Larceny requires a specific intent to steal. Common law larceny also requires a trespassory taking and carrying away of tangible personal property of value from the superior possessory interest of another. The doctor possessed the intent to steal the watch. Even though the watch was not on the nurse's person, it was not abandoned and would legally be considered in the nurse's possession. The taking was trespassory because the doctor moved the watch off the blanket. The very slight movement of picking up the watch satisfies the carrying away requirement. The crime of larceny was completed when the doctor picked up the watch with the intent to steal it, even though the nurse later told him he could keep it. (B) is incorrect. A defendant cannot be convicted of both the completed crime and the attempt to commit that crime. Attempt merges with a completed crime. (C) is incorrect. Embezzlement is the fraudulent conversion of personal property of value from another after the defendant obtained lawful possession of the property. Here, the doctor did not have lawful possession of the watch when he took it. Larceny and embezzlement are mutually exclusive. (D) is incorrect. The fact that the nurse told the doctor to keep the watch and that he intended to give it to him does not negate the crime. The crime was completed when the doctor took the watch from the superior possessory interest of the nurse with the intent to steal it.

Answer to Question 84

(A) The nursing home is liable under the doctrine of res ipsa loquitur because the injury ordinarily would not have occurred in the absence of negligence on the part of the nursing home, such as by accepting violent patients without providing adequate security for other patients. The nursing home has assumed the duty of ordinary care for the safety and security of its patients. Because the doors were locked, the injury occurred as a result of either a nursing home employee or a patient, and the nursing home would be liable in either case. Admitting patients known for their violent behavior created a foreseeable risk of injury to all the patients, and the exercise of ordinary care would require that the nursing home provide adequate security to protect the patients. The patient's beating establishes the breach of duty by the nursing home here, making it liable for the patient's injuries. (B) is incorrect. There is no rule of law which imposes strict liability in this situation. Thus, the nursing home is not strictly liable for the patients in its care, but it has assumed a duty of ordinary care for their safety and security. (C) is incorrect. The patient need not prove that the beating was caused by an employee in order to impose liability on the nursing home, since violence by another patient was foreseeable. The nursing home has assumed the duty of ordinary care for the safety and security of its patients. (D) is incorrect. An intervening criminal act of a third party will not cut off liability if it was foreseeable and the defendant owed a duty of care to the plaintiff. The nursing home has assumed the duty of ordinary care for the safety and security of its patients, and here criminal acts were foreseeable because the nursing home accepted violent patients.

Answer to Question 85

(A) Because land is considered unique, specific performance is always appropriate for the enforcement of a valid land sale contract. This option is available to either the buyer or the seller. The contract gave the seller the option of using the liquidated damages provision if the seller wished, but the seller has sued for specific performance. Because that is appropriate, it will be granted. It is not of significance that the house burned to the ground. When a contract for the sale of land is signed, equitable conversion takes place and it is, for all practical purposes, the buyer's land and the buyer's risk. Here, the risk of loss shifted to the buyer upon the signing of the contract. (B) is incorrect because frustration of purpose is not applicable. The doctrine of equitable conversion shifted the risk of loss to the buyer when the contract of sale was signed. The fact that an improvement on the property (the house) is no longer present is not relevant to the grant of specific performance. (C) is incorrect. Based upon these facts, the seller could request as a remedy either specific performance or liquidated damages of $6,000. Because the seller elected the specific performance remedy, the court will not award liquidated damages. (D) is also incorrect because there are no facts which would indicate mutual mistake. The burning down of the house would not qualify.

Answer to Question 86

(B) If an individual could prove that he would be unable to carry on his business if he were required to purchase more than half of his goods in the state because those goods were not available in the state, then the law as applied to that individual is irrational and would put him out of business. Therefore, this is the strongest argument that the statute might be a violation of due process. (A) is incorrect. Businesses not affected with the public interest are not immune from state regulation, and such regulation does not violate due process. (C) is legally incorrect; promoting local business is a permissible purpose under the police power. Usually, though, such statutes violate a provision of the Constitution. (D) is factually incorrect; the means used by the statute are closely related to the purpose of the statute. The object of the statute is to promote local business and the means chosen is to require local purchases.

Answer to Question 87

(A) The hypnotist's proposed testimony is hearsay evidence. It would be recounting an out-of-court statement (the pedestrian's hypnotically induced recollection of the accident) for the purpose of establishing the truth of the matter asserted in the statement. Therefore, the issue in deciding upon the admissibility of the hypnotist's testimony is to ascertain whether it fits within a hearsay exception. There is no hearsay exception for out-of-court statements given under hypnosis. The only hearsay exception that seems possibly applicable is the residual or "catch-all" exception, Federal Rule 803(24). Before evidence can be admitted under this exception, however, an ***elaborate pretrial notice procedure must be followed*** to assure that the other party has an opportunity to prepare to meet the hearsay evidence. No such notice was given in this case, and so (D) is incorrect. (D) is also incorrect because the catch-all exception was ***not meant to be a broad exception*** that could be invoked whenever some semblance of reliability could be attached to a hearsay statement. It was intended to be a narrow exception. It was not meant to revolutionize the law of evidence. To admit the hypnotist's testimony would have that effect. Since hypnotically induced testimony is generally inadmissible, to allow the admission of hypnotically induced hearsay statements would indeed be a radical change in the law of evidence. Since the hypnotist's testimony would be hearsay evidence not within any recognized exception to the hearsay rule, (A) is the correct answer. Both (B) and (C) are incorrect because they fail to give proper effect to the hearsay rule. (B) implies that the hypnotist's testimony would be admissible if the jury is given a limiting instruction on the weight that should be given to testimony under hypnosis. However, no instruction to the jury can cure the hearsay defect in the hypnotist's testimony; an instruction cannot magically transform inadmissible hearsay evidence into admissible evidence. (C) asserts that the testimony is admissible because the pedestrian's accurate recollection, under hypnosis, of the driver's license plate number establishes that the testimony is reliable. That assumption is highly questionable. It does not necessarily follow that, because a person can accurately recall specific numbers (*e.g.,* a phone number), he can also accurately recall related events (*e.g.,* who placed the phone call and what was said in the phone conversation). More fundamentally, the hearsay rule cannot be avoided simply by showing that hearsay evidence might be generally reliable. The hearsay rule can be avoided only if the hearsay evidence fits within a specific exception. Otherwise, the evidence is inadmissible. Because the hearsay testimony offered by the hypnotist does not fit within an exception, it is inadmissible.

Answer to Question 88

(C) For purposes of the hearsay rule, a statement is defined by Federal Rule 801(a) as an oral or written assertion, or nonverbal conduct which is intended as an assertion. In this case, the witness's pointing at the defendant is a statement because it was intended by the witness to assert that the defendant was the criminal. The sergeant's testimony concerning the witness's identification is testimony concerning an out-of-court statement and is therefore hearsay. Since the statement comes within no exception to the hearsay rule, it is inadmissible. The evidence is not evidence of a prior identification because the witness is not present on the witness stand. (A) is incorrect. Evidence of a prior identification is nonhearsay under Federal Rule 801(d)(1)(c) in only a very narrow range of cases. For a prior identification to be nonhearsay, a witness on the stand must testify that he had previously identified the defendant after perceiving him. The offered evidence does not come within that definition of nonhearsay because the witness is not present on the witness stand. The sergeant's testimony of the witness's assertive conduct is inadmissible hearsay. (B) is incorrect. The evidence is inadmissible because it is hearsay and comes within no hearsay exception. The evidence is not evidence of a prior identification because the witness is not present on the witness stand to testify to the prior identification. (D) is incorrect. The choice correctly states that the evidence is inadmissible. But it is inadmissible because it is hearsay, not because the defendant's counsel was not present at the lineup. Under constitutional principles, the defendant's counsel would not need to be present at a preindictment lineup such as this in order to have the prior identification be admitted at trial.

Answer to Question 89

(A) Even if the assignment could be termed invalid because it involved a material change in the burden of the hotelier's obligation, the hotelier can consent to it, as he evidently did by continuing to work. For purposes of this question, the issue is the buyer's status as a delegate under a delegation by the socialite of her contractual duty to pay the hotelier. By accepting the hotelier's performance and paying him, the buyer has assumed the socialite's duties and is obligated to the hotelier under the terms of the socialite-hotelier agreement. (B) is incorrect because a novation did not occur. A novation would have occurred had the hotelier agreed to release the socialite from her contract obligation in return for the assumption of that obligation by the buyer. It is not necessary for there to be a novation for the buyer to be bound. He can be bound if he assumes the socialite's obligations as a delegate pursuant to the delegation. (C) is incorrect because, although the assignment of the original contract may have been improper, the hotelier consented to it by continuing to work, and the buyer assumed the duties of a delegate. Furthermore, the duty to pay is a delegable duty. No facts indicate that the hotelier would be prejudiced by receiving payment from the buyer rather than the socialite. (D) is incorrect because the obligor can consent to an otherwise invalid assignment, thus waiving any right to argue nonassignability.

Answer to Question 90

(D) The President's order is too broad a limit on the freedom of speech and association of government employees. No government employees were allowed to have even a conversation with the press without the permission of a supervisor. Thus, it is unconstitutional. (A) is incorrect because the President's plenary power to control executive employees is limited by the Constitution. For example, the President cannot violate the First Amendment (or other constitutional guarantees) in regulating federal employees. (B) is incorrect because the Court no longer draws a distinction between rights and privileges. Furthermore, government employees would retain their First Amendment rights even if government employment were termed a "privilege." (C) is incorrect because the President has authority to enact some regulations for federal employees. The problem with this regulation is that it unduly restricts freedom of speech.

Answer to Question 91

(B) The animal shelter will lose on both farms. As to the deed to the son conveying the 590-acre farm, delivery is presumed because the deed was validly recorded, even though the son did not physically receive it and does not seem to have known of its existence. As to the deed to the daughter conveying the 640-acre farm, the fact that she did not physically keep the deed when it was presented to her does not show lack of delivery under the circumstances. The key to delivery is the grantor's intent to pass all legal controls. Because the daughter simply asked her mother to safeguard the deed, we can presume delivery under these circumstances. But because the deed to the daughter was never recorded, we cannot rely on the rule that provided valid delivery in the son's case. (A) is incorrect. Both deliveries were valid. The son's deed was valid by reliance on the presumption that recordation shows a valid delivery, and the daughter's deed on the circumstances of the gift that show proper intent. (C) is incorrect. The animal shelter does lose on the 590-acre farm, but does not win on the 640-acre farm because the daughter's having her mother keep the deed does not show lack of delivery. (D) is incorrect. The animal shelter does lose on the 640-acre farm, but does not win on the 590-acre farm because the recordation of the son's deed gives a presumption of valid delivery.

Answer to Question 92

(B) This question turns simply on whether or not there was a valid easement. The easement granted by the owner to the telephone company 30 years ago was properly recorded. That alone would put subsequent purchasers of the property on constructive notice of the easement. The fact that the easement was not in the deed from the owner to the buyer is irrelevant. A valid easement passes with title whether or not it is mentioned in the conveyance. For the subsequent purchaser to avoid the easement, that person must have taken without notice of it. Although there was no actual notice of the easement, a proper title search would have disclosed the easement, and the buyer is bound as if he knew. (A) is incorrect. If an easement is valid, there is no need to balance the hardships in order to determine whether the holder of the easement may make proper use of it. An easement to lay cables underground reasonably carries with it the right to inspect those cables or make replacements as is necessary. Hardship to the holder of the servient estate is not relevant if the easement is proper and the excavation is considered reasonable use of that easement. (C) is incorrect because the telephone company was under no obligation to mention its underground cable easement, and its failure to do so is meaningless. (D) is incorrect. Valid easements are conveyed along with the servient estate, regardless of whether they are mentioned in the conveyance or not. Because the easement was recorded, a title search would have disclosed it, and thus the buyer will be held to have constructive knowledge of it.

Answer to Question 93

(C) This question involves the admissibility of propensity evidence. The driver's witness is prepared to testify that the driver has a reputation for being a safe and prudent driver, which the driver plans to use to prove that, because he has a propensity for driving safely, he was in fact driving safely at the time of the accident. This is a classic case of the impermissible use of propensity evidence. The general rule is that evidence of character traits (here, safety and prudence) is ***inadmissible in a civil case*** to prove that a party acted in conformity with those traits on a particular occasion. [Fed. R. Evid. 404(a)] This case fits squarely within that general rule. Thus, (C) is correct. All the other answers are wrong because they each assume that propensity evidence is admissible under some circumstances in a wrongful death action. (A) indicates that such evidence is admissible if there are no unbiased eyewitnesses to the accident. (B) indicates that such evidence is admissible because the witness has personal knowledge of the character traits (the driver's propensity for safety and prudence) that are the subject of his testimony. (D) indicates that such evidence is admissible if the plaintiff has attacked the character of the defendant. All of these answers miss the basic point—that propensity evidence is inadmissible in civil cases. Furthermore, (A) is wrong because it presumes that there are no unbiased witnesses to the accident, but the question makes clear that there was an unbiased witness: the bystander. (B) is also wrong because it indicates that the witness must first testify that he has personal knowledge of the driver's driving habits before testifying about the driver's reputation for safety and prudence. This answer confuses ***reputation*** testimony with ***opinion*** testimony. The witness's testimony pertained to the driver's reputation. To be a competent witness, the witness would have to have personal knowledge of the driver's reputation. He would not have to have personal knowledge of the driver's actual driving habits. Although perhaps not as nonsensical as (A) and (B), (D) is just as inaccurate, as it bears no similarity to anything in the rules of evidence pertaining to propensity evidence.

Answer to Question 94

(A) This question is best approached by the process of elimination, and a preliminary examination of (A) suggests that it is a correct answer. The homeowner's negligence in burning leaves during a period of relatively high winds resulted in a fire, and it is foreseeable that third persons will attempt to rescue the victims of the tortfeasor's negligent acts. To the extent that the emergency vehicle was an intervening force, it was a dependent one (also responding to the fire) and was not abnormal or unforeseeable. Thus, the homeowner's negligence was a proximate cause of the driver's injuries. (B) is incorrect. The issue upon which the homeowner's liability to the driver turns is proximate cause; it is immaterial to that analysis whether the homeowner's negligence is established by a showing that he failed to exercise due care (indicated by the facts) or that his conduct violated a statute and constituted negligence per se (also established by the facts), which still leaves causation and damages to be established. Even if no statute were applicable to the circumstances, the homeowner would still be liable to the driver, thus, (B) is not as good an answer as (A). (C) is incorrect. The homeowner's negligence was a cause in fact of the driver's injuries, since it was the homeowner's negligence which both prompted the driver to attempt a rescue of the occupants of the burning residence, and brought the emergency vehicle onto the scene. It is possible for the separate actions of two independently operating actors to combine to injure the plaintiff, and whether either of them is liable for those injuries depends on the elements of the negligence analysis, including proximate cause. Here, the homeowner breached the duty of due care, and that breach was an actual and a proximate cause of the injury to the driver. (C) is therefore inaccurate. (D) is incorrect. The bare fact that the driver attempted a rescue of the occupants of a residence negligently set on fire by the homeowner cannot establish contributory negligence on the part of the driver, which is the only significance that (D) could have in these circumstances. If, under the conditions present at the time, and including the emergency nature of a rescue, the driver was found to have failed to exercise due care in attempting the rescue, the driver might be found to have engaged in contributory negligence which would bar recovery against the homeowner, but there are no facts in this question upon which such a conclusion could be based.

Answer to Question 95

(B) If the traveler was so drunk that he did not intend to rape the woman, he cannot be found guilty of attempted rape. The crime of attempt requires a ***specific intent*** to commit the substantive offense. The mens rea for rape would require the intent to engage in sexual intercourse by force without the consent of the victim. Voluntary intoxication is a defense to an attempt charge if the defendant can show that he was so drunk that he could not form the necessary intent. Thus, (B) is a possible defense although it might be difficult to establish, given the facts set out in the question. (A) is incorrect because the facts specifically state that the woman did not consent, and in fact "violently resisted." (C) makes no sense. The fact that the woman did not intend to have sex with the traveler would not be a defense for the traveler. (D) is incorrect. Although the woman's criminal intent might appeal to the jury, it is not a legal defense to attempted rape.

Answer to Question 96

(A) The Constitution is inapplicable because the bus company is a private company. The Supreme Court has ruled that the grant of a franchise is not sufficient to create state action. [Jackson v. Metropolitan Edison (1974)] Thus, there is no basis for a First Amendment claim against the bus company. (B) is incorrect; the Constitution is inapplicable because of the lack of state action. Also, (B) is incorrect based on the facts of the question. The speech restricted was political, not commercial. Thus, even though commercial speech receives less protection than political speech, this speech cannot properly be characterized as speech that seeks to induce business transactions. (C) is wrong because the audience's opposition to a message does not justify otherwise impermissible censorship. Also, (C) wrongly assumes that the Constitution applies. (D) is wrong because the availability of alternative avenues of expression does not justify otherwise impermissible censorship. Moreover, it also wrongly assumes that the Constitution applies.

Answer to Question 97

(A) A defamatory statement is actionable only if it is false. The programmer has a complete defense if her statement about the designer is true. (B) is incorrect. There likely was publication of the statement since it was made at a crowded party and overheard by a third party; ***negligence*** is sufficient to establish this element. (C) is incorrect for the same reason. The programmer could also be liable if she was negligent in allowing third persons to overhear her statement. (D) is incorrect because the programmer's statement disparaging the designer's competence in his profession is slander per se, and therefore actionable, even without a showing of pecuniary loss.

Answer to Question 98

(A) The initial contract was for $30,000. By cashing the check with "payment in full" written on it, the wholesaler has accepted the new payment terms. An accord and satisfaction occurs when there is a contract dispute or some slight alteration of the debtor's consideration, and here the debtor (the retailer) paid the entire contract price immediately on receipt of the coats. The acceptance of the new terms constitutes an accord, the cashing of the check represents the satisfaction. (B) is incorrect because discharge of a debt on the basis of account stated occurs when one payment is made to pay for a number of earlier invoices; that has not occurred here. (C) and (D) are incorrect because the entire debt has been satisfied.

Answer to Question 99

(A) The handwriting sample is relevant to the issue of the identity of the bank robber and is admissible because it was properly obtained and violated no rule of privilege. A handwriting sample is not testimonial in nature and, therefore, does not require Fifth or Sixth Amendment protections. (B) is incorrect. The handwriting sample is evidence of physical characteristics and not testimonial in nature and, therefore, not subject to Fifth Amendment protections. Therefore, there is no requirement that *Miranda* warnings be given, advising the defendant that the sample could be used against him. (C) is incorrect. Since the privilege against self-incrimination does not apply, there is no right to refuse to give the handwriting sample, provided that the content of the writing is not used against the defendant. (D) is incorrect. The presence of counsel is not required at a scientific identification made by the police for the purposes of investigation, such as taking a handwriting sample. [Gilbert v. California (1967)]

Answer to Question 100

(C) Under the U.C.C., a seller may obtain specific performance (*i.e.,* force the goods on the buyer) where the buyer has not yet accepted the goods only if the seller is unable to resell the goods at a reasonable price or the goods have been lost or damaged after risk of loss has passed to the buyer. Because the first farm has plenty of time to find another buyer and its apples are of a high quality, it will be able to resell the apples and obtain damages, but it cannot obtain specific performance. (A) is incorrect because mere breach of contract is not a sufficient basis for specific performance. (B) is evidence of a breach, namely that the corporation had an existing contract with the first farm at the time it signed the contract with the rival farm, but it does not address the issue of specific performance. (D) is an incorrect statement of the law. Specific performance is an equitable remedy that is available when the legal remedy is inadequate. However, because the first farm can easily resell its products, monetary damages are sufficient.

Exam Review by Subject

CONSTITUTIONAL LAW

Question 38

Due to anti-American sentiment that was sweeping through a foreign country, the President of the United States announced that unless incidents of insult and injury to American diplomatic personnel are stopped, he would sever diplomatic relations with that country. The Supreme Council of that foreign country countered with an announcement that all property of United States citizens or the United States government would be confiscated and forfeited if diplomatic relations were severed.

A naturalized American citizen who immigrated to the United States from that foreign country in 1965 now owns several businesses and a considerable amount of land in that country. He wants to bring a suit to prevent the President from severing diplomatic relations with the country, asserting that such an act would deprive him of property without due process of law.

As his attorney, you should advise him that a federal court would probably:

(A) Refuse to hear the suit, because the naturalized citizen lacks standing to sue.

(B) Refuse to hear the suit, because there is no diversity of citizenship between the naturalized citizen, who lives in Washington, D.C., and the President.

(C) Refuse to hear the suit, because it involves a political question.

(D) Hear the suit on the merits.

Question 11

A husband and wife were both professors at the United States Naval Academy. The husband made a speech criticizing United States foreign policy with respect to a Middle Eastern country and was dismissed from his teaching position soon thereafter. Six months later, he accepted new employment in another state.

The man's wife has commenced suit in federal court claiming that the Naval Academy violated her husband's right to due process and his right of free speech when it fired him.

The most likely ground on which the court will dismiss the suit is:

(A) The political question doctrine, because foreign policy is in the domain of the executive branch.

(B) The case is moot, because the husband has a new job.

(C) The plaintiff has no standing.

(D) There is no federal question presented.

Question 23

A state is operating a nuclear power plant on a river. The plant uses river water for cooling and discharges water back into the river 10 degrees warmer than when it was taken in. While the discharged water quickly cools, it has adversely affected the business of a downstream ice cutting operator, located in a neighboring state. The ice cutter successfully urged his state to bring suit in the United States Supreme Court against the state operating the power plant, alleging damage to its environment and seeking an injunction against the thermal discharge.

The United States Supreme Court should:

(A) Dismiss the action, because the suit is really one by the ice cutter against the state operating the power plant and is barred by the Eleventh Amendment.

(B) Hear the matter on the merits, because the ice cutter's state is suing in its own right and jurisdiction is proper.

(C) Dismiss the action, because it does not have original jurisdiction.

(D) Remand the case to the district court for trial, because it does not have the time to function as a trial court.

Question 22

A small group of terrorists hijacked a foreign airliner. Ten prominent bankers from the United States were among the airline passengers. The terrorists demanded that three individuals imprisoned in a state prison be released. Although these individuals were properly convicted of violation of state laws, the terrorists contended that they were political prisoners and that their convictions were merely a subterfuge to prevent them from inciting the local populace. The President of the United States agreed to release the three prisoners in return for the freedom of the 10 bankers. He issued official pardons and ordered the state governor to release the prisoners. The governor refused to do so, contending that the President had overreached his constitutional powers and had violated the concept of federalism.

The best argument for the governor's position is that:

(A) The President had no power to make an agreement with the terrorists because his treaty power extended only to dealings with the legitimate governments of other nations.

(B) The Constitution immunizes a governor acting pursuant to a state constitution from inconsistent orders by a federal official.

(C) The President's duty to see that the laws are faithfully executed prevents him from ordering state officials to release prisoners.

(D) The President's constitutional powers to grant pardons extends only to prisoners who have violated federal laws.

Question 10

The federal government has complete jurisdiction over certain parkland located within a state. To conserve the wildlife inhabiting that land, the federal government enacts a statute forbidding all hunting of animals in the federal park. That statute also forbids the hunting of animals that have left the federal park and have entered the state. A hunter has a state hunting license, authorizing him to hunt deer anywhere in the state. On land within the state located adjacent to the federal park, the hunter shoots a deer he knows has recently left the federal land.

The hunter is prosecuted for violating the federal hunting law. The strongest ground supporting the constitutionality of the federal law forbidding the hunting of wild animals that wander off federal property is that:

(A) This law is a necessary and proper means of protecting United States property.

(B) The animals are moving in the stream of interstate commerce.

(C) The police powers of the federal government encompass protection of wild animals.

(D) Shooting wild animals is a privilege, not a right.

Question 65

Under a program created by Congress, the federal government allocated $5 million to one of the nation's leading energy producing states "to be used solely for the development of synthetic materials to replace petroleum." The state accepted the funds and distributed $3 million from those funds to a state university, an agency of the state government. The university applied the $3 million to its ongoing energy research program, which included projects investigating the creation of synthetic replacements for petroleum products, solar power, geothermal power, biomass, and fusion power generation. The Justice Department brings suit in federal district court seeking to enjoin the expenditure of the funds in the University research programs.

The court should rule that:

(A) The University expenditure is unconstitutional because Congress has improperly delegated its power to spend for the general welfare to a state government.

(B) The expenditure is unconstitutional as a violation of the Supremacy Clause.

(C) The expenditure is constitutional because it conforms substantially with the purpose and goals of the federal program.

(D) The expenditure is constitutional because the federal government's attempt to control the actions of a state agency violates the concepts of federalism.

Question 39

A tire company is the manufacturer of, and owns the patent for, a new and unique type of truck tire. The company is the largest employer in the state in which it is located. That state enacted a law requiring all trucks using its highways to be equipped with the company's unique truck tires. An out-of-state trucking company filed suit against the state, and eventually the United States Supreme Court held that the state's statute violated the Commerce Clause.

Subsequently, Congress enacted a law that required all trucks engaged in interstate commerce to use the company's unique tires. This federal law should be held:

(A) Constitutional, because Congress's control over interstate commerce is plenary.

(B) Constitutional, only if Congress can demonstrate that the use of tires of another design somehow unduly burdens interstate commerce.

(C) Unconstitutional, if most states permit tires of another design.

(D) Unconstitutional, because the federal law reverses a decision of the Supreme Court, and the Supreme Court is the sole arbiter of constitutional issues.

Question 72

Of the following, which power is not specifically given to the Senate in the Constitution?

(A) To raise revenue.

(B) To declare war.

(C) To impeach.

(D) To regulate commerce.

Question 79

In order to protect its citizens from "loan sharks" and unscrupulous business practices, a state had enacted an anti-usury statute prohibiting loans for an interest rate in excess of 12%. Over time, interest rates rose slowly throughout the nation and the federal reserve began lending money to banks at 11.5%. As a result, banks in the state could not profitably make mortgage loans. Consequently, only extremely wealthy persons who could afford to pay cash for a home were able to purchase homes or farms in the state.

Is the anti-usury statute constitutional?

(A) Yes, because the statute does not conflict with a specific federal statute.

(B) Yes, because the state acted properly under its police power in enacting the statute.

(C) No, because the statute denies the nonwealthy equal protection of the law.

(D) No, because it restrains interstate commerce.

Question 86

A state statute requires all corporations doing business in the state and making over $1 million per year in purchases to make at least 50% of their purchases from vendors located in the state.

Which of the following arguments is most likely to succeed if the plaintiff is alleging that the statute deprives him of due process of law?

(A) It applies to businesses not affected with the public interest.

(B) Materials needed for some businesses cannot be purchased locally.

(C) The object of the statute is not within the scope of the police power.

(D) The means used by the statute are unrelated to the law's objective.

Question 49

On January 1, state legislation was enacted that prohibited private employers, under penalty of civil fines, from hiring any person who had not been a resident of that state for 10 years. The legislation also required private employers to immediately discharge any employee who had not resided in the state for a minimum of 10 years. The new statutes additionally provided that the applicable civil fines would be assessed by the state department of employment inspectors, at their sole discretion, any time they believed that an employer had hired or failed to discharge a person not meeting the residency requirements, and that the civil fines would be imposed on any employer who had hired or failed to discharge such persons on or after January 1.

An employee within the state, who is a nonresident, brought suit challenging the state statute. Which of the following arguments would most likely result in a favorable result for the challenger?

(A) The statute is an unconstitutional Bill of Attainder.

(B) The statute violates the Privileges and Immunities Clause of Article IV.

(C) The statute violates the Equal Protection Clause of the Fourteenth Amendment.

(D) The statute violates the Ex Post Facto clause.

Question 17

A Hispanic woman was a citizen of a foreign country but had lived in the United States for 10 years. She had properly acquired resident alien status and regularly complied with all regulations pertaining to resident aliens, such as annual registration at the local post office. Several of her friends had been called for jury service and she thought it would be interesting to serve on a jury. Thus, she went to the county courthouse and asked the clerk how she could apply to be a juror. The clerk replied, "You can't. We draw names, and if we want you we'll call you." Nevertheless, she was very diligent, and after tedious research she discovered that no Hispanic female alien had ever served on a jury in the county where she lived; in fact, no person of that class had ever been in a venire panel.

May she compel the county officials to include her and other persons of her class in venire panels through a lawsuit in federal district court?

(A) Yes, because there is a consistent pattern of discrimination against persons of her class.

(B) Yes, because alienage is a suspect category.

(C) No, because certain privileges, such as jury service, may be constitutionally denied to aliens.

(D) No, because she lacks standing, in that she is not involved in a case or controversy where the lack of jurors in her class might prejudice her right to a fair trial.

Question 41

Several years ago a number of employees of the state transportation department formed a workers' organization, a voluntary association incorporated under the laws of the state. The organization has grown in size over the years and has become very powerful politically. Nearly 85% of all state highway maintenance workers are members of the organization, which is supported entirely by the dues of its members. Membership is not required as a condition of employment or advancement in the state transportation department. After a vote of its entire membership on the question, a member was expelled from the organization solely because she is an active, knowing member of an organization that seeks to propagate the concept of white racial supremacy. The expelled member brings suit in an appropriate court seeking reinstatement of her membership. The suit alleges that her expulsion violates rights guaranteed her by the First and Fourteenth Amendments.

Which of the following is the strongest constitutional defense that the organization may assert to this suit?

(A) The First and Fourteenth Amendments do not apply to the actions of the organization.

(B) Active, knowing membership in organizations with overtly racist objectives is not protected by the First and Fourteenth Amendments.

(C) The organization could reasonably believe that it has a compelling interest in eliminating from its membership active, knowing members of organizations with overtly racist objectives.

(D) The expulsion of the member took place only after a vote of the organization's entire membership.

Question 96

A bus company was a private corporation that operated over fixed city routes under a franchise granted to it by the city council. To enhance revenues, the bus company rented advertising space on its vehicles. Although the city received a certain fixed percentage of the fare revenues from the company, it received nothing from the advertising fees. The management of the bus company had learned through bitter experience that any advertising that could be characterized as "controversial" led to complaints from riders and sometimes to losses in revenue. To that end, management employs a firm "no controversial advertising" policy. Thus, they refused to take ads for X-rated movies, abortion clinics, political candidates, and anything else that might be deemed "controversial." A candidate for city council was waging a populist campaign for the job and among his targets were the local utilities and the bus company. The candidate demanded that he be allowed to buy advertising on the buses, but the company's advertising manager refused, citing the company ban on all political ads. The candidate filed suit in federal district court, asking that the court require the company to accept his ads.

Which of the following is the company's best argument against the candidate's constitutional claim?

(A) The company is a privately owned company, and thus there is insufficient "state action" to invoke the United States Constitution.

(B) Commercial speech receives less protection under the First Amendment than most other forms of speech.

(C) Bus riders have First and Fourteenth Amendment rights to see the type of advertising they desire, and past experience has shown that there is substantial opposition by riders to controversial ads.

(D) The candidate has many other sources of advertising available and he does not need ads on the company's vehicles to get his message to the public.

Question 90

The President of the United States issued an executive order banning conversation by all executive employees with members of the press unless prior permission had been obtained from a supervisor. Executive Department employees were subject to dismissal for violation of the order. An employee of the United States Department of Agriculture spoke to a reporter and told the reporter that the USDA sanctioned the approval of a dangerous pesticide because of payoffs made by lobbyists to a high-ranking USDA official. The newspaper printed the story and quoted the employee by name. After a hearing in line with civil service regulations, the employee was found to have violated the executive order barring unauthorized conversations with news media reporters, and the employee was fired. The employee brought suit in federal court for reinstatement, back pay, and other benefits and also prayed that the court should strike down the executive order as unconstitutional.

If the employee's case reaches the United States Supreme Court, the justices should rule that the executive order is:

(A) Constitutional, because the President has plenary power to control Executive Department employees.

(B) Constitutional, because government employment is a privilege and not a right.

(C) Unconstitutional, because Congress, rather than the President, has authority to set the terms of federal employment.

(D) Unconstitutional, because the President cannot broadly limit all executive employees' freedom of speech and association.

Question 54

A speaker was addressing an audience in a city park on a subject that was highly offensive to many in the crowd that gathered to hear him speak. After awhile, the crowd became unruly and there was muttering and pushing, so the dozen police officers that were present formed a cordon around the speaker. A few members of the crowd indicated that if the police did not get "that S.O.B." to stop, they would do it themselves. At this point, two spectators picked up pieces of lumber from a construction site next door. The police officer in charge stepped in and demanded that the speaker stop speaking, to keep a fight from breaking out. When he refused, the police officer arrested him and he was convicted of disorderly conduct.

If the speaker appeals his conviction on constitutional grounds, it will be:

(A) Reversed, because the speaker's arrest constituted an interference with his First Amendment right to freedom of speech.

(B) Reversed, because the speaker's arrest constituted undue interference with the audience's right to assemble peaceably under the First Amendment.

(C) Sustained, because this speech caused an immediate and substantial threat to public order.

(D) Sustained, because it was the speaker's duty to obey a police officer where there were other times and places to convey his message.

CONTRACTS

Question 42

A large oil producer wanted to expand into the oil refinery business. It contacted a small oil refinery company and offered to purchase the company's refining facilities as well as its output of petroleum products from its remaining production facilities.

Lawyers for the oil producer prepared a written agreement specifying the sale price for the smaller company's refining business. The agreement also included provisions permitting the oil producer, at its option, to purchase 100% of all petroleum products removed from the earth by the smaller company for the following 15 years, at current market prices. The agreement was signed by both parties. One month after the sale of the refining facilities, the oil producer sent a fax to the smaller company stating that it would be exercising its option to purchase the smaller company's oil output for the next 15 years.

The written agreement between the oil producer and the smaller company is:

(A) Unenforceable, because the provision permitting the oil producer to purchase all of the smaller company's output was not supported by any consideration.

(B) Unenforceable, because the provision permitting the oil producer to purchase all of the smaller company's output for 15 years was indefinite and uncertain.

(C) Enforceable as to the sale of the smaller company's refining facilities, but unenforceable as to the output provision.

(D) Enforceable in its entirety.

Questions 28

A hotelier who operated a string of inns across the country decided to open a new inn in the Pacific Northwest. On June 1, he sent letters to all known hotel and motel suppliers, alerting them to his need for such items as ashtrays, televisions, linen, and mattresses. The hotelier received a letter dated June 8 from an ashtray company, stating that the company had 250 ashtrays left in stock and will sell them to the hotelier for $1 each. The company added that it must receive the hotelier's answer by November 1 and will hold the ashtrays for the hotelier until then. On July 1, the company sold 200 of the ashtrays to a competing hotel chain, who had recently opened a hotel on the East Coast. On July 2, the company sent the hotelier a fax stating it had only 50 ashtrays left for sale. The hotelier received the fax that day, but put it aside and never read it. On July 10, the hotelier notified the company that he was accepting the company's offer to sell 250 ashtrays. The company, upon receiving the hotelier's acceptance, shipped the remaining ashtrays. The hotelier sues the company for failing to deliver all 250 ashtrays.

Will the hotelier prevail?

(A) No, because the hotelier is not an ashtray merchant.

(B) No, because the company's offer was to remain open for more than three months.

(C) Yes, because the company promised in a signed writing to hold the offer open.

(D) Yes, because the hotelier never read the company's July 2 fax.

Question 37

A gardener entered into a contract with a landowner under which, for a monthly fee of $200, the gardener would provide the landowner with monthly gardening services for the calendar year. On June 1, the gardener told the landowner that she could no longer afford to work for $200 a month and demanded that she be paid $400 a month. The landowner refused, stating that he already had a valid contract with her and that he did not have to pay any more. The gardener again insisted that she would not work for less than $400. As a result, the gardener and the landowner agreed in writing on July 1 that the gardener would thereafter be paid $400 a month for the gardening services and that the term of the agreement would be extended through the end of next year.

Is the gardener legally entitled to receive a monthly fee of $400 from the landowner after July 1 of this year?

(A) Yes, but only for the period from January 1 to December 31 of next year.

(B) Yes, because the gardener and the landowner mutually agreed to modify their original contract.

(C) No, because the gardener used economic duress in order to obtain the landowner's agreement to the modification.

(D) No, because the gardener was under a preexisting duty to perform the gardening services for $200 a month.

Question 55

A mechanic noticed that his neighbor had a "for sale" sign on his old car. The mechanic thought it would be fun to have an old car to fix up and customize, and he asked his neighbor how much he wanted for the car. The neighbor told him that he would sell the car for $400, and the mechanic responded that he would buy the car for $400. They agreed that the mechanic would come to the neighbor's house by 6 p.m. the next day with the money. At 9:15 the next morning, the neighbor called the mechanic and told him that when he agreed to the sale the preceding day, he forgot that he had just put two new tires on the car and, therefore, would need to be paid an extra $50. The mechanic agreed to bring $450 in cash to his neighbor's house at six o'clock that night.

Is the mechanic legally bound to pay his neighbor the additional $50?

(A) Yes, because the original contract was not in writing.

(B) Yes, because the contract, as modified, does not exceed the minimum dollar amount required to invoke the Statute of Frauds.

(C) No, because no additional consideration was given for the oral modification.

(D) No, because contracts for the sale of goods can only be modified by merchants.

Question 18

On September 1, after lengthy negotiations, an import company agreed to sell to a clothing retailer, and the retailer agreed to buy, 10,000 imported, plaid woolen earmuffs for $8 apiece, to be delivered to the retailer's principal place of business no later than October 31. The agreement was reduced to a writing signed by both parties. A month later, the importer telephoned the retailer and explained that a strike in the manufacturer's main factory had reduced the number of earmuffs available. The parties agreed in that same phone call that the importer would deliver 7,000 earmuffs instead of the 10,000 originally called for in the contract, but that the price would still be $8 per earmuff. However, no earmuffs were delivered to the agreed-upon location on or before the contract date, and repeated telephone calls to the importer went unanswered. Finally, the retailer brought an action for breach of the modified agreement against the importer.

Which of the following is the strongest justification for the trial court to dismiss the complaint?

(A) The retailer will be unable to prove the terms of the modification, due to the parol evidence rule.

(B) The Statute of Frauds renders the modification unenforceable.

(C) The modification is unenforceable because it is not supported by adequate consideration.

(D) A written contract may not be modified by a subsequent oral agreement.

Question 98

A large wholesaler of European clothing sent out a circular to all of its customers advertising fine quality coats for sale at a price of $300 each when purchased in lots of 100 coats. The circular also stated that payment for each lot was to be made in three $10,000 installments, the first payment due within 10 days of delivery and the subsequent installments within 40 and 70 days of delivery, respectively. The day after receiving the circular, a retailer sent the wholesaler a standard order form with price, quantity, and delivery date terms filled in by the retailer, clearly indicating that the retailer was ordering one lot of 100 coats. The wholesaler shipped the coats to the retailer, and they arrived on September 10. The retailer accepted delivery of the coats and, on September 11, mailed to the wholesaler a check for $29,400. The check had the words "payment in full" written on it conspicuously. In addition, the retailer enclosed a letter with the check stating, in relevant part, "By cashing the enclosed check in the amount of $29,400, we assume that you accept our standard policy of taking a 2% discount for early payment." The wholesaler received the check on September 13 and cashed it on September 14.

Assuming that the relevant common law rules have not been modified by the check cashing rules of Article 3 of the Uniform Commercial Code in the jurisdiction, what is the legal effect of the wholesaler's cashing of the retailer's check?

(A) The entire debt is discharged, because there has been an accord and satisfaction.

(B) The entire debt is discharged on the basis of account stated.

(C) The retailer remains liable for the unpaid portion of the debt, because the discount provision was never accepted as part of the contract.

(D) Cashing the check merely satisfied a portion of the debt, and the retailer remains liable for the unpaid portion.

Question 29

A bathroom fixture company, in a signed writing, contracted with the developer of an apartment building for the sale to the building of 50 identical sets of specified bathroom fixtures, 25 sets to be delivered on March 1, and the remaining 25 sets on April 1. The agreement did not specify the place of delivery, or the time or place of payment. On March 1, the fixture company tendered 24 sets to the developer and explained that one of the 25 sets was damaged in transit from the manufacturer to the company. The fixture company also promised to deliver a replacement within five days.

Which of the following statements is correct?

(A) The developer is entitled to accept any number of the 24 sets, reject the rest, and cancel the contract both as to any rejected sets and the lot due on April 1.

(B) The developer is entitled to accept any number of the 24 sets and to reject the rest, but is not entitled to cancel the contract as to any rejected sets or the lot due on April 1.

(C) The developer must accept the 24 sets but is entitled to cancel the rest of the contract.

(D) The developer must accept the 24 sets and is not entitled to cancel the rest of the contract.

Question 7

On January 30, a company that designs and builds generators to standard industrial specifications received a telephone call from a buyer who ordered two generators at a price of $25,000 each. The parties agreed that delivery of the first generator would be on March 15, and the second on April 30. Payment was to be made no more than 30 days after delivery. On March 12, the company delivered the first generator, which the buyer accepted. On April 22, the company completed the second generator but had not yet notified the buyer. On April 23, the buyer, having made no payment to the company, canceled the agreement. The company brings an action against the buyer for breach of contract.

How much should the company recover in damages?

(A) Nothing.

(B) $25,000 only.

(C) Damages for total breach of contract for the sale of two generators, because the buyer accepted part performance.

(D) Damages for total breach of contract for the sale of two generators, because the goods were made for the buyer.

Question 8

A manufacturer of washing machines telephoned a company that built motors and asked for a price quote on an order for 250 washing machine motors built according to the specifications that the manufacturer had sent to the motor-building company the previous week. The company responded that it would sell the motors to the washing machine manufacturer at a cost of $20 apiece, with delivery in 30 days. The washing machine manufacturer agreed to the terms and instructed that its order be entered. The motor-building company immediately started work on the motors, and had made a substantial beginning on their manufacture (having completed 110 motors) when the washing machine manufacturer notified the company that it would not honor the contract. The motor-building company stopped work on the motors and sued the washing machine manufacturer, who raised the Statute of Frauds as a defense. The motor-building company responded that the specially manufactured goods exception takes the contract out of the Statute of Frauds.

If the motor-building company loses, it will be because:

(A) It had not substantially completed work on the contract.

(B) It had completed work on less than half of the motors.

(C) It stopped work on the motors before the job was completed.

(D) It could have sold the motors in the ordinary course of its business.

Question 66

A famous chef entered into a written agreement with his friend, a very famous interior decorator respected for his unique designs. The decorator agreed, for a fixed fee, to design the interior of the chef's new restaurant, and, upon the chef's approval of the design plan, to decorate and furnish the restaurant accordingly. The agreement was silent as to assignment or delegation by either party. Before beginning the work, the decorator sold his decorating business to a rival third party. Under their agreement, the decorator assigned to the third party, and the third party agreed to complete, the chef-decorator contract. The rival third party, also an experienced decorator of excellent repute, advised the chef of the assignment, and supplied him with information confirming both the third party's financial responsibility and past commercial success.

Is the chef obligated to permit the third party to perform the chef-decorator agreement?

(A) Yes, because the agreement contained no prohibition against assignment or delegation.

(B) Yes, because the chef received adequate assurances of the third party's ability to complete the job.

(C) No, because the decorator's duties were of a personal nature, involving his reputation, taste, and skill.

(D) No, because the decorator's purported delegation to the third party of his obligations to the chef affected a novation.

Question 89

A socialite purchased a hotel and hired an experienced hotelier to manage the property. The hotelier signed a three-year management contract for an annual salary of $150,000 per year, payable in monthly checks. After a year of hotel ownership proved too demanding on her social schedule, the socialite told the hotelier she was selling the hotel to a buyer. Along with the sale, the socialite assigned to the buyer the hotelier's management contract. The written contract between the socialite and the hotelier had no clause dealing with assignment of the contract. After the sale, the hotelier worked for the buyer for one year, for which the buyer paid the hotelier his $150,000 salary. The buyer then dismissed the hotelier for no apparent cause. The hotelier asserted that he is owed $150,000 for the year remaining on his contract, but the buyer refused to pay him. The hotelier has been unable to obtain further employment.

Can the hotelier recover in a suit for breach against the buyer?

(A) Yes, because the buyer accepted the hotelier's services and paid him for a year; that constituted an implied acceptance of the terms of the contract between the socialite and the hotelier.

(B) Yes, because a novation occurred, binding the buyer.

(C) No, because the assignment of the original contract was improper, and no contract existed between the buyer and the hotelier; hence, there could be no breach.

(D) No, because the original contract between the socialite and the hotelier was not assignable, even with the hotelier's consent.

Question 43

A successful stockbroker and his best friend, a land developer, were pleased that their only children were about to marry each other. The stockbroker and the developer wanted to get the marriage off to a good start. Thus, on July 1, the two agreed in writing that, on July 15, the stockbroker would deliver to the land developer a check for one-half of the market value of a two-bedroom condominium owned by the developer, and the developer would simultaneously deed the condominium to the bride and groom.

On July 10, the newlyweds learned of the agreement but neither assented to it nor changed their position in reliance on it. On July 12, the stockbroker and the developer mutually agreed to cancel their agreement.

If the newlyweds were to sue the developer and the stockbroker for breach of contract:

(A) The newlyweds would prevail because their rights as intended beneficiaries vested when the contract was made on July 1 and a later revision was ineffective in affecting their rights.

(B) The newlyweds would prevail because they received notice of the contract on July 10, and the rescission thereafter was ineffective.

(C) The stockbroker and developer would prevail because they had the right to mutually rescind their agreement.

(D) The stockbroker and developer would prevail because the newlyweds were incidental beneficiaries and had no right to enforce the contract.

Question 77

On April 4, a homeowner hired an electrician to evaluate his home's wiring. The electrician found the wiring to be faulty, called it a fire hazard, and urged the homeowner to fix it soon. That day, the homeowner entered into a written contract with the electrician, whereby the electrician agreed to repair the wiring for $1,600. The contract provided that the repair would take place prior to April 30, on a day when the homeowner would be home. On April 26, the work had yet to be done so the homeowner called the electrician to pin down a date. The electrician suggested April 29, and the homeowner agreed. On the morning of April 29, the electrician arrived ready to do the repair work. However, he discovered that no one was home, and he could not get inside. Earlier that morning, the homeowner had been rushed to the hospital for an emergency appendectomy, and the homeowner did not return home from the hospital until May 1. On that day, the faulty wiring caused a fire that severely damaged the house.

Will the electrician succeed in a breach of contract action?

(A) Yes, because the homeowner made and breached an implied-in-fact promise to make the house available to the electrician before April 30.

(B) Yes, because any recovery by the electrician will be subject to a setoff by the homeowner on account of his damage from the fire.

(C) No, because the electrician did nothing about the agreement between April 4 and April 26.

(D) No, because the homeowner's obligations under the contract were subject to an express condition precedent that failed because of supervening impossibility.

Question 56

An owner of land who was also a home contractor agreed in writing with a buyer to build a house on his (the contractor's) land and then sell the house and lot to the buyer. The contract provided that the sale must be completed by March 1. On March 5, after discovering that the house had not yet been completed, the buyer notified the contractor in writing of the buyer's election to cancel the contract because of the contractor's failure to deliver title by March 1. The contractor responded that, due to an unanticipated strike in the construction industry, performance had been unforeseeably delayed and that the house would be ready by March 20. The buyer responded that he would no longer accept delivery of the home and land. The contractor then brought an action to recover damages for breach of contract.

Who will prevail?

(A) The buyer, because the express date listed in the contract indicates that time was of the essence.

(B) The contractor, because the strike was truly an unforeseeable intervening event.

(C) The buyer, because there is a showing of good faith in the buyer's efforts to terminate the contract.

(D) The contractor, because he acted with due diligence in completing the house.

Question 78

A developer purchased a downtown lot on which she intended to have an office building constructed. She entered into a written agreement with a construction company to build a 50-story office tower for $250 million. The agreement specified that monthly progress payments of $20 million were to commence one month after the foundation was in place, with all remaining amounts due upon approval of the completed structure by the developer's architect. Construction commenced on March 10, and by April 1 the foundation was completed. On the night of April 30, a terrorist group detonated 500 pounds of explosives in the partially completed structure, totally destroying the building plus all of the construction equipment involved in the project. The construction company was forced into bankruptcy when its casualty insurer classified the loss as having occurred in an "undeclared war," and refused to replace the lost equipment. The developer engaged another construction company to construct the 50-story tower as originally planned at a price of $260 million. The trustee in bankruptcy has now brought an action against the developer to recover all payments due the company for the work completed prior to the terrorist act.

The trustee will probably recover:

(A) $20 million.

(B) The difference between $20 million and the cost to the construction company of the work completed at the time of the terrorist attack.

(C) The reasonable value of the labor and materials expended by the construction company at the time of the terrorist attack.

(D) Nothing.

Question 100

A large apple farm sells its product to various producers in the area who market apple products for commercial use. Prior to the harvesting season—the period when apple producers normally negotiate with processors and wholesalers for sale of the apples to be harvested—the farm was contacted by a health foods corporation that agreed in writing to purchase all of the farm's harvested apples. After the contract was signed, but before the harvest had begun, a rival apple farm offered to sell its apples to the corporation for 20% less than the price agreed to by the first farm. The corporation signed a contract with the rival farm for the purchase of raw apple products early enough before the beginning of the harvest so that the first farm had plenty of time to obtain another buyer for its apples. The corporation informed the first farm that its requirements for apples for the next year would be about 5% of the farm's total production.

If the first farm seeks specific performance of its contract with the corporation, the court should find for:

(A) The farm, because performance of the corporation-rival farm contract will automatically breach the first farm's contract.

(B) The farm, because its contract was prior in time to the rival farm's contract.

(C) The corporation, because the first farm can resell its apples elsewhere and then seek damages, if any, from the corporation.

(D) The corporation, because a seller of goods cannot obtain specific performance.

Question 13

For many years, a farmer has grown and harvested a sizeable wheat crop on his land. On May 1, the farmer entered into an agreement with a bakery to supply the bakery with 10,000 bushels of wheat at $15 a bushel. The agreement called for the farmer to deliver the bushels to the bakery's plant on or before September 1. In mid-July, it became apparent that the year's wheat crop grown in the United States was going to be substantially smaller than originally anticipated. As a result, the price of wheat on August 1 rose to $35 a bushel. On August 10, the farmer informed the bakery that he would be unable to deliver any bushels to the bakery on September 1, because he had sold his entire harvested crop to other consumers.

If the bakery sues the farmer for breach of contract, the bakery will:

(A) Prevail, as long as it files suit on or after September 1.

(B) Prevail, regardless of whether it sues before or after September 1.

(C) Lose, because the sharp increase in the price results in a commercial frustration of the original deal, which excuses the farmer's performance.

(D) Lose, because the unforeseen rise in price is a substantial change of circumstances which excuses both parties.

CRIMINAL LAW

Question 57

A hunter drove to one of his old spots for target shooting. When he arrived at the spot, he noticed that an adjacent area that had formerly been an open field now contained a new housing tract with a playground where children were playing. The hunter tacked a paper target to a tree that was located between the playground and the point from which he planned to shoot. He fired a number of shots at the target, and all but one hit the target. The one shot that missed that went wide of the target, ricocheted off a tree, and flew into the playground, striking a child in the head, killing the child.

If the hunter is tried for the death of the child, the most serious crime that he can be convicted of is:

(A) Murder, because the hunter's intent to shoot the child can be inferred from his conduct.

(B) Murder, because the hunter acted with wanton recklessness when he chose to shoot the gun in an area near the playground.

(C) Manslaughter, because the hunter did not intend to kill the child.

(D) Neither murder nor manslaughter, because the hunter's shooting was negligent, and mere negligence is insufficient to support conviction for a homicide crime.

Question 30

The victim's home was not well maintained, which caused much conflict with his neighbors. The neighbors to the north and south of the house, a mechanic and a doctor, had finally had enough and planned to place a smoke bomb on the victim's front porch. The doctor and mechanic consulted with another neighbor, an army veteran who was known to be an explosives expert, to help them. The army veteran agreed, but unbeknownst to the two neighbors, the army veteran manufactured a bomb containing a lethal quantity of explosives. He gave the bomb to the mechanic and doctor, along with a timed fuse. In the middle of the night, the two men set the bomb on the victim's porch. A few minutes later, a huge explosion rocked the neighborhood. Although nobody was injured, the blast blew away the front of the victim's house.

Who, of the following, is likely to be found guilty of attempted murder?

(A) The doctor, mechanic, and the army veteran.

(B) The army veteran and the mechanic, but not the doctor.

(C) The army veteran, but not the doctor and the mechanic.

(D) Neither the mechanic nor the doctor nor the army veteran.

Question 81

A gangster was threatening to inflict a "disfiguring injury" on a shopkeeper if the shopkeeper didn't accept "gang protection." The shopkeeper refused to pay and told the gangster to get out of his store. The gangster pulled out a switchblade and he flipped it at the shopkeeper. The knife thunked into the wall a few centimeters from the shopkeeper's left ear. "Oops. I slipped," said the gangster. "This is your last chance. Without my protection, you're a dead man." The gangster turned and began to walk from the store. The shopkeeper took a revolver from under the cash register, aimed it at the gangster, and shot. However, the shopkeeper missed, killing a delivery person instead.

At the shopkeeper's subsequent trial for the murder of the delivery person, which of the following is the strongest argument that the shopkeeper can only be convicted of manslaughter?

(A) The shopkeeper did not intend to kill or seriously injure the delivery person.

(B) The shopkeeper was acting in self-defense when he shot at the gangster.

(C) The shopkeeper was acting under duress when he shot the delivery person.

(D) The shopkeeper was reacting to a sufficient provocation to mitigate the homicide.

Question 46

While walking down the street, a pedestrian accidentally bumped into a street performer. The performer told the pedestrian to pay attention to where she was going. The pedestrian got mad and slapped the performer across the face. The performer, afraid that the pedestrian would continue the assault and escalate it to the point of murdering him, pulled out a gun and shot the pedestrian, killing her instantly.

The performer is most likely to be convicted of manslaughter in a state that:

(A) Recognizes the heat of passion resulting from adequate provocation as a mitigating circumstance.

(B) Applies the doctrine of diminished responsibility.

(C) Recognizes the misdemeanor-manslaughter rule.

(D) Recognizes the imperfect self-defense doctrine.

Question 83

A doctor and nurse were coworkers. The doctor admired the nurse's wristwatch and frequently said how much he wished he had one like it. The nurse decided to give the doctor the watch for his birthday the following week. On the weekend before the doctor's birthday, the two attended a hospital picnic. The nurse took his watch off and left it on a blanket when he went off to join in a touch football game. The doctor strolled by, saw the watch on the blanket, and decided to steal it. He bent over and picked up the watch. Before he could pocket it, however, the nurse returned. When he saw the doctor holding the watch, he said, "Doc, I know how much you like that watch. I was planning to give it to you for your birthday. Go ahead and take it now." The doctor kept the watch.

The doctor has committed:

(A) Larcency.

(B) Attempted larcency.

(C) Embezzlement.

(D) No crime.

Question 5

During the nighttime, a woman broke into the house of the victim with the intention of stealing his diamond ring. When she could not find the diamond ring, she became angry, lit a match to a newspaper and threw it on the victim's bed, setting the mattress on fire. The flames destroyed the bed and a portion of the floor under the bed.

In a common law jurisdiction, the woman is guilty of:

(A) Burglary only.

(B) Arson only.

(C) Burglary and attempted arson.

(D) Burglary and arson.

Question 36

After being fired from his job, an accountant drank heavily and decided to ride the bus home. While on the bus, he saw a briefcase that he mistakenly thought was his own. So, he picked up the briefcase. The owner of the briefcase tried to take the briefcase back from the accountant, and a struggle for the briefcase ensued. During the struggle, the accountant knocked the passenger to the floor, took the briefcase, and fled. The accountant was arrested and charged with robbery.

He should be:

(A) Acquitted, because he used no threats and was intoxicated.

(B) Acquitted, because his mistake negated the required specific intent.

(C) Convicted, because his intoxication was voluntary.

(D) Convicted, because mistake is no defense to robbery.

Question 95

A business traveler met a woman at a bar in the town the traveler was visiting. After an evening of drinking, when the traveler was very drunk, the woman went with the traveler to his hotel room. The woman did not intend to have sexual intercourse with the traveler; rather, she intended to drug him and steal his money. When they arrived at his room, the traveler attempted to have sexual intercourse with the woman. She told him that before they had sex they had to have one more drink. The traveler did not want another drink and used force in attempting to have intercourse with the woman. She violently resisted, and when it became clear to the traveler that she was strong enough to physically resist, he agreed to have another drink first. The woman drugged his drink, he passed out, and she completed the theft.

If the traveler is charged with attempted rape, his best defense would be:

(A) The woman consented to sexual intercourse.

(B) The traveler was too drunk to form the mens rea necessary for the crime.

(C) It was impossible to complete the crime of rape, as the woman never intended to have sex with the traveler.

(D) The woman is a thief.

Question 12

After having much too much to drink at the corner bar, the defendant decided it was time to go home. However, because of her intoxication, she did not notice that she grabbed an expensive and distinctive fur coat instead of her inexpensive cloth coat from the bar's coat room. The owner of the fur coat, who noticed the defendant staggering out of the bar and down the street, ran out of the bar and shouted for the defendant to stop. A police officer on foot patrol heard the shout and immediately apprehended the defendant.

If charged with larceny of the fur coat, the defendant should be found:

(A) Guilty, because her mistake was unreasonable.

(B) Guilty, because voluntary intoxication is not a defense to a charge of larceny.

(C) Not guilty, because the defendant did not reach a place of temporary safety and thus did not complete the crime.

(D) Not guilty, because she was too intoxicated to realize the property did not belong to her.

Question 63

At 3 a.m. on the state turnpike, a driver was stopped for driving 30 m.p.h. over the posted speed limit. Because of the speed at which she was traveling and because the driver possessed an out-of-state driver's license, the officer decided to place the driver under arrest and take her to the station house. Under state law, such an arrest is valid. At the time of the arrest, the officer searched the passenger area of the automobile, and under the front seat he found a small package containing what he immediately determined to be marijuana.

If the driver is charged with possession of marijuana, her motion to suppress the marijuana will most likely be:

(A) Granted, unless the officer had probable cause to believe the car contained items that were legitimate to seize.

(B) Granted, because the search was of an area outside the control of the arrestee.

(C) Denied, because the search was incident to a valid arrest.

(D) Denied, if the court determines the officer had a reasonable fear of the driver.

Question 64

Two police officers stopped an automobile for improperly proceeding through a red light. When one of the officers approached the car, he observed some hand-rolled cigarettes on the dashboard. He ordered the driver out of the car, examined the cigarettes, and determined that they were joints of marijuana. The officer then arrested the driver and guarded him in the back seat of the police cruiser while the second officer searched the entire car, including the trunk. In the trunk, he found two rare paintings that had recently been stolen from the city's art museum.

The driver was charged with possession of stolen goods and brought a motion to suppress the introduction of the paintings into evidence.

This motion is most likely to be denied because the second officer properly conducted:

(A) A search incident to an arrest.

(B) An automobile search.

(C) A custody search.

(D) An inventory search.

Question 34

The police had long suspected that an appliance store owner was selling stolen merchandise, but were unable to prove it. One night, under the direction of the police, an informant approached the store owner and offered to sell him a microwave that was represented as stolen. In fact, the oven belonged to one of the officers. The store owner indicated that he was interested and suggested meeting at a local park to complete the sale. The informant showed up at the scheduled time, but the store owner did not. When the informant saw the owner again, he asked why he had not shown up. The owner replied, "I wanted to make sure you were not working for the police." The two men then set up another meeting in the park, at which time the owner purchased the microwave for $25. Shortly thereafter, the owner was arrested by the police with the microwave in his possession.

On the issue of entrapment, the court should find:

(A) The conduct of the police amounted to entrapment, because it directly implanted a criminal intent in the mind of the owner.

(B) The conduct of the police amounted to entrapment, because the informant was not a member of the police department.

(C) The conduct of the police amounted to entrapment, because he performed a necessary act for the crime of knowingly receiving stolen property by making the property available to the owner for purchase.

(D) The conduct of the police did not amount to entrapment, because the owner already had a preexisting criminal intent to buy stolen property, and the action of the informant merely afforded him an opportunity to carry out his criminal intent.

Question 35

The police suspected that an 18-year-old living with his mother was selling marijuana to his high school classmates. The police went to the house without a search warrant and secured the mother's permission to search the teen's bedroom. In the bedroom, they found a locked suitcase under the teen's bed. The mother said that it was her son's suitcase but that they could search it. The police then broke the lock, opened it and found a substantial amount of marijuana. The police charged the teen with possession of marijuana with intent to distribute it.

If the teen should bring a pretrial motion to suppress the marijuana, that motion should be:

(A) Granted, because the mother was not informed of her right to refuse consent to the search.

(B) Granted, because the mother's consent to search the suitcase was invalid.

(C) Denied because the mother had authority to consent to a search of anything within her home.

(D) Denied, under the doctrine of in loco parentis.

Question 75

A defendant shot and wounded a victim in the victim's home late one night. The defendant was subsequently prosecuted for burglary under a statute that defined burglary as "the trespassory entering of the dwelling house of another with intent to commit a felony therein." At trial, the prosecution attempted to prove that the defendant had picked the lock on the victim's front door while the victim slept, crept into the house, awakened the victim at gunpoint, and demanded money, shooting the victim when he attempted to wrest the gun from the defendant's hand. The defendant testified on his own behalf, and told the jury that he had been invited into the house by the victim, who then pulled a knife and attempted to force him to pay an asserted debt. The defendant explained that he had shot the victim when the victim attempted to stab him after he denied owing any money. The judge then instructed the jury, among other things, that they should find the defendant not guilty if they believed, by a preponderance of the evidence, either that the victim had invited the defendant into the house or that the defendant had shot the victim when the latter attempted to stab him with a knife. The defendant was convicted of burglary and appealed.

The appellate court should:

(A) Reverse, because the jury instruction as to the trespassory entering was unconstitutional.

(B) Reverse, because the jury instruction as to self-defense was unconstitutional.

(C) Reverse, because both jury instructions were unconstitutional.

(D) Affirm, because both jury instructions were constitutional.

Question 99

A suspect was captured in a high-speed police chase five minutes after a bank robbery. The robbers had handed the teller a handwritten note demanding the money. The suspect was taken to the police station where, over his protests, he was required to write out the words of the note. After introducing the robbers' note to the teller, the prosecution also offered in evidence the writing which the suspect had been required to make by the police.

On appropriate objection, the court should rule the writing to be:

(A) Admissible.

(B) Inadmissible, because he was not advised that his handwriting sample could be admitted into evidence against him.

(C) Inadmissible, because he was not advised of his right to refuse to give a handwriting sample.

(D) Inadmissible, because he had not been informed he had a right to have counsel present.

Question 60

A defendant was on trial before a jury for murder. The state's prosecuting attorney had six witnesses prepared to testify against the defendant. After three of these witnesses completed their testimony, but before the prosecutor called her other witnesses to testify, the presiding judge called the prosecutor and the defense attorney to the bench. The judge told the prosecutor, "Frankly, your case stinks! You don't have enough evidence to convict this man of first degree murder. You are wasting our time. Reduce the charge to manslaughter and maybe you can strike a bargain with the defendant." The prosecutor replied, "No, your honor, I want to finish my case." The defendant heard the conversation, rose to his feet, and said, "Your honor, I'll plead guilty to manslaughter!" The judge, over the prosecutor's protestations, agreed to accept the plea and found the defendant guilty of manslaughter. The state appealed and the case was remanded for retrial.

Can the state retry the defendant for murder?

(A) Yes, because double jeopardy does not attach until the jury retires for deliberations.

(B) Yes, because the judge unconstitutionally forced a plea bargain, violating the Separation of Powers Clause.

(C) No, because double jeopardy attaches when the first witness is sworn.

(D) No, because the defendant was actually convicted of a lesser-included offense.

Question 15

A drug dealer was convicted in federal court of possession of 10 kilos of cocaine with intent to distribute. She was sentenced to a prison term. Subsequently, a federal grand jury indicted the dealer under a separate statute for conspiracy to distribute the same 10 kilos of cocaine. She moved to dismiss the indictment.

Her motion should be:

(A) Granted, because the Double Jeopardy Clause protects her against a second prosecution for the same criminal conduct.

(B) Granted, because the Due Process Clause protects her against double punishment for the same criminal conduct.

(C) Denied, because the Double Jeopardy Clause does not apply when the second prosecution is for violation of a separate statute.

(D) Denied, because each prosecution requires proof of an element that the other does not.

EVIDENCE

Question 50

The police set up an undercover "sting" operation in which they posed as fences of stolen property and bought and sold such property to anyone who came into their downtown warehouse. A defendant is being prosecuted for receiving stolen property in connection with his arrest by the undercover operatives, and the prosecution attempts to introduce a videotape showing the defendant offering to sell a television set to one of the police officers.

If this evidence is held to be inadmissible, the most likely reason is that:

(A) It is hearsay not within any exception.

(B) It violates the defendant's privilege against self-incrimination.

(C) A proper foundation was not established for its introduction into evidence.

(D) Criminality may not be proven by specific instances of misconduct.

Question 44

A tool producer was in the business of manufacturing and selling various hardware. The owner of a retail hardware store ordered 1,000 hammers from the tool producer, using the standard form that the tool producer's sales personnel used. Shortly after the hardware store placed their order, the tool producer's headquarters caught fire. All the purchase and sale records were destroyed in the fire. Afterwards, the hardware store owner asserted that the salesperson had agreed that the price for the hammers would be $5,000. The tool producer maintained that the price was $5,500. The tool producer then sued the hardware store. At the trial, the tool producer's director of the order department took the stand. After establishing that the original order had been destroyed by fire, the director sought to testify that the price of the order was $5,500.

Such testimony is:

(A) Inadmissible, because it is self-serving and untrustworthy.

(B) Inadmissible, because of the best evidence rule.

(C) Inadmissible, because it is not the best degree of secondary evidence.

(D) Admissible.

Question 45

A candidate was running for state senator. His campaign manager made the following statement to a potential contributor: "If you want to maintain high moral standards in this community, you should donate to my client's campaign. His opponent is a child molester and a thief, but all of that has been hushed up." A journalist overheard these statements and took detailed notes while the campaign manager was speaking, recording verbatim what the campaign manager said. The potential contributor also told several friends what the campaign manager had said, and the candidate's opponent sued the campaign manager for defamation.

At the trial, the candidate's opponent called the journalist to testify. The journalist is prepared to testify as to what he heard, but he is not willing to produce his notes containing the campaign manager's statement. The defense objects to the journalist's testimony.

The testimony is:

(A) Inadmissible under the best evidence rule.

(B) Inadmissible as hearsay not covered by an exception.

(C) Admissible as relevant evidence based on firsthand knowledge.

(D) Admissible, because the journalist's notes are protected by the journalist's privilege.

Question 16

A defendant calls a secretary present at a meeting between the defendant and the plaintiff in which attempts were made to negotiate a settlement. The secretary offers to testify that the plaintiff said at the meeting, "Well, maybe it wasn't fraud—I'll settle for refund of the purchase price plus $50,000." The plaintiff objects.

The offered testimony is:

(A) Admissible hearsay (under the admission exception to the hearsay rule) to show the plaintiff's recognition of the weakness of his case.

(B) Admissible, because statements made in the course of settlement negotiations are admissible where relevant, even though offers to compromise are excluded.

(C) Inadmissible, because of public policy.

(D) Inadmissible, because the statement was made in the office of the defendant, an attorney, and hence privileged.

Question 25

A defendant is on trial for robbing a liquor store. The store clerk testified that the defendant came into the store at about 11 p.m., pointed a .45 automatic pistol at him, and demanded that he give him all the money in the cash register. The clerk testified that the store was well-lit and that the defendant was not wearing a mask. The defendant's attorney called the clerk's employer to testify that when the clerk gave her a report of the robbery, he told her that the defendant pointed a .38 revolver at him.

The trial judge should find this testimony:

(A) Admissible, because it tends to show that the clerk is an unreliable witness.

(B) Admissible, because it has bearing on the clerk's truthfulness and veracity.

(C) Inadmissible, because it is extrinsic evidence of a collateral matter.

(D) Inadmissible, because it is hearsay not subject to any exceptions.

Question 62

A biker sued a driver for injuries allegedly sustained in an automobile accident. The driver's defense was that the biker was the cause of the accident, since the biker ran a red light and crashed into the driver's car. The driver's principal witness testified that he was standing on the corner when the accident occurred, and he observed the biker run the red light and crash into the driver's car. On cross-examination of the witness, the biker's lawyer asked, "Isn't it true that on the day of the accident you were 300 miles away from the scene attempting to extract protection money from the owner of a seaside restaurant?" The driver's attorney objected to the question, but the objection was overruled by the court. The witness then refused to answer the question, invoking the privilege against self-incrimination.

The biker's attorney moved to have the witness's direct testimony stricken from the record.

The court should:

(A) Grant the motion, because the privilege against self-incrimination is not applicable to civil cases.

(B) Grant the motion, because the biker has not had an adequate opportunity for meaningful cross-examination.

(C) Deny the motion, because the witness has a right to refuse to answer.

(D) Deny the motion, because the jury can assess the weight to be given to the witness's testimony.

Question 93

A tourist was hit at a street crossing by an automobile. The accident was witnessed by a bystander and by the tourist's wife. The tourist was hospitalized for several weeks and when it was apparent that he was about to die, the tourist cried out in anguish, "Why didn't the driver stop for the red light?" The tourist died immediately thereafter. The wife later brought an action against the driver for wrongful death, alleging excessive speed, failure to observe traffic signals, and defective brakes.

A witness for the driver was called to testify that the driver enjoyed a reputation for being a safe and prudent driver based on his personal knowledge of the driver's driving habits. The trial judge should rule the witness's testimony:

(A) Admissible, because, where there are no unbiased eyewitnesses to an accident, reputation as a safe driver may be used to prove the driver acted in conformity with that reputation at the time in question.

(B) Admissible, because the witness first testified that he has personal knowledge of the driver's driving habits.

(C) Inadmissible, because evidence of a reputation as a safe and prudent driver cannot be used to prove that the driver acted in conformity with that reputation at the time in question.

(D) Inadmissible, because, in a civil case, character evidence may be used only after the plaintiff has attacked the character of the defendant.

Question 76

During a defendant's trial for murder, the state introduced circumstantial evidence tending to establish her guilt, but could not provide direct evidence that she had committed the murder. No one had seen the killer going into or coming out of the victim's office around 2:30 p.m., the time of the victim's death by strangulation. During her defense case, the defendant took the stand and testified that she could not have committed the charged murder, because on the day of the victim's death she had been on a business trip 3,000 miles away. The prosecution then called a rebuttal witness. The witness will testify that, at 1 p.m. on the day of the charged murder, he had put his hand on the defendant's knee while both sat at a bar across town. The defendant had then coquettishly removed his necktie and attempted to strangle him with it until bystanders pulled her away and she left the bar. The defendant objects to admission of the witness's testimony.

How should the trial judge rule?

(A) For the defendant, because she did not place her character at issue in the trial.

(B) For the defendant, because the testimony is character evidence not directed at her character for truth and veracity.

(C) For the state, because the testimony established that the defendant had the opportunity to commit the charged crime.

(D) For the state, because the testimony established that the defendant has a character for violence.

Question 87

A pedestrian suffered serious injuries and amnesia after being struck by a car. The pedestrian sued the driver of the car. During case preparation, the pedestrian's attorney was frustrated by his client's inability to remember any of the facts surrounding the accident. He therefore hired a qualified hypnotist to question the pedestrian. While hypnotized, the pedestrian described details of the accident, stating that the car that struck him ran a red light, and the car's license plate number was XYZ356. It so happens that XYZ356 is the license number of the driver's vehicle. At trial, the driver stipulated that his car struck the pedestrian, but asserts a defense that he was not negligent and that the light was green when he entered the intersection. Because the pedestrian's amnesia persists at the time of trial, the pedestrian's attorney wishes to call the hypnotist to the stand to testify as to the statements made by the pedestrian under hypnosis. The driver's attorney objects.

How should the court rule on the objection?

(A) Sustained, because the hypnotist's testimony would be hearsay not within any recognized exception to the hearsay rule.

(B) Sustained, because the jury was not given a limiting instruction on the weight that should be given to testimony under hypnosis.

(C) Overruled, because the accuracy of the license plate number establishes that the testimony is reliable.

(D) Overruled, because the testimony falls within the catch-all exception to the hearsay rule.

Question 88

A witness who was unable to speak was an eyewitness to a robbery in the park. He went to the police station shortly after the crime was committed, and when asked who committed the robbery, pointed to the defendant in a police lineup in which there were several men who were dressed like the defendant and were the defendant's size. The defendant was then indicted for robbery. The witness died before trial, and the sergeant in charge of the lineup desires to testify at the defendant's trial that the witness pointed to the defendant at the lineup.

His testimony is:

(A) Admissible as evidence of prior identification.

(B) Admissible to prove the defendant committed the crime.

(C) Inadmissible, because the sergeant's testimony is hearsay.

(D) Inadmissible, because the defendant's counsel was not present at the lineup.

Question 20

A man and woman who shared an apartment were arrested and charged with murder. The woman's attorney moved to have the defendants tried separately. The motion was granted. The woman was tried first and was acquitted of the crime. The man's trial began one month later. The man's attorney called a witness, who was now living with the man, to testify that, shortly after she was acquitted of murder, the woman had told the witness that she (the woman) had killed the victim because the victim owed her money, and that the man was not involved at all in the victim's death.

The witness's testimony should be:

(A) Admissible as an admission by a co-conspirator.

(B) Admissible as a declaration against penal interest.

(C) Inadmissible, because it is hearsay not within any exception.

(D) Inadmissible, because the woman is estopped from contradicting the jury verdict of acquittal.

Question 3

In a writer's copyright suit against various publishers of versions of his book, the writer's interrogatories asked for information concerning total sales of versions of the book by the defendant publishers the previous year. The defendants replied to the interrogatories by referring the writer to a current edition of a publication industry journal for the information.

If, at trial, the writer offers that publication as evidence of the defendants' sales volume, this evidence is:

(A) Inadmissible as hearsay not within any exception.

(B) Inadmissible as lacking sufficient authentication.

(C) Admissible as an adoptive admission of the defendants.

(D) Admissible as a business record.

Question 4

Two men who had long hated each other got into a violent argument in a restaurant one night. The result of the argument was that the first man pulled out a gun and shot the second. The prosecution calls a witness to testify that he was standing in the parking lot, and, as the first man was leaving the restaurant, he dropped the gun into a nearby garbage can.

The witness's testimony regarding the first man's conduct would be:

(A) Admissible hearsay falling within the state-of-mind exception.

(B) Admissible, because nonassertive conduct is not hearsay, and it is otherwise admissible.

(C) Inadmissible, because nothing was said.

(D) Inadmissible, because the first man's acts constitute assertive conduct.

Question 31

A defendant is on trial for robbing a state bank. She testified that she was in another state at the time of the robbery. The defendant calls her friend as a witness to testify that two days before the robbery the defendant told him that she was going to spend the next three days in the other state.

The witness's testimony is:

(A) Admissible, because the statement falls within the present sense impression exception to the hearsay rule.

(B) Admissible, because a statement of plans falls within the hearsay exception for then-existing state of mind.

(C) Inadmissible, because it is offered to establish an alibi by the defendant's own statement.

(D) Inadmissible, because it is hearsay not within any exception.

Question 70

A bank executive was on trial for embezzling $10,000 from the bank where he worked. A key witness for the prosecution was called to testify, but on the stand he had difficulty remembering the specifics of a conversation he had with the executive regarding the executive's accounting procedures. To refresh the recollection of the witness, the prosecutor showed the witness a memorandum that the witness had written for his file, detailing the conversation. The witness reviewed the memorandum, and then testified that he recalled the conversation. He proceeded to testify about the specifics of the conversation.

The defense counsel then asks that the memorandum be introduced into evidence. The court should:

(A) Exclude the evidence if it determines that the witness's memory was refreshed.

(B) Exclude the evidence if it determines that a reasonable jury would conclude that the witness's memory was refreshed.

(C) Admit the evidence if it determines that the witness's memory was not refreshed.

(D) Admit the evidence if it was used to refresh the witness's recollection.

Question 71

A boater and a water skier were involved in a boating accident. Shortly after the accident, the water skier prepared a written summary of the events surrounding the accident. At trial two years later, the water skier is on the stand and is unable to accurately recall the details of the accident so she is asked to read to the jury the aforementioned account of the accident. The trial judge should rule her proposed testimony:

(A) Inadmissible, because the best evidence is the writing itself.

(B) Admissible, because her memory of the actual event is imperfect.

(C) Admissible, because it refreshes her recollection.

(D) Admissible, even though hearsay, because the out-of-court declarant is on the stand and is capable of being cross-examined.

REAL PROPERTY

Question 52

A husband purchased a cabin with his separate property. The husband provided in his will that the cabin be devised "to my sister-in-law for so long as my wife is alive, remainder to my son." Shortly thereafter, the husband died. When the sister-in-law learned of her interest in the cabin, she decided to lease the property. She entered into a valid written lease for a term of three years with a tenant, who agreed to pay $3,000 per year rent, with $1,500 due in advance every six months. The tenant paid the first $1,500 and took possession of the property. Two years later, one week after the tenant had paid the $1,500 due for the ensuing six-month period, the wife died. The son demanded that the tenant surrender possession of the cabin, but the tenant refused.

In an appropriate action for possession of the disputed property, the son will probably:

(A) Prevail, because his rights are superior to the tenant's.

(B) Prevail, if he reimburses the tenant for the portion of the six months' rent already paid to the sister-in-law that is attributable to the period after the tenant surrenders possession.

(C) Lose, because he did not wait to bring the action until the period for which the tenant had already paid rent had elapsed.

(D) Lose, because the tenant has the right to remain in possession for the last year of his lease as long as he pays the final $1,500.

Question 32

A rancher deeded his ranch "to my son so long as he lives, and on his death to my son's widow for the remainder of her life, and on her death to each of her lineal descendants who are living on her death, to share and share alike." The deed was validly executed, delivered, and recorded. At the time of the conveyance, the son was married but had no children. Three years later, the rancher died. His will left all of his estate to his sister. Two years after the rancher's death, the son was killed in an automobile accident, leaving his widow with twin girls. Upon the widow's death many years later, she was survived by both girls, her only lineal descendants.

Who now owns the ranch?

(A) The girls are tenants in common, with each owning an undivided one-half; their interest vested on the son's widow's death, well within the period of lives in being plus 21 years.

(B) The girls are tenants in common, with each owning an undivided one-half; they received a vested remainder, which is not subject to the Rule Against Perpetuities.

(C) The sister owns the ranch in fee simple, because the Rule Against Perpetuities voided the gift over to the son's widow and the following gift to her lineal descendants.

(D) The sister owns the ranch in fee simple, which she received upon the death of the son's widow.

Question 33

A landowner conveyed his parcel of land "to my sister and her heirs so long as it is used for residential purposes, but if it is ever used for other than residential purposes, then to the local community center."

Five years later, the landowner died, devising all of his real estate to his friend and leaving his daughter as his only heir.

The following year, the landowner's sister and the landowner's daughter entered into a contract with a third party to sell the parcel to him in fee simple for $100,000. After examining title, the third party refused to perform under the contract because he believed the sister and the daughter could not deliver good title.

The jurisdiction follows the common law Rule Against Perpetuities and has a statute providing that all future estates and interests are alienable, descendible, and devisable in the same manner as possessory estates and interests.

If the sister and the daughter sue the third party for specific performance, their request will be:

(A) Granted, because the sister owns the parcel in fee simple.

(B) Granted, because the sister and the daughter together own the parcel in fee simple.

(C) Denied, because the local community center has a valid interest in the parcel.

(D) Denied, because the friend has a valid interest in the parcel.

Question 80

Twenty years ago, four brothers inherited their father's 360-acre farm as joint tenants with right of survivorship. The oldest brother immediately moved onto the south 60 acres and began farming it. The two middle brothers formed a partnership and began farming the northern 200 acres. The fourth brother had no interest in farming and stayed in the city. The remaining 100 acres were vacant and unoccupied.

Eight years ago, a creditor sued and obtained a judgment lien on the oldest brother's interest in the farm. This interest was sold to a farmer at a judicial sale in order to satisfy the lien. Two years later, the third brother died, leaving a son as his only heir. The second brother continued farming the northern 200 acres. Five years later, the fourth brother died, leaving a daughter as his only heir. Soon afterwards, the farmer who purchased the first brother's interest at the judicial sale decided he wanted to start farming the land. He wants a clarification of exactly how much land he owns. There is a seven-year statute for adverse possession in the state.

If the 360 acres were allocated to each owner in accordance with each owner's fractional interest, how many acres would each own?

(A) The farmer owns 60 acres; the second brother, the third brother's son, and the fourth brother's daughter each own 100 acres.

(B) The farmer owns 90 acres, the second brother and the third brother's son each own 100 acres, and the fourth brother's daughter owns the remainder.

(C) The farmer, the second brother, the third brother's son, and the fourth brother's daughter each own 90 acres.

(D) The farmer owns 90 acres, and the second brother owns 270 acres.

Question 14

Two partners bought a commercial building from an owner. They paid cash for the building and took title as joint tenants with right of survivorship. Several years later, the first partner executed a mortgage on the building to secure a personal loan to a bank. The second partner had no knowledge of the mortgage to the bank. The state in which the commercial building is located recognizes the lien theory of mortgages. The first partner died before paying off his loan. He left all of his property by will to his daughter, his only heir.

Who has title to the commercial building?

(A) The second partner has title free and clear of the mortgage.

(B) An undivided one-half is held by the second partner free and clear of the mortgage, and the other one-half is held by the daughter, subject to the mortgage.

(C) An undivided one-half is held by the second partner and the other one-half by the daughter, with both halves subject to the mortgage.

(D) The second partner has title to the entire property, with an undivided one-half being subject to the mortgage.

Question 74

A landlord entered into a written four-year lease with a tenant for an apartment in the landlord's apartment house. The tenant's lease, and all leases in the apartment house, prohibited the playing of musical instruments between 10 p.m. and 8 a.m. The lease required the tenant to pay the rent on a monthly basis. Two years into the lease, the tenant assigned the lease to a nurse with the landlord's permission. The nurse then assigned the lease to his brother with the landlord's permission. The brother went into possession. A neighboring tenant in the same apartment house insisted upon playing a trumpet in a loud manner between 2 a.m. and 4 a.m. The brother complained to the landlord without success. Unable to sleep each night, the brother abandoned his apartment after occupying it for two months.

If the landlord sues the nurse for the rent due during the period after the nurse's brother left, the nurse's best defense would be:

(A) A breach of the landlord's covenant of quiet enjoyment.

(B) Estoppel, because the landlord consented to a further assignment.

(C) Lack of privity of estate.

(D) Constructive eviction.

Question 92

Thirty years ago, a telephone company purchased an easement from an owner to install, inspect, repair, replace, and maintain underground transmission cables within a specified portion of the owner's property. The deed granting the easement was validly recorded, and the telephone company shortly thereafter laid underground long distance lines traversing the owner's land beneath the area described in the easement deed.

Fifteen years later, the owner sold a 50-acre portion of his land to a buyer. This portion included part of the easement granted to the telephone company. The buyer erected a residence on the purchased land and planted 49 acres of walnut trees. He granted an easement to the telephone company to string aerial telephone wires. The underground easement was never disclosed.

Last year, the telephone company informed the buyer that it would have to excavate underground cables and replace them with new ones. This was the first the buyer knew of the cables lying under his land. The cables, lying within the easement, are directly beneath a row of black walnut trees running the length of the buyer's property. Black walnuts have become extremely valuable, and the buyer estimates that their value is approximately $400,000.

The buyer seeks an injunction prohibiting the telephone company from undertaking the planned excavation. The trial court should rule for:

(A) The telephone company, because the benefits of installing the new cables outweigh the harm done to the buyer.

(B) The telephone company, because ownership of the easement permits it to make the excavation.

(C) The buyer, because the telephone company concealed the existence of the underground easement from the buyer when it acquired the overhead easement from him.

(D) The buyer, because the deed by which he purchased his property made no mention of the easement, and he had no actual knowledge of it.

Question 47

An owner of 40 acres of mountain land sold the western 20 acres to a buyer. Because no access to any public road existed on the western side of the property, the deed conveying title to the buyer included an easement for ingress and egress that ran along the southern border of the owner's land. This deed was duly recorded.

About the same time that this sale took place, the county extended the public road so that it abutted on the buyer's 20 acres. The buyer then built a cabin on the property.

Later, the owner and the buyer both sold their 20 acres to the owner's cousin. The cousin then sold the 20 acres acquired from the buyer to his lawyer and sold the other 20 acres to a doctor. All deeds involved in the various conveyances of the 20-acre parcels were validly recorded. Neither the cousin-lawyer deed nor the cousin-doctor deed made any mention of easements or rights-of-way. In fact, no use was ever made of the easement.

A few years later, the lawyer sold his 20 acres to a development company that wished to build a hunting lodge on the property. The development company now wants to construct a road across the doctor's property in the manner contemplated in the deed from the original owner to the buyer.

What is the strongest argument as to why the development company should not be permitted to construct the road?

(A) Any easement that might have existed was extinguished by abandonment because of nonuse.

(B) Any easement that once existed was terminated by merger.

(C) The county's subsequent expansion of the public road removed the necessity of using the easement across the eastern parcel.

(D) Neither the cousin-doctor deed nor the cousin-lawyer deed made any mention of the easement.

Question 48

Twenty-five years ago, a property owner placed a large sewer line (to service a single-family house he built on the property) across a neighbor's property without the neighbor's permission. Three years ago, the owner tore down the house in preparation for the construction of an apartment building on the land, and made an agreement with municipal authorities to take an easement across the neighbor's property and install a new sewer line to service the apartment building. The municipal authorities failed to perform their agreement, and the owner constructed the apartment building last year using the existing sewer line. The state has a 20-year statute for acquiring property interests by adverse use.

If the neighbor attempts to enjoin the use of the sewer line to service the apartment building, she will:

(A) Prevail, because the agreement with the municipal authorities estopped the owner from using the existing line to service the apartment building.

(B) Prevail, because the increased flow of sewage from the apartment building was beyond the prescriptive rights acquired.

(C) Not prevail, because the original sewer line was a license which ripened into an implied easement.

(D) Not prevail, because the use was within the scope of the prescriptive easement acquired.

Question 9

A developer prepared and recorded a subdivision plan, calling for 100 home sites on half-acre lots. There were five different approved plans from which a purchaser could choose the design of the home to be built on his lot. Each deed, which referred to the recorded plan, stated that "no residence shall be erected on any lot that has not been approved by the homeowners' association."

A lawyer purchased a lot and built a home based on one of the approved designs. However, many of the lots were purchased by investors who wanted to hold the lots for investment purposes. Two years after the lots went on the market, one such investor sold her lot to an architect by a deed that did not contain any reference to the recorded plan nor the obligation regarding approval by the homeowners' association. In fact, because very few residences had been built in the subdivision since the lots were first available for purchase, no homeowners' association meetings had been held in two years.

The architect, at a great expense, built a very modernistic house on her one-half acre. The lawyer, who had been unaware of the fact that this house was being built, brings an action to have the house torn down.

The probable result of this action will be in favor of:

(A) The architect, because her deed contained no restrictive covenants.

(B) The architect, because any restrictive covenant in her deed can only be enforced by the opposite party to the covenant or that person's successor in title.

(C) The lawyer, because the recorded subdivision plan, taken with the fact that all lots were similarly restricted and the architect had notice of this, gave him the right to enforce the covenant on her property.

(D) The lawyer, because his deed contained the restrictive covenant.

Question 85

A seller entered into a written land sale contract with a buyer on May 20, whereby the seller agreed to sell a home to the buyer for $60,000. The closing date was set at August 1. The buyer put up $6,000 as earnest money, as provided by the contract. The contract stated that if the buyer failed to perform by tendering the balance due on the house on August 1, the $6,000 could be treated as liquidated damages "at the option of the seller."

On July 21, the week before the closing, the house burned to the ground because of a freak lightning strike during a thunderstorm. When August 1 arrived, the buyer refused to tender $54,000 to the seller. The buyer asked the seller for the refund of his earnest money because the house had been destroyed. The seller refused and filed suit, asking for specific performance. The buyer countersued, demanding refund of the $6,000 earnest money.

How should the court rule on the suits?

(A) The court will order specific performance by the buyer.

(B) The court will order the seller to return the $6,000 to the buyer because of frustration of purpose of the contract.

(C) The court will award the seller $6,000 as liquidated damages.

(D) The court will award neither party the relief sought because of mutual mistake.

Question 61

A homeowner leased his home to a tenant for three years. The following year, the homeowner conveyed the house to a buyer, who never recorded her deed nor did anything with regard to the house. The tenant continued paying rent to the homeowner.

Three months after the conveyance to the buyer, the homeowner conveyed the property to his proctologist, who knew nothing of the prior conveyance to the buyer. The homeowner took the proctologist's money and skipped town. The proctologist told the tenant he now owned the house and that all rents should be paid to him. The tenant complied.

Six months later, the proctologist went to his local bank for a loan. He offered to put up the property as security. One of the bank's title searchers discovered that the proctologist had never recorded his deed and that, just two weeks prior to his loan application, the buyer had recorded a deed to the house that bore an earlier date than the deed the proctologist had shown the bank. Because of this cloud on the title, the bank refused the loan request. When the tenant discovered this, she quit paying rent to the proctologist. The state has a notice recording statute.

If the proctologist sues the tenant to compel the payment of rent, the proctologist will likely:

(A) Win, because the tenant is estopped from denying a landlord-tenant relationship with the proctologist, since she had paid rent for many months.

(B) Win, because the proctologist was a bona fide purchaser when he bought the property from the homeowner.

(C) Lose, because the proctologist failed to record his deed to the property.

(D) Lose, because the proctologist did not have good title to the property and cannot demand rent from tenants in possession.

Question 91

A mother had her lawyer prepare and execute two deeds: one conveying a 640-acre farm to her daughter and the other conveying a 590-acre farm to her son. The mother produced the deed to the daughter, who told her mother to keep the deed just in case the daughter misplaced it. The mother held on to the deed. The next day, the mother went to her lawyer's office to have the deeds recorded, but she forgot the daughter's deed at home. The mother gave the lawyer the son's deed and promised to bring the daughter's deed in the next day. Later that afternoon, the lawyer recorded the son's deed. That night, the mother suffered a stroke and died in her sleep. The daughter's deed was never recorded but was found in the mother's home after her death. In her will, the mother left all of her property to her daughter, her son, and the local animal shelter, in three equal shares. Aside from her modest home and some small bank accounts, the mother had no appreciable estate.

If the animal shelter challenges the deeds to the farms on grounds of lack of proper delivery, it will:

(A) Win on both farms.

(B) Lose on both farms.

(C) Win on the 640-acre farm but lose on the 590-acre farm.

(D) Win on the 590-acre farm but lose on the 640-acre farm.

Question 24

A homeowner agreed to sell his home to an accountant. He gave the accountant a general warranty deed and the accountant gave him S86,000, his asking price. The deed was recorded. A few years later, the accountant sold the property to a doctor, who paid her $125,000 for the property. To save on attorney's fees, the accountant went to her local office supply store to purchase a general warranty deed form. The store was out of those forms, but the clerk suggested that she use the form labeled "Quit-claim Deed," asserting that it would transfer the title just as well as the other form. The accountant purchased the form and filled in the blanks with the appropriate information she copied from her old deed. The doctor did not hire a lawyer to represent him in the purchase of the house.

The doctor accepted the deed from the accountant and gave her $125,000. Soon after the doctor moved into the house, it was discovered that the homeowner's title was not good. The true owner now demands that the doctor vacate. Title is judicially determined to be with the true owner, and the doctor is forced out.

Does the doctor have any action against the homeowner or the accountant based on any covenant for title?

(A) Yes, the doctor can sue both and can recover $125,000.

(B) Yes, the doctor can sue the homeowner, but not the accountant, and can recover his full $125,000.

(C) Yes, the doctor can sue the homeowner, but not the accountant, and can recover only $86,000.

(D) No, the doctor can sue neither the homeowner nor the accountant.

Question 67

A landowner in fee simple signed a promissory note for $10,000 to a bank, and secured the note by a mortgage of her land to the bank. The mortgage was duly recorded. The landowner then sold the property to an attorney, who assumed and agreed to pay the mortgage to the bank on the land. The attorney did not make payments on the mortgage note to the bank. The bank, following appropriate statutory procedures, foreclosed the mortgage and gave notice to both the landowner and the attorney that it intended to sue for any deficiency. At the foreclosure sale, the property sold for $6,000. The bank now sues both the landowner and the attorney for $5,000, which is the remaining amount of the unpaid principal and interest on the note plus costs of foreclosure.

The bank will be successful in obtaining a judgment against:

(A) Only the landowner.

(B) Only the attorney.

(C) Either the landowner or the attorney.

(D) Both the landowner and the attorney.

Question 68

A developer owned an office building subject to a first mortgage with a creditor in the amount of $1 million. Subsequently, the developer borrowed $100,000 from a bank secured by a second mortgage on the building to help pay the first mortgage and other expenses of the building. The developer's financial condition worsened, and he was unable to make the required payments on the first mortgage to the creditor. The developer approached the creditor and offered to give her a deed to the building in satisfaction of all of his obligations to the creditor. The developer delivered to the creditor a quitclaim deed to the building, which recited as consideration the release of the developer from all liability on the mortgage to the creditor. The deed was duly recorded.

Shortly thereafter, the office market greatly improved, and the building was worth $1.5 million. The developer then brought an action against the creditor, claiming that the deed was an equitable mortgage, and the bank served notice on the creditor that it was preparing to foreclose its mortgage on the building.

In appropriate actions, the creditor will prevail against:

(A) The developer only.

(B) The bank only.

(C) Both the developer and the bank.

(D) Neither the developer nor the bank.

Question 2

For several years, a landowner supplied water to the factory located on his land from a pump located on that same land. The pump drew water from a nearby creek, which provided plenty of water for all the factory's needs. Subsequently, a developer purchased property abutting the northern boundary of the landowner's land and constructed a large apartment building upstream from the creek, which also ran through her property. The building's water supply was pumped from the creek. Once the developer's building was fully occupied by tenants, there remained insufficient water to meet the needs of the factory.

If the jurisdiction follows the prior appropriation theory of water rights, when the landowner sues to stop the developer's use of the water, the result will be:

(A) The developer wins, because prior appropriation always protects upstream owners.

(B) The developer wins, because of the exception for domestic uses.

(C) The landowner wins, because he was the first to use water from the stream as a riparian owner.

(D) The landowner wins, because he first made beneficial use of the water.

TORTS

Question 53

A motorcyclist had just bought a new motorcycle. One week later, while still learning how to ride the motorcycle, he saw a classmate from school that he did not like walking along the sidewalk. He tried to scare him by swerving onto the sidewalk at a driveway, planning to swerve back onto the street at the next driveway just in front of the classmate. As the motorcyclist attempted to swerve back onto the street, the motorcycle's front tire blew because of a latent defect, causing him to lose control of the steering. He attempted to apply the brakes, but due to his inexperience, hit the accelerator by mistake. The motorcycle struck and seriously injured the classmate. The classmate sues the motorcyclist for battery.

Who is likely to prevail?

(A) The classmate, because the motorcyclist intended to frighten the classmate.

(B) The classmate, unless the motorcyclist's negligence in hitting the accelerator was the proximate cause of the accident.

(C) The motorcyclist, because he did not intend to inflict bodily harm on the classmate.

(D) The motorcyclist, because the injury was proximately caused by the defective front tire.

Question 27

A textile company and the local textile union were involved in a bitter labor dispute that had required the governor to use the National Guard. The Guard took up positions surrounding the company's main plant and issued orders that no more than 20 picketers could picket at any one time and that all employees who were on strike were forbidden to cross the perimeter established by the Guard. In spite of this order, union marchers approached the plant and refused to obey the commander's order to disperse. As they crossed the perimeter, the Guard was ordered to fire on the marchers. As a result, seven strikers were injured.

The seven strikers brought a claim for damages against the state, which has abolished governmental immunity. Evidence indicates that the use of weapons was not necessary to protect anyone, but that the Guard used the weapons because it had previously experienced trouble in controlling civil disorders.

The best basis for recovery by the strikers is a claim based on:

(A) Battery.

(B) Unusually dangerous activity.

(C) Negligence.

(D) Strict liability in tort.

Question 21

A farmer crossing a cattle breeder's land with permission noticed that the breeder had forgotten to put the prize bull in his barn as usual, and the bull noticed the farmer at the same time and charged. The farmer bolted for the nearest safety—the fence between the pen and a melon grower's melon patch. Leaping over, the farmer landed on and shattered several melons. Hearing the melee, the melon grower ran from a hiding place where he had been waiting to try to catch some children who had been stealing melons. He pointed his shotgun, which was loaded with rock salt, and exclaimed, "Stop or I'll shoot." Just then two juvenile melon thieves decided to make their escape and ran from where they had been crouching. The melon grower aimed his shotgun at them and prepared to fire but slipped on the shattered and slimy melons, and the load of rock salt struck the farmer, whom the melon grower had recognized and had not intended to hit.

Has the melon grower committed an assault against the farmer?

(A) Yes, because he actually pointed the shotgun at the farmer.

(B) Yes, if the farmer reasonably believed that the melon grower might shoot him.

(C) No, because the shotgun was only loaded with rock salt.

(D) Yes, because assault is included within the tort of battery, and the melon grower committed a battery when he shot the farmer in the shoulder.

Question 58

After a bitter breakup with his ex-girlfriend, a man sank into a dark depression. It was deepened when he bumped into her at a store and she shouted at him, "Get away from me and stay away from me! You have the characteristics of a garden slug." He decided to commit suicide, which was a crime in the jurisdiction, by sitting in his running car in a closed garage. However, a neighbor discovered him and dragged him unconscious from the vehicle. The man was hospitalized for carbon monoxide poisoning but survived.

If the man sues the ex-girlfriend for his injuries, he is likely to:

(A) Prevail, because the ex-girlfriend's comments caused the man to suffer emotional distress.

(B) Prevail, if the ex-girlfriend intended to cause the man emotional distress.

(C) Lose, because the man's injuries resulted from his own voluntary choice.

(D) Lose, because the man's injuries resulted from his attempt to commit an illegal act.

Question 26

A mountain lodge catered to cross-country skiing enthusiasts. Every winter, the owner of the lodge, along with his assistants, marked and groomed trails on his extensive lands. He charged a fee for a day's use of the trails. He also supplied equipment for those who needed it and provided lodging and meals for skiers staying more than one day. A woman on her first cross-country skiing outing was striding along a groomed trail when, with a loud crack, the rotten limb of a huge oak under which the trail passed separated from the tree because of the load of ice and snow it bore. It came crashing down on top of the woman, killing her instantly. The woman's heirs brought a wrongful death action against the lodge owner.

If the lodge owner prevails, it will be because:

(A) The oak limb was a natural condition of the land.

(B) The lodge owner did not know that the oak limb was rotten and was likely to fall.

(C) The lodge owner could not reasonably have discovered the rotten limb by inspecting his property.

(D) The ice and snow was an intervening force that caused the limb to fall.

Question 40

A pregnant woman visited her family doctor to seek relief from arthritis in her hips. The doctor prescribed a steroid-type drug. The pregnant woman took the drug as prescribed and obtained relief from her pain. The pharmaceutical company which manufactured the drug enclosed information concerning the drug in the packages it shipped to drugstores and with samples provided to physicians. This literature warned that the drug should not be prescribed for pregnant women because it caused enlargement of the ears of male children. The enlargement occurred when the children reach puberty. Studies confirming this result were published in various medical journals. The pregnant woman gave birth to a son soon thereafter. Although the son had a normal early childhood, his ears grew disproportionately large when he reached age 16, and he has suffered severe emotional distress because of his appearance. Now 17, the son has brought suit against the doctor for malpractice.

In that lawsuit:

(A) The son will prevail if he can prove that most doctors would not have prescribed the drug for his mother.

(B) The son will prevail unless the doctor establishes that he had not read the journals reporting on the side effects of the drug.

(C) The doctor will prevail because the statute of limitations has run on the son's claim.

(D) The doctor will prevail because no duty is owed to an unborn child.

Question 94

A homeowner raked up numerous dead, dry leaves that had fallen on his yard and set fire to the pile, even though the wind was blowing at 15-20 miles per hour that day, and a county ordinance made it unlawful to burn leaves on any day when the wind speed exceeded 10 miles per hour. After the homeowner went into his house, the wind whipped the burning leaves into the air and deposited some of them, still burning, on the wood-shingled roof of a neighboring house, setting the house on fire. A driver was passing by and saw the burning roof of the neighbor's house. He pulled over, got out of his car and ran across the street towards the neighbor's yard so that he could warn the occupants of the house. The driver was struck by a paramedic's vehicle just arriving in response to a telephone report of the fire. In a jurisdiction that follows the traditional common law rules applicable to contributory negligence, the driver brought an action against the homeowner to recover for the injuries he suffered from being struck by the emergency vehicle.

How should the court rule in this action?

(A) For the driver, because the homeowner's negligence was a proximate cause of the driver's injuries.

(B) For the driver, because the homeowner's conduct constituted negligence per se.

(C) For the homeowner, because the emergency vehicle was the actual cause of the driver's injuries.

(D) For the homeowner, because the driver would not have been injured if he had not stopped and run across the street.

Question 84

A nursing home, as a matter of policy, admitted patients known for violent behavior. Each night before the patients went to bed, all doors were locked so that intruders could not enter the premises without forcing an entry. One morning an elderly and docile patient was found beaten in her bed. The doors had been locked and there were no signs of forced entry into the building during the previous night.

If the patient should sue the nursing home for her injuries and establishes the above facts, she is likely to:

(A) Recover, because an occurrence such as this would not ordinarily happen unless the nursing home was negligent.

(B) Recover, because the nursing home is strictly liable for the patients in its care.

(C) Not recover, unless the patient can prove that the beating was caused by an employee of the nursing home.

(D) Not recover, because the beating was caused by the criminal act of a third party.

Question 69

A driver negligently drove his car into a pedestrian, breaking her leg. The pedestrian's leg was put in a cast, and she used crutches to get about. While shopping at the market, the pedestrian did not notice when she put one of her crutches on a piece of banana peel, even though she was using her crutches with care. The peel had been negligently left on the floor by the manager of the produce department. The pedestrian's crutch slipped on the peel and she fell to the floor, breaking her arm. Had the pedestrian stepped on the peel when she did not have to use crutches, she would have regained her balance.

If the pedestrian sues the driver and the market for her injuries, she will be able to recover from:

(A) The driver, for her broken leg only.

(B) The driver, for both of her injuries.

(C) The market, for both of her injuries.

(D) The driver, for her broken leg only, and the market, for her broken arm only.

Question 82

A pilot had given her 15-year-old son informal piloting lessons, including practice on takeoffs and landings on their farm's landing strip. Confident in her son's ability, she agreed to the son's request to fly by himself to his uncle's ranch, which also had a landing strip, to attend his cousin's high school graduation party. The son took off safely, but about five minutes later the aircraft's engine stopped running; the plane stalled and then crashed, killing the son. It was later determined that the engine ran out of fuel because a burst fuel line had been overlooked during a routine maintenance check of the pilot's plane the week before the crash. An airplane mechanic at the small private airport where the pilot went for fuel and maintenance had performed the maintenance check.

The pilot brought a wrongful death action against the mechanic's employer, the private airport, in a jurisdiction that retains traditional contributory negligence rules. At trial, the airport raises a contributory negligence defense.

This defense will prevent the pilot's recovery if the jury finds that a contributing factor in causing the accident was negligence by:

(A) The pilot in permitting her son to fly the airplane.

(B) The son in his handling of the plane after the engine quit.

(C) Both the pilot in permitting her son to fly and the son in handling the plane.

(D) Either the pilot in permitting her son to fly or the son in handling the plane.

Question 51

A driver left her car parked on the side of a hill. Two minutes later, the car rolled down the hill and struck and injured a pedestrian. In the pedestrian's negligence action against the driver, the pedestrian introduced into evidence the facts stated above, which are undisputed. The driver testified that, when she parked her car, she turned the front wheels into the curb and put on her emergency brakes, which were in good working order. She also introduced evidence that, in the weeks before this incident, juveniles had been seen tampering with cars in the neighborhood. The jury returned a verdict in favor of the driver, and the pedestrian moved for a judgment notwithstanding the verdict.

The pedestrian's motion should be:

(A) Granted, because it is more likely than not that the driver's negligent conduct was the legal cause of the pedestrian's injuries.

(B) Granted, because the evidence does not support the verdict.

(C) Denied, because, given the driver's evidence, the jury was not required to draw an inference of negligence from the instances of the accident.

(D) Denied, if the driver was in no better position than the pedestrian to explain the accident.

Question 19

A stockbreeder kept his prize bull in a fenced enclosure on his property. The stockbreeder's neighbor, who raised sheep, was driving his tractor inattentively and drove the tractor over the stockbreeder's fence, creating a four-foot hole in the fence. The neighbor was unaware of the damage he caused and drove the tractor to another part of his farm. Later, the bull wandered through the hole in the fence onto the neighbor's property. The bull was peacefully munching on hay left out for the sheep when the neighbor's sheepdog began barking loudly and harrying the bull, nipping at the bull's heels. The bull became enraged and stampeded over the neighbor's property. Several sheep had the misfortune of finding themselves in the bull's path and were either gored or trampled to death. The neighbor sued the stockbreeder for the death of his sheep.

Which of the following is most helpful to the neighbor?

(A) A bull is livestock and its owner is strictly liable for damages caused by its trespass.

(B) The neighbor was unaware that he knocked the fence down.

(C) The fence was down for several hours before the bull wandered through it.

(D) A bull is a dangerous animal and its owner is strictly liable for damages caused by its actions.

Question 6

A consumer purchased an air compressor, designed for powering tools and inflating tires, to use in a remodeling project. The consumer discovered that the reservoir and nozzle for a paint compressor gun he owned fit the threads on the nozzle of his air compressor. He decided to use the manufacturer's compressor rather than buying the compressor that went with the spray gun because he needed to paint a fence. After painting for a few minutes, the paint reservoir on the spray gun exploded, causing severe injuries to the consumer. The consumer subsequently brought a strict products liability action against the air compressor manufacturer to recover for his damages.

Evidence at trial revealed the following: (i) The spray gun reservoir had exploded because the air compressor developed too much air pressure for use in a spray device; it was for this reason that the manufacturer did not manufacture a spray painting attachment for its compressor. (ii) The manufacturer purposefully chose an unusual threading for its compressor nozzle to prevent its use with most spray painting systems, but the spray gun that the consumer had was a foreign-manufactured model that happened to use the same threading. (iii) When used with the tools and attachments produced by the air compressor manufacturer, the air compressor was completely safe and suffered from no design or manufacturing defects.

If the jury finds for the manufacturer, it will be because:

(A) The manufacturer exercised due care in the design and manufacture of the paint sprayer.

(B) It was not foreseeable that the compressor would be used by consumers to attach power spray devices.

(C) The compressor suffered from no design or manufacturing defects when used in the intended manner.

(D) The consumer misused the compressor when he attached it to his spray-painting gun.

Question 73

A local farm switched from vehicular application of pesticide to aerial spraying. When the aerial spraying began, the farm foreman discovered that, for the first time, the farm was experiencing appreciable drift of the insecticide, a portion of which drifted onto a nearby private school. The school filed an action seeking to have the aerial spraying enjoined as a nuisance.

If the farm prevails, it will be because:

(A) The farm's aerial spraying is in conformity with the general practices in the industry and was conducted with reasonable care.

(B) One landowner may not maintain an action for nuisance.

(C) The maintenance of vehicular application systems will greatly increase the farm's costs of operation.

(D) The drift of the insecticide does not substantially interfere with the use and enjoyment of the school's property.

Question 1

A "wind farm" was constructed on the open land next to a gas station where a mechanic is employed. The huge windmills generated electrical power and oscillated at low speeds, resulting in very low-frequency but high-amplitude sound waves which caused extreme discomfort in a substantial minority of people. The mechanic is one of the people adversely affected by such sound waves; the vibrations from the windmills give him severe headaches and upset his immune system.

If the mechanic brings an action for nuisance against the owners of the wind farm and loses, it will be because:

(A) Sound waves are not the kind of physical phenomenon on which liability for nuisance can be based.

(B) The owners of the wind farm cannot generate power without producing the offending sound waves, despite their best efforts to find an alternative technology.

(C) At lease six out of 10 people are not affected by low-frequency sound waves.

(D) The mechanic neither owns nor rents the gas station at which he works.

Question 59

A somewhat portly executive who was very prominent in business and social circles was aghast when he saw an article in the local paper describing the growing popularity of nude beaches. It was accompanied by a photograph of people enjoying themselves at a nearby nude beach. The picture was cropped so that nothing inappropriate was revealed, but the bather in the foreground of the picture was clearly the executive. The executive did enjoy visiting the nude beach on occasion, but he had never mentioned this to people in his social circle. Needless to say, he was quite embarrassed by the publication of the photograph, and he filed suit against the newspaper demanding damages from the newspaper for violation of his privacy rights.

Which of the following is the newspaper's best defense?

(A) There was no intrusion by the newspaper into the executive's private affairs.

(B) The newspaper did not place the executive in a false light.

(C) The picture was taken in a public place and appropriately accompanied by a newsworthy story.

(D) The newspaper did not use the photograph in any way to promote its circulation or advertising revenue.

Question 97

A software designer and software programmer ran into each other at a crowded software convention. The designer suggested to the programmer that they become partners. The programmer quickly retorted, "Look buddy, I like you, you're a nice guy and all that, but I'd never become your business partner, because when it comes to software design, you are totally incompetent." This remark was overheard by the private secretary to the CEO of a major software company that often subcontracted portions of jobs to smaller software design businesses, although it had never used this designer before.

If the designer sues the programmer for defamation, who is likely to prevail?

(A) The programmer, if her statement about the designer's competence is true.

(B) The programmer, because there was no publication.

(C) The designer, unless the programmer did not know her statement could have been overheard.

(D) The designer, if he suffered pecuniary loss as a result of the programmer's statement.